Principles and Standards for School Mathematics Navigations Series

NAVIGATING *through* NUMBER *and* OPERATIONS *in* GRADES 3–5

Natalie N. Duncan
Charles Geer
DeAnn Huinker
Larry Leutzinger
Ed Rathmell
Charles Thompson

Francis (Skip) Fennell
Volume Editor

Peggy A. House
Navigations Series Editor

NATIONAL COUNCIL OF
TEACHERS OF MATHEMATICS

Copyright © 2007 by
The National Council of Teachers of Mathematics, Inc.
1906 Association Drive, Reston, VA 20191-1502
(703) 620-9840; (800) 235-7566; www.nctm.org

Second Printing 2010

Library of Congress Cataloging-in-Publication Data

Navigating through number and operations in grades 3-5 / Natalie N. Duncan ... [et al.] ;
Francis (Skip) Fennell, volume editor.
  p. cm. — (Principles and standards for school mathematics navigations series)
 Includes bibliographical references and index.
 ISBN 978-0-87353-584-7
 1. Mathematics--Study and teaching (Elementary)--United States. 2. Mathematics--Study
and teaching (Elementary)--Activity programs. 3. Numeration--Study and teaching
(Elementary) 4. Numerical calculations--Study and teaching (Elementary) 5. Problem solving
in children. 6. Reasoning in children. I. Duncan, Natalie N. II. Fennell, Francis M., 1944-
 QA13.N3845 2006
 372.7--dc22
                              2006029838

The National Council of Teachers of Mathematics is a public voice of mathematics
education, supporting teachers to ensure equitable mathematics learning of the
highest quality for all students through vision, leadership, professional development,
and research.

Printed in the United States of America

In memory of

JOHN VAN DE WALLE,

who helped initiate this volume and served as a chapter reviewer.
We will all miss John's dedication, tenacity, compassion, and vision.

TABLE OF CONTENTS

CONTENTS OF THE CD-ROM

Introduction

Table of Standards and Expectations, Number and Operations, Pre-K–12

Applets

Fraction Models

Splitting Arrays to Solve Multiplication

Make Ten to Add

Blackline Masters and Templates

All the blackline masters listed above, plus the following:

Base-Ten Blocks

Inch Grid Paper

Fraction Circles

Fraction Strips

Pattern Blocks

Shaded Grids

16 × 25 Array

Multiplication Concept Cards

Readings from Publications of the National Council of Teachers of Mathematics

"Fractions Attack! Children Thinking and Talking Mathematically"
Patricia C. Alcaro, Alice S. Alston, and Nancy Katims
Teaching Children Mathematics

"Using Manipulative Models to Build Number Sense for
Addition of Fractions"
Kathleen Cramer and Apryl Henry
Making Sense of Fractions, Ratios, and Proportions
2002 Yearbook of the National Council of Teachers of Mathematics

"Misconceptions about Multiplication and Division"
Anna O. Graeber
Arithmetic Teacher

"The Decimal Dilemma"
Robert Glasgow, Gay Ragan, Wanda M. Fields, Robert Reys,
and Deanna Wasman
Teaching Children Mathematics

"Examining Dimensions of Fraction Operation Sense"
DeAnn Huinker
Making Sense of Fractions, Ratios, and Proportions
2002 Yearbook of the National Council of Teachers of Mathematics

"Multiplication and Division Word Problems: Improving
Students' Understanding"
DeAnn M. Huinker
Arithmetic Teacher

"Investigating Students' Conceptual Understanding of Decimal Fractions
Using Multiple Representations"
Sherri L. Martinie and Jennifer M. Bay-Williams
Mathematics Teaching in the Middle School

About This Book

Number and operations is the first of five content strands identified by *Principles and Standards for School Mathematics* (National Council of Teachers of Mathematics [NCTM] 2000). *Navigating through Number and Operations in Grades 3–5* is the second of four volumes on teaching about number and operations in the Navigations Series. These four Navigations volumes reflect the vision of number and operations concepts that *Principles and Standards* presents. Through selected instructional activities, they illustrate ideas in *Principles and Standards* about how to introduce these concepts, how they develop, what to expect of students during and at the end of each grade band, how to assess what students know, and how selected instructional activities can contribute to learning these concepts.

Learning about number and operations builds on children's earliest experiences with numbers and representations of numbers. After children enter school, they begin exploring relationships among numbers and number systems. They move gradually toward an understanding of the four basic operations—their meanings and their relationships with one another—and ultimately they develop computational fluency. The expectations of the Number and Operations Standard evolve as students grow and mature.

In elementary school, classroom teachers devote a large portion of their time to developing students' familiarity with number and operations. Conceptual understanding and computational fluency with whole numbers, fractions, and decimals form the bedrock of mathematics learning in both early and later years. In short, experience with number and operations is crucial, and most teachers recognize the importance of this topic in grades 3–5. At this level, the ultimate goal of work in number and operations is for students—*all* students—to develop a sense of number. This elusive yet critical set of understandings implies comfort and flexibility with numbers—wholes, fractions, and decimals —as well as with operations involving such numbers.

Teachers of grades 3–5 are responsible for much of their students' comprehension of the representation of numbers and the meanings of operations—particularly multiplication and division—and finally for their development of computational fluency. *Principles and Standards* notes that students in grades 3–5 should continue to develop a sense of number with a focus on multiplication and division: "Their understanding of the meanings of these operations should grow deeper as they encounter a range of representations and problem situations, learn about the properties of these operations, and develop fluency in whole-number computation" (NCTM 2000, p. 149).

This book focuses on the key topics relating to number that all teachers of grades 3–5 must address. Chapter 1 presents activities that stress the importance of understanding and representing numbers—in this case, whole numbers, fractions, and decimals. The emphasis here is on concepts of place value and comparing and ordering numbers. In

The activities in this book also support the core topics suggested for emphasis in grades 3–5 in NCTM's recently released *Curriculum Focal Points for Prekindergarten through Grade 6 Mathematics: A Quest for Coherence* (NCTM 2006). This new publication specifies by grade level essential content and processes that *Principles and Standards* discusses in depth by grade band.

addition, number theory makes an appearance in an activity involving prime, composite, and square numbers.

Chapter 2 emphasizes the importance of understanding operations. For students in grades 3–5, these operations include the multiplication and division of whole numbers, addition and subtraction of fractions, and multiplying and dividing numbers close to 1. Representation is once again an extremely important component of the chapter's activities.

Teaching basic facts—the fundamental number combinations of the integers 0–10 for addition and multiplication—may be one of the most challenging—and perhaps frustrating—topics for teachers of grades 3–5. Chapter 3 presents a problem-based approach to basic facts, with an emphasis on fact strategies and the use of arrays and other representations.

Chapter 4 focuses on algorithms and developing fluency in using them. Activities include the use of "adding up" in subtraction, applying the distributive property in the multiplication of whole numbers, using mental mathematics in division, making estimates, and visualizing operations involving fractions by using a clock as a representation tool.

Every chapter begins with a brief introduction to the five activities in the chapter. Each activity includes a summary, and recommended grade levels, student goals, prior knowledge or experience, and materials and equipment for the activity are specified. Most activities require one or more activity pages, which are identified in the materials list and signaled by an icon (see the key in the margin). These activity pages appear as reproducible blackline masters in the book's appendix and can also be printed directly from the CD-ROM that accompanies the book. Material on the CD-ROM, also signaled by an icon, includes three applets for students to use as well as suggested supplemental readings for teachers' professional development.

All the activities unfold in sections. An "Engage" section introduces important ideas and presents tasks intended to capture students' interest. An "Explore" section explains the core investigation that all students should be able to do. Some activities then present a "Reflect" section, suggesting how to guide students in thinking back on their work and consolidating their learning. Other activities integrate these ideas into the "Extend" section, which concludes every activity by offering ideas for helping students take the activity further or in a new direction. Throughout, the activities present questions that teachers can pose to stimulate students to think more deeply about mathematical ideas. Possible responses appear in parentheses after some questions. Margin notes include teaching tips and resources, as well as quotations from *Principles and Standards*, which are also signaled by an icon.

Like the other volumes in the Navigations Series, *Navigating through Number and Operations in Grades 3–5* does not offer a complete curriculum for number and operations in this grade band. Rather, teachers should use the book in conjunction with other instructional materials.

Three different icons appear in the book, as shown in the key. One alerts readers to materials quoted from *Principles and Standards for School Mathematics*, another points them to supplementary materials on the CD-ROM that accompanies the book, and a third signals the blackline masters and indicates their locations in the appendix.

Key to Icons

Principles and Standards

CD-ROM

Blackline Master

Three different icons appear in the book, as shown in the key. One alerts readers to material quoted from *Principles and Standards for School Mathematics,* another points them to supplementary materials on the CD-ROM that accompanies the book, and a third signals the blackline masters and indicates their locations in the appendix.

NAVIGATIONS SERIES

GRADES 3–5

NAVIGATING *through* NUMBER *and* OPERATIONS

Introduction

What could be more fundamental in mathematics than numbers and the operations that we perform with them? Thus, it is no surprise that Number and Operations heads the list of the five Content Standards in *Principles and Standards for School Mathematics* (NCTM 2000). Yet, numbers and arithmetic are so familiar to most of us that we run the risk of underestimating the deep, rich knowledge and proficiency that this Standard encompasses.

Fundamentals of an Understanding of Number and Operations

In elaborating the Number and Operations Standard, *Principles and Standards* recommends that instructional programs from prekindergarten through grade 12 enable all students to—

- understand numbers, ways of representing numbers, relationships among numbers, and number systems;
- understand meanings of operations and how they relate to one another;
- compute fluently and make reasonable estimates.

The vision that *Principles and Standards* outlines in the description of this Standard gives Number and Operations centrality across the entire mathematics curriculum. The *Navigating through Number and Operations*

1

volumes flesh out that vision and make it concrete in activities for students in four grade bands: prekindergarten through grade 2, grades 3–5, grades 6–8, and grades 9–12.

Understanding numbers, ways of representing numbers, relationships among numbers, and number systems

Young children begin to develop primitive ideas of number even before they enter school, and they arrive in the classroom with a range of informal understanding. They have probably learned to extend the appropriate number of fingers when someone asks, "How old are you?" and their vocabulary almost certainly includes some number words. They are likely to be able to associate these words correctly with small collections of objects, and they probably have been encouraged to count things, although they may not yet have mastered the essential one-to-one matching of objects to number names. During the years from prekindergarten through grade 2, their concepts and skills related to numbers and numeration, counting, representing and comparing quantities, and the operations of adding and subtracting will grow enormously as these ideas become the focus of the mathematics curriculum.

The most important accomplishments of the primary years include the refinement of children's understanding of counting and their initial development of number sense. Multiple classroom contexts offer numerous opportunities for students to count a myriad of things, from how many children are in their reading group, to how many cartons of milk their class needs for lunch, to how many steps they must take from the chalkboard to the classroom door. With experience, they learn to establish a one-to-one matching of objects counted with number words or numerals, and in time they recognize that the last number named is also the total number of objects in the collection. They also discover that the result of the counting process is not affected by the order in which they enumerate the objects. Eventually, they learn to count by twos or fives or tens or other forms of "skip counting," which requires that quantities be grouped in certain ways.

Though children initially encounter numbers by counting collections of physical objects, they go on to develop number concepts and the ability to think about numbers without needing the actual objects before them. They realize, for example, that five is one more than four and six is one more than five, and that, in general, the next counting number is one more than the number just named, whether or not actual objects are present for them to count. Through repeated experience, they also discover some important relationships, such as the connection between a number and its double, and they explore multiple ways of representing numbers, such as modeling six as six ones, or two threes, or three twos, or one more than five, or two plus four.

Young children are capable of developing number concepts that are more sophisticated than adults sometimes expect. Consider the prekindergarten child who explained her discovery that some numbers, like 2 and 4 and 6, are "fair numbers," or "sharing numbers," because she could divide these numbers of cookies equally with a friend, but numbers like 3 or 5 or 7 are not "fair numbers," because they do not have this property.

As children work with numbers, they discover ways of thinking about the relationships among them. They learn to compare two numbers to determine which is greater. If they are comparing 17 and 20, for example, they might match objects in two collections to see that 3 objects are "left over" in the set of 20 after they have "used up" the set of 17, or they might count on from 17 and find that they have to count three more numbers to get to 20. By exploring "How many more?" and "How many less?" young children lay the foundations for addition and subtraction.

Continual work with numbers in the primary grades contributes to students' development of an essential, firm understanding of place-value concepts and the base-ten numeration system. This understanding often emerges from work with concrete models, such as base-ten blocks or linking cubes, which engage students in the process of grouping and ungrouping units and tens. They must also learn to interpret, explain, and model the meaning of two- and three-digit numbers written symbolically. By the end of second grade, *Principles and Standards* expects students to be able to count into the hundreds, discover patterns in the numeration system related to place value, and compose (create through different combinations) and decompose (break apart in different ways) two- and three-digit numbers.

In addition, students in grade 2 should begin to extend their understanding of whole numbers to include early ideas about fractions. Initial experiences with fractions should introduce simple concepts, such as the idea that halves or fourths signify divisions of things into two or four equal parts, respectively.

As students move into grades 3–5, their study of numbers expands to include larger whole numbers as well as fractions, decimals, and negative numbers. Now the emphasis shifts from addition and subtraction to multiplication and division, and the study of numbers focuses more directly on the multiplicative structure of the base-ten numeration system. Students should understand a number like 435 as representing $(4 \times 100) + (3 \times 10) + (5 \times 1)$, and they should explore what happens to numbers when they multiply or divide them by powers of 10.

The number line now becomes an important model for representing the positions of numbers in relation to benchmarks like 1/2, 1, 10, 100, 500, and so on. It also provides a useful tool at this stage for representing fractions, decimals, and negative integers as well as whole numbers.

Concepts of fractions that the curriculum treated informally in the primary grades gain new meaning in grades 3–5 as students learn to interpret fractions both as parts of a whole and as divisions of numbers. Various models contribute to students' developing understanding. For example, an area model in which a circle or a rectangle is divided into equal parts, some of which are shaded, helps students visualize fractions as parts of a unit whole or determine equivalent fractions.

Number-line models are again helpful, allowing students to compare fractions to useful benchmarks. For instance, they can decide that 3/5 is greater than 1/3 because 3/5 is more than 1/2 but 1/3 is less than 1/2,

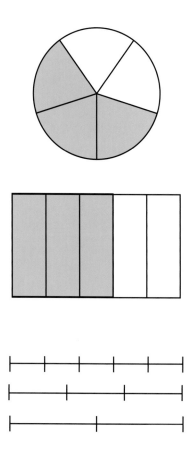

or they can recognize that 9/10 is greater than 7/8 because 9/10 is closer to 1 than 7/8 is. Parallel number lines, such as one marked in multiples of 1/3 and another in multiples of 1/6, can help students identify equivalences.

During these upper elementary years, students also encounter the concept of percent as another model for a part of a whole. Their work should help them begin to develop benchmarks for common percentages, such as 25 percent, $33\frac{1}{3}$ percent, or 50 percent.

In grades 6–8, students expand their understanding of numbers to include the integers, and now they learn how to add, subtract, multiply, and divide with negative as well as positive numbers. Developing a deeper understanding of rational numbers is another very important goal for these students, who must increase their facility in working with rational numbers represented by fractions, decimals, and percents.

At this level, the curriculum places particular emphasis on developing proportional reasoning, which requires students to understand and use ratios, proportions, and rates to model and solve problems. Fraction strips, circles, number lines, area models, hundreds grids, and other physical models provide concrete representations from which students can draw conceptual meaning as they hone their understanding of rational numbers. Exposure to these models develops students' abilities to translate fluently from one representation to another, to compare and order rational numbers, and to attach meaning to rational numbers expressed in different but equivalent forms.

The concept of proportionality, which is a central component of the middle-school curriculum, serves to connect many aspects of mathematics, such as the slope of the linear function $y = mx$ in algebra, the scale factor in measurements on maps or scale drawings, the ratio of the circumference to the diameter of a circle (π) in geometry, or the relative frequency of a statistic in a set of data. Thus, students have numerous opportunities to develop and use number concepts in multiple contexts and applications. In some of those contexts, students encounter very large or very small numbers, which necessitate scientific notation and a sense of orders of magnitude of numbers.

Finally, students in grades 6–8 are able to focus more directly on properties of numbers than they were at earlier stages of development. They can investigate such key ideas as the notions of factor and multiple, prime and composite numbers, factor trees, divisibility tests, special sets (like the triangular and square numbers), and many interesting number patterns and relationships, including an introduction to some irrational numbers, such as $\sqrt{2}$.

When students move on to grades 9–12, their understanding of number should continue to grow and mature. In these grades, students customarily encounter many problems, both in mathematics and in related disciplines like science or economics, where very large and very small numbers are commonplace. In working such problems, students can use technology that displays large and small numbers in several ways, such as 1.219 E17 for 1.219 (10^{17}), and they need to become fluent in expressing and interpreting such quantities.

High school students also have many opportunities to work with irrational numbers, and these experiences should lead them to an understanding of the real number system—and, beyond that, to an understanding of number systems themselves. Moreover, students in grades 9–12 should develop an awareness of the relationship of those systems to various types of equations. For example, they should understand that the equation $A + 5 = 10$ has a whole-number solution, but the equation $A + 10 = 5$ does not, though it does have an integer solution. They should recognize that the equation $10 \cdot A = 5$ requires the rational numbers for its solution, and the equation $A^2 = 5$ has a real-number solution, but the equation $A^2 + 10 = 5$ is solved in the complex numbers.

Students should also understand the one-to-one correspondence between real numbers and points on the number line. They should recognize important properties of real numbers, such as that between any two real numbers there is always another real number, or that irrational numbers can be only approximated, but never represented exactly, by fractions or repeating decimals.

In grades 9–12, students also encounter new systems, such as vectors and matrices, which they should explore and compare to the more familiar number systems. Such study will involve them in explicit examination of the associative, commutative, and distributive properties and will expand their horizons to include a system (matrices) in which multiplication is not commutative. Using matrices, students can represent and solve a variety of problems in other areas of mathematics. They can find solutions to systems of linear equations, for instance, or describe a transformation of a geometric figure in the plane. Using algebraic symbols and reasoning, students also can explore interesting number properties and relationships, determining, for example, that the sum of two consecutive triangular numbers is always a square number and that the sum of the first N consecutive odd integers is equal to N^2.

Understanding meanings of operations and how operations relate to one another

As young children in prekindergarten through grade 2 learn to count and develop number sense, they simultaneously build their understanding of addition and subtraction. This occurs naturally as children compare numbers to see who collected more stickers or as they solve problems like the following: "When Tim and his dad went fishing, they caught seven fish. Tim caught four of the fish. How many did his dad catch?" Often, children use concrete materials, such as cubes or chips, to model "joining" or "take-away" problems, and they develop "counting on" or "counting back" strategies to solve problems about "how many altogether?" and "how many more?" and similar relationships.

Even at this early stage, teachers who present problems in everyday contexts can represent the problem symbolically. For example, teachers can represent the problem "How many more books does Emily need to read if she has already read 13 books and wants to read 20 books before the end of the school year?" as $13 + \square = 20$ or as $20 - \square = 13$. Such expressions help students to see the relationship between addition and subtraction.

Young children also build an understanding of the operations when they explain the thinking behind their solutions. For example, a child who had just celebrated his sixth birthday wondered, "How much is

6 and 7?" After thinking about the problem for a moment, he decided that 6 + 7 = 13, and then he explained how he knew: "Well, I just had a birthday, and for my birthday I got two 'five dollars,' and my $5 and $5 are $10, so 6 and 6 should be 12, and then 6 and 7 must be 13."

As young students work with addition and subtraction, they should also be introduced to the associative and commutative properties of the operations. They should learn that when they are doing addition, they can use the numbers in any order, but they should discover that this fact is not true for subtraction. Further, they should use the commutative property to develop effective strategies for computation. For example, they might rearrange the problem 3 + 5 + 7 to 3 + 7 + 5 = (3 + 7) + 5 = 10 + 5 = 15.

Early work with addition and subtraction also lays the conceptual groundwork for later study of operations. Multiplication and division are all but evident when students repeatedly add the same number—for example, in skip-counting by twos or fives—or when they solve problems requiring that a collection of objects be shared equally among several friends. The strategies that young children use to solve such problems, either repeatedly adding the same number or partitioning a set into equal-sized subsets, later mature into computational strategies for multiplication and division.

The operations of multiplication and division, and the relationships between them, receive particular emphasis in grades 3–5. Diagrams, pictures, and concrete manipulatives play important roles as students deepen their understanding of these operations and develop their facility in performing them.

For example, if an area model calls for students to arrange 18 square tiles into as many different rectangles as they can, the students can relate the three possible solutions (1 by 18, 2 by 9, and 3 by 6) to the factors of 18. Similar problems will show that some numbers, like 36 or 64, have many possible rectangular arrangements and hence many factors, while other numbers, like 37 or 41, yield only one solution and thus have only two factors. By comparing pairs of rectangular arrangements, such as 3 by 6 and 6 by 3, students can explore the commutative property for multiplication. As illustrated in the three examples below,

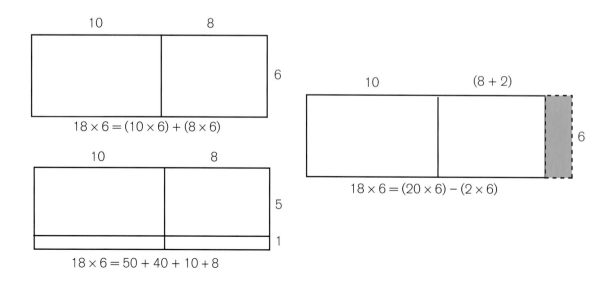

by decomposing an 18-by-6 area model, students can develop an understanding of the distributive property.

Other models for multiplication might involve rates or combinations. In grades 3–5, a typical problem involving a rate might be, "If 4 pencils cost 69¢, how much will a dozen pencils cost?" Problems involving combinations at this level are often similar to the following: "How many different kinds of meat-and-cheese sandwiches can we make if we have 2 kinds of bread (white and wheat), 4 kinds of meat (beef, ham, chicken, and turkey), and 3 kinds of cheese (Swiss, American, and provolone)?" (See the tree diagram below.)

To develop students' understanding of division, teachers should engage them in working with two different models—a partitioning model ("If you have 36 marbles and want to share them equally among 4 people, how many marbles should each person receive?") and a repeated-subtraction model ("If you have 36 marbles and need to place 4 marbles into each cup in a game, how many cups will you fill?"). Students should be able to represent both models with manipulatives and diagrams.

In exploring division, students in grades 3–5 will inevitably encounter situations that produce a remainder, and they should examine what the remainder means, how large it can be for a given divisor, and how to interpret it in different contexts. For example, arithmetically,

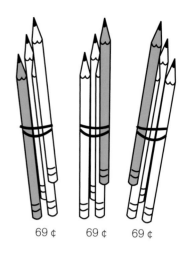

69 ¢   69 ¢   69 ¢

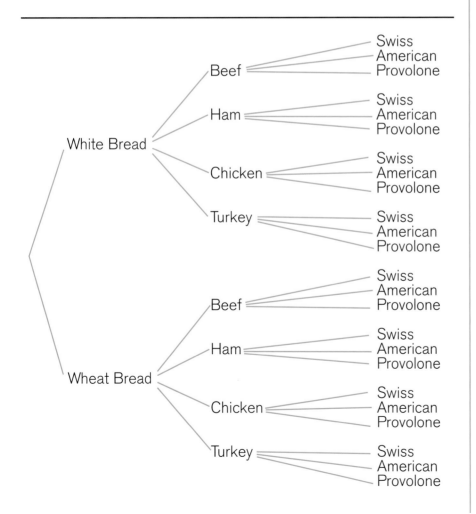

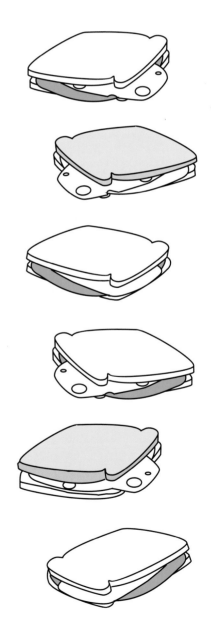

$28 \div 5 = 5\frac{3}{5}$, but consider the solutions to each of the following problems:

- "Compact disks are on sale for $28 for 5 disks. How much should one disk cost?" ($5.60)
- "Muffins are packaged 5 to a box for the bake sale. How many boxes can you make up if you bake 28 muffins?" (5).
- "Parents will be transporting children in minivans for the class field trip. Each van can take 5 children. The class has 28 children. How many vans will parents need to drive for the trip?" (6).

The understanding of all four operations that students build with whole numbers in the upper elementary grades broadens during grades 6–8, when they apply those operations to fractions, decimals, percents, and integers. Moreover, as students operate with rational numbers and integers, they encounter new contexts that may challenge their conceptual foundations. For example, when students are multiplying or dividing with fractions or decimals between 0 and 1, they see results that expose as misconceptions the commonly held beliefs that "multiplication makes larger" and "division makes smaller."

Other challenges that middle-grades students must confront include understanding when the result of a computation with integers is positive and when it is negative, knowing how to align decimals in computations with decimal fractions, and recognizing where in an answer to place a decimal point. Operating with fractions has proven difficult for many students. Lacking conceptual understanding, many have tried to get by with rote application of procedures that they don't understand. In the middle grades, therefore, it is important that students develop an understanding of the meaning of such concepts as numerator, denominator, and equivalent fractions and their roles in adding and subtracting fractions.

Middle school students need to model and compare expressions that are frequently subject to confusion, such as "divide by 2," "multiply by 1/2," and "divide by 1/2," and they must see that different models of division are sometimes required to give meaning to such ideas. For example, "divide by 2" can be modeled by a partitioning model ("separate the amount into two equal quantities"), but "divide by 1/2" is more appropriately represented by a repeated-subtraction model:

"You made $2\frac{3}{4}$ gallons of lemonade. How many $\frac{1}{2}$-gallon bottles can you fill?"

$$\left(2\frac{3}{4} \div \frac{1}{2} = 5, \text{ with a remainder of } \frac{1}{4} \text{ gallon}\right)$$

Encouraging students to estimate and evaluate the reasonableness of the results of their computations is important in helping them expand their number sense.

As students' algebraic concepts grow during grades 6–8, they will also frequently face computations involving variables, and they will need to extend their understanding of the operations and their properties to encompass simplification of and operations with algebraic expressions. Understanding the inverse relationship between addition and subtraction, between multiplication and division, and between "square" and "square root" will be important in such tasks.

In grades 9–12, students should go beyond producing the results of specific computations to generalize about operations and their properties and to relate them to functions and their graphs. For example, they should describe and compare the behavior of functions such as $f(x) = 2x$, $g(x) = x + 2$, $h(x) = x^2$, or $j(x) = \sqrt{x}$. They should reason about number relations, describing, for instance, the value of $a \cdot b$ where a and b are positive numbers and $a + b = 50$. They should understand and correctly apply the results of operating with positive or negative numbers when they are working with both equations and inequalities.

In addition, high school students should learn to perform operations in other systems. They should find vector sums in the plane, add and multiply matrices, or use multiplicative reasoning to represent counting problems and combinatorics.

Computing fluently and making reasonable estimates

Although an understanding of numbers and the meanings of the various operations is essential, it is insufficient unless it is accompanied by the development of computational proficiency and a sense of the reasonableness of computational results. Computational skills emerge in the prekindergarten and early elementary years in conjunction with students' developing understanding of whole numbers and counting.

Young children's earliest computational strategies usually involve counting. As they think about number problems involving addition or subtraction, young students devise different solution schemes, and teachers should listen carefully to their students' explanations of these thinking strategies. Encouraging children to explain their methods and discussing different students' strategies with the class helps students deepen their understanding of numbers and operations and refine their computational abilities.

At first, young children rely heavily on physical objects to represent numerical situations and relationships, and they use such objects to model their addition and subtraction results. Over time, they learn to represent the same problems symbolically, and eventually they carry out the computations mentally or with paper and pencil, without needing the actual physical objects. Students should have enough experience and practice to master the basic one-digit addition and subtraction combinations, and they should combine that knowledge with their understanding of base-ten numeration so that, by the end of grade 2, they can add and subtract with two-digit numbers.

As students become more proficient with addition and subtraction, teachers can help them examine the efficiency and generalizability of their invented strategies and can lead them to an understanding of standard computational algorithms. When students understand the procedures that they are employing, they are able to carry them out with accuracy and efficiency.

In grades 3–5, students should extend their knowledge of basic number combinations to include single-digit multiplication and division facts, and by the end of the upper elementary years they should be able to compute fluently with whole numbers. As students develop their computational proficiency, teachers should guide them in examining and explaining their various approaches and in understanding algorithms for addition, subtraction, multiplication, and division and employing them effectively. In turn, teachers must understand that there is more than one algorithm for each of the operations, and they should recognize that the algorithms that are meaningful to students may not be the ones that have traditionally been taught or that some people have come to assume offer "the right way" to solve a problem.

In grades 3–5, students are beginning to work with larger numbers, and it is important for them to develop a strong sense of the reasonableness of a computational result and a facility in estimating results before computing. It will often be appropriate for students to use calculators when they are working with larger numbers. At other times, paper and pencil may be appropriate, or it may be reasonable for teachers to expect mental computation. Teachers and students should discuss various situations to assist students in developing good judgment about when to use mental arithmetic, paper and pencil, or technology for whole-number computation.

Other aspects of computational fluency in the 3–5 grade band involve understanding the associative, commutative, and distributive properties and seeing how those properties can be used to simplify a computation. Students at this level will also encounter problems that require the introduction of order-of-operations conventions.

While students in grades 3–5 are honing their skills with whole-number computation, they also will be spending a great deal of time developing an understanding of fractions and decimals. However, computing with rational numbers should not be the focus of their attention yet. Rather, students should apply their understanding of fractions and decimals and the properties of the operations to problems that include fractions or decimals. For example, "How many sheets of construction paper will Jackie need to make 16 Halloween decorations if each decoration uses $2\frac{1}{4}$ sheets of paper?" General procedures for calculating with rational numbers and integers will be the focus of instruction in the next grade band.

In grades 6–8, students learn methods for computing with fractions and decimals as extensions of their understanding of rational numbers and their facility in computing with whole numbers. As with whole-number computation, students develop an understanding of computing with fractions, decimals, and integers by considering problems in context, making estimates of reasonable expectations for the results, devising and explaining methods that make sense to them, and comparing their strategies with those of others as well as with standard algorithms. When calculating with fractions and decimals, students must learn to assess situations and decide whether an exact answer is required or whether an estimate is appropriate. They should also develop useful benchmarks to help them assess the reasonableness of results when they are calculating with rational numbers, integers, and percents. Computational fluency at the middle grades also includes a facility in reasoning about and solving problems involving proportions and rates.

In grades 9–12, students should extend their computational proficiency to real numbers and should confidently choose among mental mathematics, paper-and-pencil calculations, and computations with technology to obtain results that offer an appropriate degree of precision. They should perform complex calculations involving powers and roots, vectors, and matrices, as well as real numbers, and they should exhibit a well-developed number sense in judging the reasonableness of calculations, including calculations performed with the aid of technology.

Numbers and Operations in the Mathematics Curriculum

Without numbers and operations there would be no mathematics. Accordingly, the mathematics curriculum must foster the development of both number sense and computational fluency across the entire pre-K–12 continuum. The Number and Operations Standard describes the core of understanding and proficiency that students are expected to attain, and a curriculum that leads to the outcomes envisioned in this Standard must be coherent, developmental, focused, and well articulated across the grades. At all levels, students should develop a true understanding of numbers and operations that will undergird their development of computational fluency.

The *Navigating through Number and Operations* books provide insight into the ways in which the fundamental ideas of number and operations can develop over the pre-K–12 years. These Navigations volumes, however, do not—and cannot—undertake to describe a complete curriculum for number and operations. The concepts described in the Number and Operations Standard regularly apply in other mathematical contexts related to the Algebra, Geometry, Measurement, and Data Analysis and Probability Standards. Activities such as those described in the four *Navigating through Number and Operations* books reinforce and enhance understanding of the other mathematics strands, just as those other strands lend context and meaning to number sense and computation.

The development of mathematical literacy relies on deep understanding of numbers and operations as set forth in *Principles and Standards for School Mathematics*. These *Navigations* volumes are presented as a guide to help educators set a course for the successful implementation of this essential Standard.

NAVIGATING *through* NUMBER *and* OPERATIONS

Chapter 1
Understanding and Representing Numbers

The importance of understanding and representing numbers expands during grades 3–5. Students encounter larger whole numbers as well as numbers in different systems, such as rational numbers and negative integers. They learn to judge the relative sizes of numbers. An important step in building a sense of number is discerning relationships among common representations of rational numbers—fractions, decimal numbers, and percentages. Students begin work with number theory, encountering prime and composite numbers. They learn about factorization, examining such ideas as greatest common factor and common multiples. They also become acquainted with square numbers.

As students encounter larger whole numbers in grades 3–5, developing *benchmarks* for such large numbers as 100, 1,000, and even 10,000 becomes helpful. Consider the number 10,000. You might ask your students:

- "How could you express this number in dollars? You could say $10 \times \$1,000$ or $100 \times \$100$."

- "How about distance? How far is 10,000 meters? Did you know that a 10K race is 10 kilometers, or 10,000 meters? How far is that? Could you run or walk that distance? Really fast runners can run that distance in a half hour. A person could drive that distance in about ten minutes."

Placing large numbers in a familiar context helps students understand their size or magnitude.

Benchmarks are important for rational numbers as well. Halves, fourths, and thirds are obvious benchmarks. Motivate the students to think about the magnitude of rational numbers and relationships among them with such questions as the following:

- "How much of that pie is $\frac{1}{2}$?"

- "How many of the apples in the basket would equal one-half?"

- "How long would half the clothesline be? Can you represent this length by using a number line?"

- "Which is the least time—a half hour, a quarter hour, or one-third of an hour? How can you show this on a clock?"

- "How can you think of $\frac{1}{2}$ as a decimal? As a percentage?"

- "Supermarkets sell 2 percent milk. How could you write this percentage as a decimal? As a fraction?"

At the heart of the students' work with numbers in grades 3–5 is *place value*. Noting the position and value of a number and naming the number are important skills. Students benefit from experiences that require them to read, write, and name numbers. The ability to represent numbers includes the ability to think *flexibly* about numbers; students should recognize, for example, that $134 = 100 + 30 + 4 = (25 \times 5) + 9 = 150 - 16 = (100 + 25) + (10 - 1)$, and so forth.

Activities that ask the students to represent a special "number of the day"—a whole number, fraction, or decimal number—in a variety of ways can help build such flexibility, which at this level is particularly important with whole numbers. At the same time, similar attention to related rational numbers is also essential.

The five activities in this chapter are intended to develop students' understanding of whole numbers, fractions, and decimals through the use of a variety of representations. Several of the content areas reflected in the activities are quite broad. A single, one-day lesson could not include all the content encompassed by that area. Also, because the amount of time that teachers spend on mathematics each day varies, it is not possible to develop a one-day lesson that will fit the time for all classes in grades 3–5. You may develop a one-day or multi-day lesson from the activities. Alternatively, depending on your students' needs and your preferences, you may selectively choose tasks that the students can complete during a one-day lesson.

"In grades 3–5, students' study and use of numbers should be extended to include larger numbers, fractions, and decimals."
(NCTM 2000, p. 149)

Place Value in Whole Numbers and Decimals

Grades 3 and 4

Summary

Students expand their understanding of place value in both whole numbers and decimals.

Goals

- Understand place value within the base-ten number system
- Represent whole numbers and decimals by using concrete models and number symbols
- Compare and order whole numbers and decimals by using concrete models and number symbols

Prior Knowledge or Experience

- Experience with base-ten blocks

Materials and Equipment

For each student—
- A set of base-ten blocks—40 units (ones), 30 rods (tens), and 5 flats (hundreds)—per student or pair of students (can be made from the template "Base-Ten Blocks" on the CD-ROM)
- A copy of each of the following blackline masters:
  - "Spin to Win"
  - "Place-Value Mat—Whole Numbers"
  - "Place-Value Mat—Decimal Numbers"
- One or two sheets of paper

For every 3–4 students—
- A pair of dice

For the teacher—
- Two sets of overhead base-ten blocks (can be cut from transparencies of the template "Base-Ten Blocks" on the CD-ROM)
- Transparencies of the following blackline masters:
  - "Spin to Win"
  - "Spinner Master"
  - "Place-Value Mat—Whole Numbers"
  - "Place-Value Mat—Decimal Numbers"
- A "clicker" or other device for producing a sound (a block of wood that you can tap on, or two wooden sticks that you can strike together, for example)
- *A Place for Zero* (LoPresti 2003)

"Students who understand the structure of numbers and the relationship among numbers can work with them flexibly."
(NCTM 2000, p. 149, referring to Fuson [1992])

pp. 158, 159, 160, 161

A ones-block ("unit" or "single")

A tens-block ("rod" or "long")

A hundreds-block ("flat")

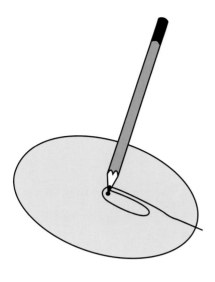

The accompanying CD-ROM includes the template "Base-Ten Blocks," which you can reproduce on cardstock or paper (and laminate for greater durability if you wish) to make base-ten manipulatives for your students. If commercial overhead base-ten blocks are unavailable, you can also reproduce the template on transparencies, cut out transparent base-ten-blocks, and color them with markers for use on an overhead projector.

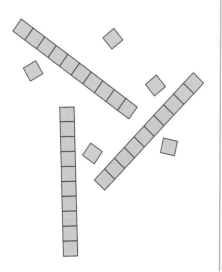

- A paper clip and pencil
- Overhead projector

Activity

Engage

Engage the whole class in a quick game to introduce the concept of *place value*. Give each student a copy of the blackline master "Spin to Win." You will need an overhead spinner, which you can make from the template "Spinner Master." Reproduce the template on a transparency, and use a paper clip and a pencil to produce a workable spinner (see the margin).

For each game, you will spin five numbers. Your students must place each number that you spin in one of the five game circles on their "Spin to Win" sheets. Use a transparency of the blackline master to explain the game. Be sure that the students understand that their goal is to make the largest four-digit whole number that they can without moving or erasing a number once they have placed it in a circle. Each game includes a "Reject" circle, which allows the students to discard one number instead of placing it in a game circle.

At the end of a game, help the students compare their numbers to determine which number is the largest. Ask, "What strategies could you use to create the largest number? The smallest number?" Discuss the students' responses.

Another good starting point for teaching about *place value* in whole numbers is a "Tell Me" activity. For example, using transparent copies of base-ten blocks, you can display unit pieces (ones) on the overhead projector. Say to your students, "Tell me how many units you see." Add or remove unit pieces or arrange them in different patterns on the overhead projector. Each time say, "Tell me how many units you see."

Next, add rods (tens-blocks). Place three rods and five units on the overhead. Say, "Tell me the place-value name of this number." (3 tens and 5 ones) Then say, "Tell me the standard base-ten name of this number." (35) Use different combinations of tens- and ones-blocks, as well as different patterns and groupings of blocks (see the illustration in the margin). Say, "When you use base-ten blocks, 3 rods and 5 units will always equal 3 tens and 5 ones. This is another way of saying 35, regardless of the way you arrange the blocks."

Now show a two-digit number—for example, 54—on the overhead projector. You could represent this number as 5 rods and 4 units. Ask the students to tell you the number. Then ask them to suggest other ways of representing 54 with tens- and ones-blocks (for examples, 4 rods and 14 units, 54 units, and so on). Show other two-digit numbers and have the students tell you what the numbers are.

Then add a flat (hundreds-block), and continue the activity with three-digit numbers. Some students may benefit from using the blackline master "Place-Value Mat—Whole Numbers." The mat serves as a graphic organizer for the representations of the hundreds, tens, and ones in numbers used by the students. If you think the mat would be helpful, distribute copies of it and show how to use it.

Next, show one flat, five rods, and three units to represent the number 153 on the overhead projector. Ask the students to use pencil and paper and write the number that the blocks represent. Have them first use standard or expanded base-ten notation (153 or 1 hundred, 5 tens, and 3 ones) and then have them use hundreds, tens, and ones notation to name this number in a *different* way—for example, 15 tens and 3 ones; 12 tens and 33 ones; 1 hundred, 4 tens, and 13 ones, and so forth.

Note that in addition to base-ten blocks, teachers can use other proportional manipulative materials to teach place-value concepts. These materials include bean sticks, Popsicle sticks, and various types of interlocking cubes. Ideally, students should have experience with at least one other manipulative besides base-ten blocks so that their understanding of place value and related concepts does not depend on a single representation.

Explore

After "Tell Me" activities, introduce "Show Me" activities. Distribute to the students sets of base-ten blocks and copies of the blackline master "Place-Value Mats—Whole Numbers." Say, "Use your base-ten blocks to show me a two-digit number—how about 42?" After they have represented the number successfully, continue: "Now show me that number in a different way." (For example, they could show 42 as 2 tens and 22 ones.) Let the students practice this skill with other two-digit numbers.

Next say, "Use your base-ten blocks to show me a three-digit number —how about 108?" The students might use one flat and eight units. Again ask the students to show the number in a different way. (For example, instead of using a flat, they could show 108 as ten rods and eight units, or nine rods and eighteen units, etc.) Encourage the students to use their place-value mats for this activity. Demonstrate how to arrange flats, rods, and units in the appropriate columns to construct a number. Numbers with zeroes in the ones or tens place may be especially difficult for some students to express in expanded notation or show with base-ten blocks.

As the students construct numbers and express them in different ways, monitor their work. Assist them individually as needed. This process will give you an opportunity to assess your students' understanding of place value and determine whether they need additional practice with "Show Me" activities.

Have the students organize their base-ten blocks according to ones, tens, and hundreds, and then introduce a little game called "Make a Square." Show the students a "clicker" (or another device for producing a sound—two sticks that you can tap together, for example). Say, "Listen carefully to the clicks that I'm making. How many clicks do you hear? How could you show that number on your place-value mat? Place ones-blocks on your mat to equal the number of clicks."

For example, click the clicker three times. The students should add three ones-blocks to the ones column on their place-value mats. Click the clicker another five times. The students should add five more ones-blocks to the ones column on their mats. Click the clicker another four times. When the students add four more ones-blocks to the ones column on their mats, for a total of twelve ones-blocks in the ones column, they should trade ten ones-blocks for one tens-block so that

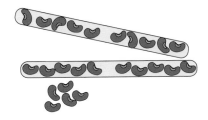

Bean sticks are a manipulative tool that you or your students can make and use to reinforce place-value concepts. Dried beans (such as pinto beans) serve as units, and ten beans glued to a craft stick serve as a ten. Complete instructions for constructing bean sticks are available at http://illuminations.nctm.org/lessons/count20/beanstick.pdf.

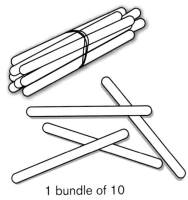

1 bundle of 10
Popsicle sticks + 4 sticks =
10 + 4 = 14

Students can count Popsicle sticks as units and bundle them as tens. They can also use interlocking cubes individually as units and snap cubes together as a ten.

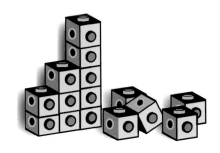

their place-value mats will show one ten and two ones (12 = one rod and two units).

As you continue clicking the clicker, the students should continue to add ones-blocks to their place-value mats. Emphasize that they should always have the fewest blocks possible in the ones column of their place-value mats. Encourage them to make all possible ten-for-one trades, converting every ten ones-blocks into one tens-block. When they have ten tens-blocks, they can trade these for a hundreds-block. Getting a hundreds-block, or a flat, "makes a square" and thus completes the game.

After the students have added blocks and made all possible trades, they should record on a sheet of paper the base-ten number that represents the total number of blocks. For four ones-blocks, they will record 4; for eight ones-blocks, they will record 8; for one tens-block and two ones-blocks, they will record 12; and for one hundreds-block, they will record 100. At the beginning of the activity and during the first few trades, demonstrate these procedures for the students on the overhead projector, focusing especially on the few times when they make ten-for-one trades.

As your students become proficient in adding units and making trades, generate larger numbers and more frequent trades by using the overhead circle spinner (for numbers up to 9) or a pair of dice (for numbers up to 12). Continue until the students reach 100 and have made enough trades to add a hundreds-block, or flat, to their mats. You could continue the activity by having the students make a second square. The students could also play "Make the Square Disappear" by removing blocks from their place-value mats according to the numbers produced by a clicker, a spinner, or a pair of dice.

The games "Make a Square" and "Make a Square Disappear" reinforce the regrouping of numbers that many addition and subtraction problems require. Students can benefit from additional experience with both games, which they should play with base-ten blocks and other manipulatives.

Another game based on place value with whole numbers is "Race for a Square." To play this game, organize your students into groups of three or four. Have students in each group take turns rolling two dice. Each player rolls a number, puts that many unit squares on his or her place-value mat, and makes all possible ten-for-one trades. The game continues until one player has enough tens and ones blocks to make a square. This player wins the race for a square.

Reflect

Have the students reflect on what their work has taught them about place value. Write a three-digit number—for example, 647—on the board. Call on some students to count forward from 647 by ones, naming the next ten numbers. Have other students count backwards from 647 by ones, naming the preceding ten numbers. Ask other students, "What is 10 more than 647? What is 10 less than 647? What is 100 more? What is 100 less?" Use the same number and see how many different ways students can express it with ones, tens, and hundreds. Repeat these questions with other numbers. For younger students, teachers should start this activity with two-digit numbers and then move to three-digit numbers.

Have the students discuss their experiences with *place value* and the base-ten number system. Questions could include the following:

- "How would you define or describe *place value*?" (The *place* of a digit tells the digit's *value* in a particular system of numeration. For example, in the case of the base-ten number 234, the 3 is in the tens place, so the value of the 3 is 3 × 10, or 30.)
- "What is the distinguishing characteristic of the base-ten number system?" (grouping by tens)
- "How would you explain the base-ten number system to someone who knew nothing about it?" (Every time you have ten of a particular quantity, you trade the group of ten for one of the next quantity. For example, if you had ten units, you would trade them for one ten. If you had ten tens, you would trade them for one hundred, etc.)
- "Why do you think we use a base-ten number system rather than a system in another base, such as base two, base five, or base twenty?" (The place value system that we customarily use is based on groups of tens. It is likely that this system became dominant because each person has ten digits on his or her own two hands. The number of objects grouped together in a number system is called its base.)

Extend

You can extend your students' learning about place value in a variety of ways. The following four strategies are examples.

Strategy 1. Expand on "Tell Me" and "Show Me" activities to give students practice in comparing and ordering numbers. "Show Me, Show Me, Tell Me" is a related game that you can play with your students. Name two numbers and ask the students to show both numbers on their place-value mats. Then have them compare the numbers and describe the relationship between them. The students can show three or more numbers on their place-value mats and order them from largest to smallest or smallest to largest.

Strategy 2 Move from manipulative models to symbolic representations of numbers. Forming a "Human Place-Value Chart" is one way to help students make this transfer, and it can be especially useful for exploring place value beyond the hundreds place. Write the

following digits on twelve sheets of paper (one number per sheet): 0, 0, 0, 1, 2, 3, 4, 5, 6, 7, 8, and 9. Make the numerals large enough for your students to see from anywhere in the classroom. Randomly distribute the sheets with the numbers 1–9 to the class. Ask the nine students with these digits to come to the front of the classroom to form a "Human Place-Value Chart." As the students come up, randomly arrange them in a straight line and have them hold their numbers in front of them. A nine-digit number—for example, 572,193,468 — should now be visible. Have the students in the class name this number.

Use the human place-value chart to review work with ones, tens, and hundreds places. Have the students name each three-digit *number period*, sometimes referred to as a "number family." Each group of three

"*The curriculum should devote substantial attention to developing an understanding of the decimal place-value system, to using its features in calculating and problem solving, and to explaining calculation and problem solving methods with decimal fractions.*" (Kilpatrick, Swafford, and Findell 2001, p. 417)

Number periods, sometimes called "number families," are groups of three digits, counting from the right, in large whole numbers. Each group takes its name from the place of the rightmost digit in the group. Thus, a number may have a "units period," "thousands period," "millions period," "billions period," and so on.

Some interesting very large numbers appear in *On Beyond a Million* (Schwartz 2001) and *Can You Count to a Googol?* (Wells 2000).

Information on number periods to 1 centillion is available at http://mathworld.com/ LargeNumber.html.

digits takes its name from the place of the rightmost digit in the group. For example, in the number 572,193,468, the three-digit group 468 is the "units period," the group 193 is the "thousands period," and the group 572 is the "millions period." The students should note that neither "tens" nor "hundreds" ever appear in the names of three-digit number periods.

Have the students in the human place-value chart randomly switch places to form another nine-digit number. Again, ask the students in the class to name the number. As time allows, extend the place-value chart to the billions period by distributing the number sheets with the three zeroes, asking those students to come up, and inserting them into various places in the human place-value chart to form a twelve-digit number—for example: 260,804,017,359. Have the place-value chart randomly show twelve-digit numbers (keeping zero out of the hundred billions place), and direct the students to name the place and value of various digits as well as the numbers.

Next, build a new human place-value chart by asking the students who were part of the original human place-value chart to give their number sheets to other students in the class and let them take their place in the chart. Write the new number on the board, ask the members of the new place-value chart to form that number, and then select someone from the class to read the number. If the students need further practice, have the human place-value chart form additional numbers.

By adding more members to the place-value chart, you can extend numbers to the trillions place and beyond. The class could even form a human place-value chart involving every student in the class and make a number that would be very large. A class with twenty-six students could make a twenty-six-digit number that would be in the septillions (10^{25})—an extremely large number! The number 13 septillion (13,000,000,000,000,000,000,000,000) represents the approximate weight of the earth in pounds. Involve all the students in the class to create a class number as close to 13 septillion as possible. Some students may need to hold a number sheet in each hand, or two students may need to share one number sheet, to have exactly twenty-six digits. Two other interesting large numbers that students can build by using the nine-digit human place-value chart are 284,365,179 (the number of seconds that a child will have lived by the end of the first week after his or her ninth birthday) and 294,817,653 (the approximate population of the United States in early 2005).

Strategy 3. Read aloud to the class the picture book *A Place for Zero* (LoPresti 2003). This story recounts the adventures that lead Zero to

Navigating through Number and Operations in Grades 3–5

the discovery of his place in the land of Digitaria. Through an interesting plot and colorful illustrations, this book describes the importance of zero as a placeholder.

Strategy 4. Modify all the activities in this lesson and use them to teach concepts of place value that relate to decimal numbers. The blackline master "Place-Value Mats—Decimal Numbers" can help extend place-value concepts to the hundredths place. Students can use a flat to represent one whole, or 1; a rod to represent one tenth, or 0.1; and a unit to represent one hundredth, or 0.01. They can assemble 1.87, for example, with one flat, 8 rods, and 7 units.

In this activity, students have worked with manipulatives to strengthen their understanding of concepts of place value for whole numbers. The next activity invites them to classify numbers by type and helps them learn about three important types of whole numbers—primes, composites, and squares.

In *A Place for Zero* (LoPresti 2003), Zero has nothing to add, so he can't play Addemup with the other numbers. Zero is sad until he discovers his own place—and value—as a place holder in Digitaria.

If you do not have access to overhead square tiles, make transparencies of the template "Inch Grid Paper" (on the CD-ROM) and cut out the squares. Shading them with colored markers will make them more visible on an overhead projector, but color is otherwise unimportant in the activity.

p. 162

If commercial square tiles are available, your students can work with them. However, if you have no access to commercial tiles, you can make usable sets for your students by reproducing the template "Inch Grid Paper" (on the CD-ROM) on cardstock (laminating for greater sturdiness if you wish) and cutting out the squares. Note that color is not important in the activity; the squares may be assorted colors or may be uncolored.

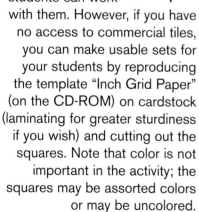

Fig. **1.1.**

Setup of a chart for identifying the shared characteristic of a group of numbers

Number Name Discoveries

Grades 4–5

Summary

Students expand their knowledge of classes of numbers, focusing on primes, composites, and squares.

Goals

- Use concrete models and number symbols to identify prime, composite, and square numbers
- Represent prime, composite, and square numbers
- Identify characteristics of prime, composite, and square numbers

Prior Knowledge or Experience

- Experience with odd and even numbers as well as factors and multiples

Materials

For each pair of students—

- 25 square tiles (can be made from the template "Inch Grid Paper" on the CD-ROM)
- One copy of the blackline master "Tile Rectangles"

For the teacher—

- 25 overhead square tiles (can be cut from a transparency of the template "Inch Grid Paper" if commercial overhead squares are unavailable)
- A transparency of the blackline master "Tile Rectangles"
- An overhead projector
- Two sheets of chart paper (optional)

Activity

Engage

Explain to the students that there are many types of numbers. They are going to explore some characteristics of numbers and learn the names of three types: *primes*, *composites*, and *squares*. On the board or a sheet of chart paper, make a chart titled "What's Our Characteristic?" (see fig. 1.1), divided into columns for "yes" and "no."

What's Our Characteristic?	
Yes	No

The following list categorizes numbers by particular characteristics. Write the list on the board, a transparency, or chart paper for all your students to see:

- Numbers that are odd (for example, 23)
- Numbers that contain the digit 7 (for example, 671)
- Numbers that are multiples of 5 (for example, 30)
- Numbers whose digits are in ascending order (for example, 567)
- Numbers that are palindromes (that is, numbers that are the same whether we read their digits from left to right or from right to left; for example, 1221)
- Numbers whose digits add up to 8 (for example, 251)

Tell the students, "I am thinking of a certain number characteristic." Do not tell them the characteristic that you have selected. Say, "On the 'yes' side of the chart, I'm going to write two numbers that have the characteristic that I'm thinking about." Enter your numbers, and then say, "On the 'no' side, I'm going to write two numbers that do not have the characteristic." Enter your numbers.

Have the students study all four numbers. Then have them name several additional numbers, and enter each one on the appropriate side of the chart. When students think that they know the characteristic of the numbers in the "yes" column, let them describe it to the class. If they are correct, select another number characteristic and write another four numbers on the chart, two in the "yes" column and two in the "no" column. Again, have the students study the numbers, suggest some additional numbers, and identify the number characteristic. If a student guesses incorrectly, have the students continue naming numbers for you to enter in the "yes" or "no" column. Repeat the activity several times, using the various categories of numbers on the list.

For a final exercise with the "What's Our Characteristic?" chart, enter two prime numbers in the "yes" column and two composite numbers in the "no" column. Proceed as before, entering numbers in the appropriate column as the students suggest them.

You may have some students who are familiar with prime numbers and composite numbers. Other students may correctly identify the characteristics of the numbers in the chart but be unable to name these types of numbers. Still other students may be unable to see what distinguishes the numbers in the "yes" column from the numbers in the "no" column.

Provide hints about the number of factors that a particular number has. Remind the students that a prime number is greater than 1 and has only two factors—itself and 1—and a composite number is also greater than 1 but is not prime. (Remember that the number 1 is neither prime nor composite, so 1 is not an appropriate number to enter in the either column for this exercise.)

At this stage, accept answers that characterize the numbers by how many or which numbers they have as factors. Encourage the students to think about how prime and composite numbers are different. Tell the students that they are going to make discoveries about prime and composite numbers and about square numbers.

A prime number is a whole number that is greater than 1 and has only two factors—itself and 1.

A composite number is a whole number that is greater than 1 and has more than two factors.

A square number is a whole number that has an odd number of factors and is the product of one of those factors and itself. (Square numbers are so named because they can be represented by rectangular arrays that are square—for example, a 5-by-5 array or a 6-by-6 array.)

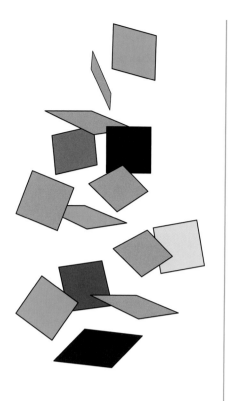

Explore

Using overhead square tiles and a transparency of the blackline master "Inch Grid Paper," demonstrate for the students all the rectangles that you can make with two tiles (see fig. 1.2a) and four tiles (see fig. 1.2b). A rectangle with a base of 2 units and a height of 1 unit is labeled 2 × 1. A rectangle with a base of 1 unit and a height of 2 units is labeled 1 × 2. For this activity, you should consider these shapes to be different rectangles.

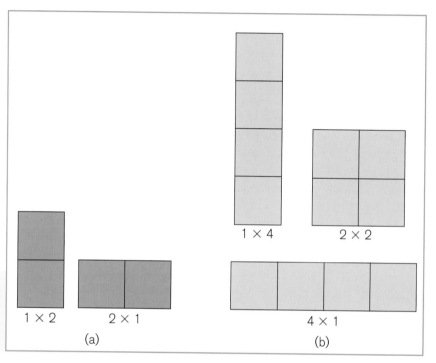

Fig. 1.2.

Rectangles formed from (a) two and (b) four square tiles

Pair the students and to each pair distribute 25 square tiles and a copy of the blackline master "Tile Rectangles." Have the students use data from your demonstration of the rectangles formed from two and four square tiles to fill in rows 1 and 2 of the table in "Tile Rectangles." Then have them use square tiles to make all possible rectangles for the numbers 1, 3, and 5–25. For each number, they should enter the dimensions and the total number of rectangles constructed. (Fig. 1.3 shows the possibilities.)

When the students have completed the activity sheet "Tile Rectangles," ask for volunteers to tell you the number of rectangles that they made for each number of square tiles. On the board or an overhead transparency, make a chart classifying the numbers 1–25 on the basis of the total rectangles that the number represents (see format of the chart in fig. 1.4). Your chart should have four columns: (1) for numbers that give only one rectangle, (2) for numbers that give only two rectangles, (3) for numbers that give more than two rectangles, and (4) for numbers that give an odd number of rectangles (the completed chart appears in the figure).

Have the students help you record the numbers 1–25 in the appropriate columns. As an extension to this activity, you might have the students predict, without using the tiles, in which column the numbers 26, 27, and 28 would go.

Ask the students to study the data in the four columns and describe the characteristics of the numbers in each. Then ask them, "Can you

Number of Tiles	Dimensions of Rectangles	Number of Rectangles
1	1 × 1	1
2	1 × 2, 2 × 1	2
3	1 × 3, 3 × 1	2
4	1 × 4, 2 × 2, 4 × 1	3
5	1 × 5, 5 × 1	2
6	1 × 6, 2 × 3, 3 × 2, 6 × 1	4
7	1 × 7, 7 × 1	2
8	1 × 8, 2 × 4, 4 × 2, 8 × 1	4
9	1 × 9, 3 × 3, 9 × 1	3
10	1 × 10, 2 × 5, 5 × 2, 10 × 1	4
11	1 × 11, 11 × 1	2
12	1 × 12, 2 × 6, 3 × 4, 4 × 3, 6 × 2, 12 × 1	6
13	1 × 13, 13 × 1	2
14	1 × 14, 2 × 7, 7 × 2, 14 × 1	4
15	1 × 15, 3 × 5, 5 × 3, 15 × 1	4
16	1 × 16, 2 × 8, 4 × 4, 8 × 2, 16 × 1	5
17	1 × 17, 17 × 1	2
18	1 × 18, 2 × 9, 3 × 6, 6 × 3, 9 × 2, 18 × 1	6
19	1 × 19, 19 × 1	2
20	1 × 20, 2 × 10, 4 × 5, 5 × 4, 10 × 2, 20 × 1	6
21	1 × 21, 3 × 7, 7 × 3, 21 × 1	4
22	1 × 22, 2 × 11, 11 × 2, 22 × 1	4
23	1 × 23, 23 × 1	2
24	1 × 24, 2 × 12, 3 × 8, 4 × 6, 6 × 4, 8 × 3, 12 × 2, 24 × 1	8
25	1 × 25, 5 × 5, 25 × 1	3

Fig. **1.3.**

Numbers of rectangles that can be formed from 1–25 square tiles

Numbers of tiles that yield—			
Exactly one rectangle	Exactly two rectangles	More than two rectangles	An odd number of rectangles
1	2, 3, 5, 7, 11, 13, 17, 19, 23	4, 6, 8, 9, 10, 12, 14, 15, 16, 18, 20, 21, 22, 24, 25	1, 4, 9, 16, 25

Fig. **1.4.**

A chart classifying each whole number from 1 to 25 on the basis of the number of rectangles that can be formed from that number of square tiles

Math Trek: Adventures in the MathZone (Peterson and Henderson 1999) engages children in exploring such topics of number theory as Mersenne primes in a series of activities with an amusement park theme.

Students use the Sieve of Eratosthenes to explore prime numbers in the investigation Discovering Primes As the Ancient Mathematicians Did (pp. 8–13; 52–54) in *Navigating through Problem Solving and Reasoning in Grade 4.* (Yeatts et al. 2005)

name the number types that these numbers represent?" The numbers that give only two rectangles are prime, the numbers that give more than two rectangles are composite, and the numbers that give an odd number of rectangles are square. Using the characteristics that they have discovered for these numbers, have the students formulate a definition for each type of number. Guide them in seeing that their work demonstrates that a prime number is a number that has only two factors—1 and the number itself, a composite number is a number that has more than two factors, and a square number is a number that has an odd number of factors.

Reflect

Have the students reflect on their work with prime, composite, and square numbers. Guide the discussion by posing such questions as the following:

- "You've seen that a few numbers belong in two columns in the chart. Can you think of any number that might belong in *three* columns?" (No; a number cannot be both a prime and a perfect square. All perfect squares greater than 1 are composite numbers.)
- "According to your definitions, the number 1 is neither a prime nor a composite number. Why?" (The number 1 has only one factor—1. Primes have exactly two factors—the number itself and 1. Composites have more than two factors.)
- "One of these numbers—373 or 376—is prime. Which one could *not* be prime?" (The number 376 must be composite because all even numbers greater than 2 are divisible by 2.)

Extend

The procedure known as the Sieve of Eratosthenes provides students with an interesting technique for determining whether a number is prime or composite. The children's book *Math Trek: Adventures in the MathZone* (Peterson and Henderson 1999) presents this procedure and explains how students can easily use it to determine the twenty-five prime numbers smaller than 100. Students can also extend explorations with prime numbers by using "The Sieve" located on the National Library of Virtual Manipulatives Web site at http://matti.usu.edu/nlvm/nav/vml_asid_158.html. This interactive Web site allows students to determine prime numbers up to 200 electronically, explore other patterns with primes, and make other discoveries with these numbers.

Square numbers are important in mathematics. To strengthen your students' understanding of the concept of a square number, have them work with their completed "Tile Rectangles" activity sheets to construct and name the first five square numbers. Show these numbers as a pattern (1, 4, 9, 16, and 25; successive differences give the odd numbers 3, 5, 7, 9, …). Challenge the students to extend the pattern so that their list includes the first twelve square numbers: 1, 4, 9, 16, 25, 36, 49, 64, 81, 100, 121, and 144.

In this activity, students have worked with properties of numbers in building representations that have helped them identify and learn to distinguish prime, composite, and square numbers. The next activity reinforces their understanding of fractions.

Fraction Models

Grades 3–4

Summary

Students expand their understanding of fractions as parts of a unit or area, parts of a collection of objects, and locations on a number line.

Goals

- Understand fractions represented as parts of a unit or area, parts of a collection of objects, and locations on a number line
- Use concrete materials to represent fractions as parts of a unit or area, parts of a collection of objects, and locations on a number line
- Name fractional parts of a unit or area, of a collection of objects, and of a number line

Prior Knowledge or Experience

- Experience in identifying common fractions ($\frac{1}{2}, \frac{1}{3}, \frac{1}{4}$) as parts of a unit or area or as parts of a collection of objects

Materials and Equipment

For each pair of students—

- A set of fraction circles (can be made from the "Fraction Circles" templates on the CD-ROM)
- 20 fraction squares or square tiles (red, blue, and at least one other color; can be made from the template "Inch Grid Paper" on the CD-ROM)
- A set of fraction strips (can be made from the "Fraction Strips" templates on the CD-ROM)
- Other manipulatives representing the three fraction models—area, set, and length (for the area model, use pattern blocks [templates on the CD-ROM] and grid paper; for the set model, use two-color counters, color cubes, and overhead counters; and for the length model, use Cuisenaire rods and fraction tower pieces)
- Three sheets of $8\frac{1}{2}$-by-11-inch paper
- A sheet of 11-by-17-inch paper
- Crayons or marking pens
- Access to the applet Fractions Models (optional; on the accompanying CD-ROM)

For the teacher—

- Overhead fraction circles, fraction squares, and fraction strips (transparent pieces can be made from the "Fraction Circles" templates, as well as the templates "Inch Grid Paper" and "Fraction Strips," on the CD-ROM, and colored with markers)

If you have access to commercial sets of fraction circles, fraction squares, and fraction strips, your students can use these materials. Likewise, you can use commercial overhead versions of the manipulatives.

If you don't have access to commercial fraction circles, you can make sturdy facsimiles for your students from the "Fraction Circle" templates (whole, halves, thirds, fourths, fifths, sixths, eighths, tenths, and twelfths) on the CD-ROM:

- Reproduce each template on cardstock of a different color, and cut out the circles and their respective sectors. (For more durable fraction circles, laminate the cardstock sheets before cutting out the circles.)

- Make fraction circle kits by putting circles of each color, separated into sectors, in a resealable plastic bag.

If commercial fraction squares or color tiles are unavailable for your students' use, you can make sets of squares by reproducing the template "Inch Grid Paper" (on the CD-ROM) on cardstock in three or four different colors (red, blue, and at least one other color), cutting out the squares, and distributing multicolored sets to pairs of students.

You can adapt the steps for making fraction circles to produce fraction strips from the "Fraction Strips" templates on the CD-ROM.

To make overhead fraction circles and fraction strips (for use on an overhead projector), reproduce the respective templates from the CD-ROM on transparencies, cut out all pieces, and shade them appropriately with colored markers.

Area Model

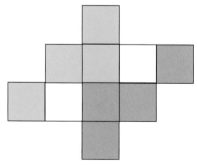

Blue squares = 4/10, or 2/5, of the area
Gray squares = 4/10, or 2/5, of the area
White squares = 2/10, or 1/5, of the area
Blue + Gray + White = Whole area
2/5 + 2/5 + 1/5 = 5/5, or 1

- An overhead transparency showing an 8-inch line segment for a number line marked with 0 at the left end and 1 at the right end
- A copy of the children's book *Apple Fractions* (Pallotta 2002)
- A copy of the children's book *Fraction Action* (Leedy 1994)
- Four or five apples of different varieties, all approximately the same size and shape (optional)
- A paring knife (optional)

Activity

Engage

Ask your students for examples of fractions that they have encountered in their everyday experiences. They might tell you about drinking half a glass of milk, needing to get to a music lesson in a quarter of an hour, eating one-third of a candy bar, and so on. Make a list of the fractions and their contexts on the board or an overhead projector.

Use the area model to show fractions as parts of a unit or region. On an overhead projector, make a 2 × 3 rectangle with any combination of red and blue overhead fraction squares. Ask the students, "How many red squares do you see?" Then ask, "How many squares are in the whole rectangle?" Explain that you are thinking about the rectangle as equal to one unit or a whole region, and ask, "What part of the rectangle is made up of red squares?" When the students have answered this question correctly, ask the same question about the blue squares.

To give the students additional practice, have them help you make different shapes with red and blue squares on the overhead projector, and guide them in naming parts of the unit or area as fractions. For example, you and your students might make a 3 × 3 rectangle with four red squares and five blue squares. Ask, "What part of the rectangle is made up of red squares? What part is made up of blue squares?"

Add squares in a third color—say, yellow—to make larger, three-colored shapes. For these shapes, ask the students to name the fractions represented by the red squares, the blue squares, and the yellow squares. Then have them name the fractions made up of the red and blue squares together, the blue and yellow squares together, ot the red and yellow squares together. Emphasize that the area model always involves a unit or region and that fractions name parts of the whole (see the margin).

Next, use the set model, showing fractions as parts of collections of objects. Scatter six red and blue squares (in any distribution of the colors) on the projector screen. Ask the students, "How many red square do you see? How many blue squares?" Emphasize that now you are thinking of the entire collection of squares as equal to one whole, or all the squares. Ask them, "What fractional part of the collection is made up of red squares? What part is made up of blue squares?" For further practice, add to the collection more red or blue squares, or yellow squares, and then ask the students to name parts of the new collections as fractions. Be sure that your students understand that the set model always involves a collection of objects and that fractions name parts of the collection (see the right margin on the next page).

Finally, use the length model, showing fractions as locations on a number line. Place a toothpick so that it bisects an eight-inch line segment on a transparency on the overhead projector. Label the left end of the segment "0" and the right end "1." Explain that the toothpick marks the point midway between 0 and 1 and thus divides the number line into halves. Next, use toothpicks to divide the line segment into thirds, and then into fourths. For further practice, have the students help you show and name other fractions as locations on the line. Ask them first to estimate and then to determine the number of squares that they must line up against the line to measure one-third of it (they will not be able to give an answer in a whole number of squares), three-fourths of it, and other fractional parts of the line. Emphasize that the length model always involves a line segment with fractional numbers naming locations on, or parts of, the segment (see below).

To make connections with real-world objects, read your students the book *Apple Fractions* (Pallotta 2002). In this book, elves have fun with fractions as they divide different kinds of apples into halves, thirds, fourths, and so on, including less conventional fractional parts. After finishing the story, show your students selected illustrations from the book again, each time asking them,

- "What fraction does this picture show?"
- "How does the picture show the fraction?
- "Does the picture use the area model (showing the fraction as part of a unit or region), the set model (showing the fraction as part of a collection of objects), or the length model (showing the fraction as a location on, or part of, a line)?"

Although most of the book's illustrations show the area model (part of a whole apple), they depict this model in various ways, and some pictures near the end of the book depict the set model for fractions.

If you wish, you can bring into the classroom four or five apples representing different varieties featured in *Apple Fractions* and slice them in front of your students to demonstrate the area, set, and length models of fractions. For example, to show the area model (fractions as parts of a

Set Model

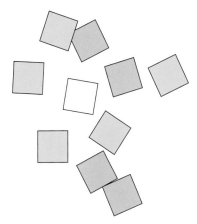

Collection, or whole = 10 squares
5 blue squares = 5/10 = 1/2 of the collection
4 gray squares = 4/10 = 2/5 of the collection
1 white square = 1/10 of the collection
1/2 + 2/5 + 1/10 = 1, or the whole collection

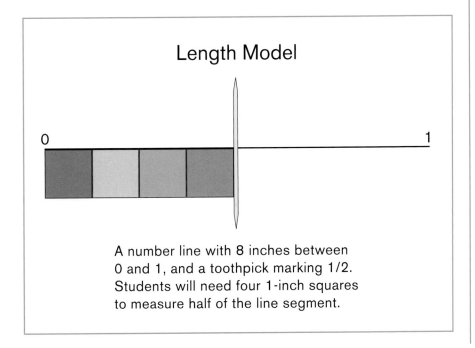

Length Model

0   1

A number line with 8 inches between
0 and 1, and a toothpick marking 1/2.
Students will need four 1-inch squares
to measure half of the line segment.

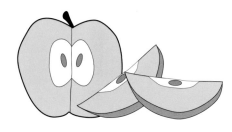

unit or region), you might slice an apple into quarters and hold up each quarter for your students to see. Hold two quarters together to reform half the apple. Add another quarter to show three-quarters. Finally, hold all four quarters together to reform the whole apple.

For a concrete demonstration of the set model, you might select a red delicious apple and a yellow delicious apple of about the same size and shape. Cut both apples into eighths, and make a set consisting of some slices of red apple and some slices of yellow apple. Ask the students, "What part of this set of apple slices is made up of slices of yellow delicious apple? What part is made up of slices of red delicious apple?"

To reinforce understanding of the length model, line up thin slices of apple and ask the students how many slices make up half your line, one quarter of it, and so on.

Explore

You may decide to devote additional time to the ideas in the activity Fraction Models by focusing on a different fraction model each day over a period of three days. Have the students use manipulative materials or make drawings to represent various fractions with the "model of the day." The following three-day sequence can give students time to explore and experience fractions as parts of a unit or area, as parts of a collection of objects, and as locations on a number line.

Day 1—Area Model. Remind the students that the area model represents fractions as parts of a unit or region, and that they can use this model to show parts of a variety of shapes and objects—circles, triangles, pentagons, cubes, spheres, apples, and so forth. Introduce fraction circles, selecting the appropriate circles to show a whole, halves, thirds, fourths, fifths, and sixths. Distribute fraction circles made from the respective "Fraction Circles" templates (or commercial fraction circles for these fractions).

Display transparent fraction circles on the overhead projector to demonstrate how the students can use the whole circle as the base unit and can then construct representations of fractions as part of the circle. Show fraction circle pieces for $\frac{1}{2}, \frac{1}{3}$ and $\frac{2}{3}$, reviewing the fact that each fraction covers that portion of the whole circle.

Ask your students to sort out all their fourths, fifths, and sixths pieces and use them to make representations of all the fractions they can that are less than a whole. Tell them, "Twelve fractions are possible, though you won't be able to show them all at the same time, because you'll need some pieces for more than one fraction. But see if you can make and name all twelve fractions." The twelve fractions are

$$\frac{1}{4}, \frac{2}{4}, \frac{3}{4}, \frac{1}{5}, \frac{2}{5}, \frac{3}{5}, \frac{4}{5}, \frac{1}{6}, \frac{2}{6}, \frac{3}{6}, \frac{4}{6}, \text{ and } \frac{5}{6}.$$

Next, distribute a sheet of paper to each student, and direct the students to fold the sheets into fourths. Then ask them to tell you four fractions that they showed with fraction circles—for example, $\frac{3}{4}, \frac{2}{5}, \frac{1}{6},$ and $\frac{1}{4}$. Display the four fractions on the board or an overhead transparency.

Ask the students to write each one in one quarter of their paper and draw a visual representation of it, using the "part of a whole," or area, model. Challenge them to use at least three different shapes or objects in drawing their fractions (see the margin).

Day 2—Set Model. As necessary, review the area model for fractions from day 1. Then turn to the set model, reminding the students that this model represents fractions as parts of a collection of objects. Distribute appropriate manipulative materials, such as plastic tiles in different colors, colored counters, or colored squares cut from cardstock. Ask the students to show such fractions as

$$\frac{1}{4}, \frac{2}{4}, \frac{3}{4}, \frac{1}{5}, \frac{2}{5}, \frac{3}{5}, \frac{4}{5}, \frac{1}{6}, \frac{2}{6}, \frac{3}{6}, \frac{4}{6}, \text{ and } \frac{5}{6},$$

this time working with the set model.

As before, ask the students to tell you the names of four fractions from their work, and display them on the board or the overhead projector. Again distribute sheets of paper for the students to fold into fourths, and have them draw collections of objects to represent specific fractions. For example, a student might draw four circles and shade three of them to represent the fraction $\frac{3}{4}$ (see the margin).

Day 3—Length Model. Review the set model of fractions if necessary. Remind the students that the length model shows fractions as locations on, or parts of, a line. Distribute to each pair of students a set of manipulative strips for a whole, halves, thirds, fourths, fifths, and sixths made from the "Fraction Strips" templates on the CD-ROM (or commercial strips for these fractions). Again, distribute paper to the students and ask them to fold it into fourths. List four fractions on the board or an overhead transparency and ask the students to use the "fractions as a location on a line" model to represent these fractions (see the margin).

Reflect

On the board or an overhead transparency, set up a "Fraction Models" chart like that in figure 1.5. Show the chart to your students, pointing out that someone can fill in the blank in the heading with any fraction. Distribute sheets of 11-by-17-inch paper (other sizes will work) to each student or pair of students, and help them fold the paper into three roughly equal columns. Tell them to copy the main heading and column headings from the chart that you have made.

Area Model

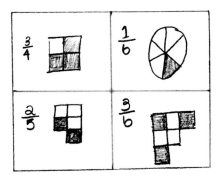

Set Model

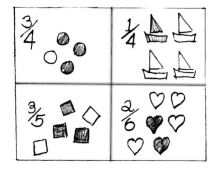

Length Model

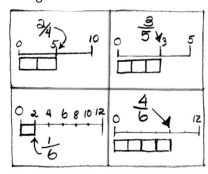

Fig. **1.5.**

Setting up a "Fraction Models" chart to use to represent any fraction

Fraction Models for _____		
Area Model	Set Model	Length Model

Assign each student or pair of students a fraction from those that they have used in their work. Have them write the fraction in the blank and then use the area, set, and length models to show the fraction in three different ways.

After all the students have drawn the fractions assigned to them according to the models named in the column headings, ask them to talk about their charts and explain their work. Figure 1.6 shows sample charts from students. You might organize your students' charts according to denominators and display them on a bulletin board to provide ongoing exposure to fractions and fraction models.

Return to the list of fractions in everyday contexts generated by your students at the beginning of the activity. Ask the students to reflect on

Fig. **1.6.**

Sample "Fraction Models" charts from students

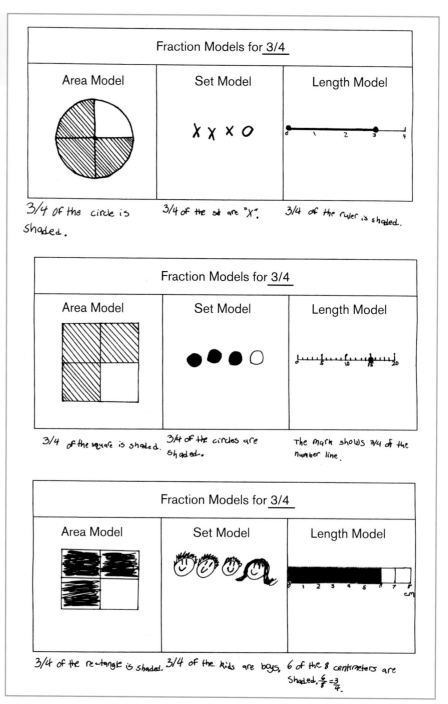

similarities and differences among these fractions. On the board or a transparency, make a three-column chart and list the three fraction models at the top of the columns. Ask the students to try to classify one of the fractions-in-context as an example of a fraction represented with the area model, another as an example of a fraction represented with the set model, and a third as an example of a fraction represented with the length model. Have them explain their thinking. Record the fraction in the correct column on the table. Have the students categorize the other fractions on the list.

Extend

For further practice with the area model, distribute fraction circles for eighths, tenths, and twelfths made from the appropriate "Fraction Circles" templates (or use commercial circles). Emphasize that eight eighths, ten tenths, and twelve twelfths all equal one whole. You can also use fraction strips for eighths, tenths, and twelfths (or other manipulative materials mentioned in the materials list) to extend students' understanding of the meaning of each fraction model.

Another way to give your students additional experience with fraction models is to read them stories from the children's book *Fraction Action* (Leedy 1994). The book includes five stories in all, with colored illustrations in cartoon format, featuring Miss Prime and her students and their experiences with fractions. The stories, all with surprise endings, help students understand fraction models. You can extend your students' work to include the language arts by having them attempt to write similar stories incorporating fraction models in illustrations.

Students can also strengthen their understanding by working with the applet "Fraction Models" on the accompanying CD-ROM. This applet explores the three models for representing fractions (with numerators from 0 to 20 and denominators of 1, 2, 4, 5, 8 10, and 20). Students name a fraction by selecting a numerator and a denominator from the lists, and then they select the area, set, or length model. The applet then shows the named fraction by using the selected model.

Emphasize to the students that area, set, and length representations of fractions are everywhere in everyday experience. To underscore the point, surprise the students with a Fraction Models snack break. To present fractions with the area model, offer chocolate bars and graham crackers marked for breaking into equal-sized pieces. Set out an assortment of jelly beans, M&Ms, or different kinds of dry cereal to present fractions with the set model. Parts of licorice sticks, fruit-flavored candy sticks, breadsticks, or long pretzel sticks can illustrate fractions presented with the length model. This experience can provide a tasty and memorable conclusion to the students' study of fraction models.

This activity has provided a hands-on exploration of the three fraction models—area, set, and length. In the next activity, students continue to use the models to help them compare and order fractions.

"Representations should be treated as essential elements in supporting students' understanding of mathematical concepts and relationships." (NCTM 2000, p. 67)

Actions on Fractions

Grades 3–5

Summary

Students expand their understanding of processes for comparing and ordering fractions.

Goals

- Compare fractions by using concrete models
- Compare fractions by using benchmarks
- Order fractions by using concrete models, benchmarks, and parallel number lines

Prior Knowledge

- Some preliminary experience in comparing and ordering fractions

Materials

p. 163

If you have access to commercial sets of fraction circles and fraction strips, your students can use these materials. Likewise, you can use commercial overhead versions of these manipulatives.

For each pair of students—

- A set of fraction circles (can be made from the "Fraction Circles" templates on the CD-ROM)
- A set of fraction strips (can be made from the "Fraction Strips" templates on the CD-ROM)
- A sheet of unlined paper ($8\frac{1}{2}$-by-11 inches)
- A copy of the blackline master "Parallel Number Lines"
- One deck of cards

For the teacher—

- An overhead projector
- Overhead fraction circles (can be made from transparencies of the "Fraction Circles" templates on the CD-ROM)
- A transparency of the blackline master "Parallel Number Lines" (*Note*: Cut off or tape over the two number lines at the bottom of the sheet that show 0.1s and 0.01s.)
- A copy of the children's book *The Hershey's Milk Chocolate Fraction Book* (Pallotta 1999)

Activity

Engage

Ask your students the following "Which is more?" questions:

- "Which is more—$\frac{5}{12}$ or $\frac{7}{12}$ of a dozen doughnuts?"
- "Which is more—$\frac{1}{2}$ or $\frac{1}{4}$ of a pie?"

- "Which is more— $\frac{5}{6}$ or $\frac{5}{12}$ of a chocolate candy bar?"

- "Which is more— $\frac{1}{6}$ or $\frac{2}{3}$ of a pizza?"

The students' responses will provide a quick check of their skill in comparing and ordering fractions. For students who have some previous experience, change the fractions in the third and fourth questions to make the comparisons more difficult. Tabulate the students' responses on the board.

Using an overhead projector and a set of overhead fraction circles, review the ways in which fractions are named. Show the students two complete fraction circles—for example, the circle divided into halves and the circle divided into thirds. Remove one sector from each circle— a half and a third, respectively. Ask a student to name the fraction represented by each sector, and then have the student say which fraction is larger. Continue with other pairs of sectors from the fraction circles, connecting each sector with its symbolic name.

Demonstrate how to use fraction circles to compare two fractions— for example, $\frac{2}{3}$ and $\frac{3}{4}$, determining the larger or smaller fraction by placing sectors for one fraction on top of sectors for the other. Ask the students to name two other fractions (limit the choices to fractions with denominators of 2, 3, 4, 6, or 12). Have them predict which fraction is larger or whether the fractions are equivalent. Have students come up to the overhead projector and use the fraction circles to check their predictions.

Comparisons of three fractions shift the focus to the idea of *ordering* fractions. Have the students name three or more fractions. Ask them to predict the order of the fractions. Then have students come to the overhead projector and guide them in using fraction circles to order the fractions from smallest to largest.

Distribute to each pair of students a set of fraction circles made from the "Fraction Circles" templates (on the CD-ROM) or commercial circles. Return to the four "Which is more?" questions, this time having the students use fraction circles to determine the correct answers. Discuss each question, asking the students about any differences between their original responses and the answers that they have now obtained.

Explore

Introduce the term *benchmark*. Explain that a benchmark is a numerical reference point that can help someone compare and order numbers. Write the fraction $\frac{1}{3}$ on the board or an overhead transparency. Ask the students, "Can you explain what $\frac{1}{3}$ means?" If your students have completed the preceding activity, Fraction Models, they may say that $\frac{1}{3}$ means one of three equal parts of a unit or a region, one of three equal elements of a collection, or one of three equal sections of a line segment. If they do not offer these explanations on their own, use the

If you don't have access to commercial fraction circles, you can make sturdy facsimiles for your students from the "Fraction Circle" templates (whole, halves, thirds, fourths, fifths, sixths, eighths, tenths, and twelfths) on the CD-ROM:

- Reproduce each template on cardstock of a different color, and cut out the circles and their respective sectors. (For more durable fraction circles, laminate the cardstock sheets before cutting out the circles.)

- Make fraction circle kits by putting circles of each color, separated into sectors, in a resealable plastic bag.

You can adapt the steps for making fraction circles to produce fraction strips from the "Fraction Strips" templates on the CD-ROM.

To make overhead fraction circles and fraction strips (for use on an overhead projector), reproduce the respective templates from the CD-ROM on transparencies, cut out all pieces, and shade them appropriately with colored markers.

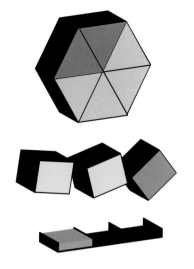

three fraction models—area, set, and length—to show $\frac{1}{3}$ in three different ways. Have the students describe how they would divide an object or a set of objects into thirds. Then have the students give examples of objects that they could divide into thirds.

On the board, set up a chart similar to the one shown in figure 1.7. Place an overhead fraction-circle sector for $\frac{1}{3}$ on the overhead projector. Say to the students, "We are going to use $\frac{1}{3}$ as a benchmark to determine whether other fractions are less than or greater than $\frac{1}{3}$."

Then have the students name the following fractions one at a time—

$$\frac{1}{1} \text{ (or 1)}, \frac{2}{3}, \frac{1}{2}, \frac{1}{4}, \frac{2}{4}, \frac{3}{4}, \frac{1}{6}, \frac{4}{6}, \frac{5}{6}, \text{and } \frac{1}{12}.$$

Do not show them the corresponding sectors of fraction circles. For each fraction, ask the students, "Is this fraction less than $\frac{1}{3}$? Or is it greater than $\frac{1}{3}$?" As the students give their best prediction of where each fraction will go on the chart, record the fraction in the column that they indicate. At this time, do not comment on any fractions that the students place incorrectly.

Fig. **1.7.**

Setup of a benchmark chart for 1/3

Fractions Less than $\frac{1}{3}$	Fractions Greater than $\frac{1}{3}$

After the students have predicted the places of all ten fractions, have them fold a sheet of unlined paper in half lengthwise, and ask them to make their own benchmark chart for $\frac{1}{3}$. Taking the $\frac{1}{3}$ sector as a benchmark, students should use appropriate sectors from their sets of fraction circles to verify the placement of the ten fractions on the chart. Let them determine for themselves whether the fraction is larger or smaller than $\frac{1}{3}$, and direct them to record the fraction in the proper column on their chart.

When the students have finished classifying the fractions, compare their answers with their predictions on the benchmark chart on the board. Discuss the fractions whose places the students predicted incorrectly and ask them to consider possible reasons for their misconceptions.

Next, have the students fold paper for three-column benchmark charts (see fig. 1.8). They can keep records in the chart as they determine

Fractions Closest to 0	Fractions Closest to ½	Fractions Closest to 1

Fig. **1.8.**

Setup of a benchmark chart for 1/2

whether a fraction is closest to 0, 1, or a selected benchmark fraction, such as $\frac{1}{2}$.

On the board or an overhead transparency, write the following fractions:

$$\frac{1}{3} \quad \frac{3}{8} \quad \frac{7}{9} \quad \frac{5}{6} \quad \frac{11}{12} \quad \frac{2}{10}$$

$$\frac{3}{10} \quad \frac{9}{10} \quad \frac{5}{6} \quad \frac{1}{8} \quad \frac{2}{6} \quad \frac{6}{11}$$

Have the students analyze each fraction in relation to 0, $\frac{1}{2}$, and 1.

Ask them, "Is this fraction close to 0? Close to $\frac{1}{2}$? Close to 1? To which of the three numbers is it closest?" Then have them place the fraction in the appropriate column in the chart. After the students have determined the category for each of the fractions, have them explain their thinking. Ask, "Why did you place that fraction in that column?" Prompt them to examine their ideas by posing the question, "Do you see any patterns among the fractions in each column?" If time permits, select fractions that are greater than 1 (for example, $\frac{8}{5}$ and $\frac{13}{12}$) and fractions that are exactly between two of the benchmarks (for example, $\frac{1}{4}$ and $\frac{3}{4}$).

Help the students discover and describe the following patterns in the fractions in each column:

1. In the column "Fractions Closest to 0," fractions have numerators that are very small in comparison with their denominators.
2. In the column "Fractions Closest to $\frac{1}{2}$," fractions have denominators that are about twice as large as their numerators.
3. In the column "Fractions Closest to 1," fractions have numerators and denominators that are about the same size.

Reflect

Review the meaning of *fraction* and the ways in which the students can compare two fractions. Using the "Which Is More?" questions once again, explore patterns that the students have discovered for determining the larger or smaller fraction. For example, ask the students, "What helps you when you are comparing $\frac{1}{2}$ and $\frac{1}{3}$? Extend the discussion and generalize it to other pairs of fractions.

Help your students think about fractions in four groups:

1. *Fractions with the same denominators.* For such fractions, the numerators name the number of equal-sized parts of the fraction. The fraction with the larger numerator names the larger fraction. For instance, $\frac{7}{12}$ is a larger part of a dozen doughnuts than $\frac{5}{12}$. Ask the students, "Which is larger, $\frac{7}{10}$ or $\frac{9}{10}$?"

2. *Fractions with a numerator of 1.* Numerators of 1 name one part of the whole, and the denominators name the number of equal parts into which the whole is divided. The fraction with the smaller denominator names the larger fraction. For example, $\frac{1}{2}$ of a pie is more than $\frac{1}{4}$ of a pie. Ask the students, "Which is larger, $\frac{1}{3}$ or $\frac{1}{5}$?"

3. *Fractions with the same numerators (other than 1).* A fraction's denominator names the number of equal parts into which the whole is divided. If we are comparing two fractions with different denominators but equal numerators, our comparison is between equal numbers of parts that are different sizes. Because the number of parts is the same, the fraction with the smaller denominator is larger. For instance, $\frac{5}{6}$ of a chocolate candy bar is more than $\frac{5}{12}$ of the same candy bar. Ask the students, "Which is larger, $\frac{3}{5}$ of an apple or $\frac{3}{7}$ of it?"

4. *Fractions with different numerators and different denominators.* For such fractions, we can use benchmarks, equivalent fractions, or parallel number lines to determine the relative sizes of two fractions. If we place the fractions on parallel number lines, the fraction that we locate farther from 0 is the larger.

   For example, we can clearly see that $\frac{2}{3}$ of a pizza is more than $\frac{3}{6}$ of a pizza when we place both fractions on number lines. Ask the students, "Which is larger, $\frac{3}{4}$ of a candy bar or $\frac{6}{7}$ of it?"

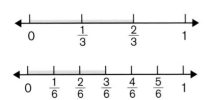

Discuss each group of fractions. Ask the students, "What is different about the fourth group? Why are fractions in this group more challenging to compare than others?"

Involve the students in a little game called "More or Less?" Select a fraction—say, $\frac{3}{4}$. This fraction will be your benchmark. Write it on the board, along with a different fraction that is close to it—say, $\frac{5}{8}$. Ask the students, "Is $\frac{5}{8}$ larger or smaller than our benchmark of $\frac{3}{4}$?" If your students say correctly that $\frac{5}{8}$ is smaller than $\frac{3}{4}$, be sure to have them explain their thinking. Prompt them to think about the comparison in a different way with the question, "Can you think of another way to explain why $\frac{5}{8}$ is less than $\frac{3}{4}$?"

Repeat the activity, using different fractions. Encourage the students to think about equivalent fractions as they compare another fraction to a selected benchmark. For example, when comparing $\frac{1}{2}$ and $\frac{5}{8}$, a student might say, "I know that $\frac{1}{2}$ equals $\frac{4}{8}$, and $\frac{5}{8}$ is greater than $\frac{4}{8}$. So I know that $\frac{5}{8}$ is greater than $\frac{1}{2}$." If $\frac{5}{8}$ is the benchmark, and a student is comparing $\frac{2}{3}$ to it, he or she might say, "I know that $\frac{2}{3}$ equals $\frac{4}{6}$, which is $\frac{1}{6}$ more than $\frac{3}{6}$, which equals $\frac{1}{2}$. I know that $\frac{5}{8}$ is $\frac{1}{8}$ more than $\frac{4}{8}$, which equals $\frac{1}{2}$. And because sixths are larger than eighths, I know that $\frac{2}{3}$ is greater than $\frac{5}{8}$."

Extend

You can have your students use fraction strips in addition to fraction circles. Experience with two or more manipulatives can help them develop facility with different models of fractions.

You can also expand your students' experiences in comparing and ordering fractions by having them locate fractions on parallel number lines. The blackline master "Parallel Number Lines" includes number lines for a whole, halves, thirds, fourths, sixths, and tenths. You can use the parallel number lines with many tasks. For example, ask the students, "Which is closer to 1: $\frac{5}{6}$ or $\frac{7}{10}$? Use the number lines to prove your answer." Number lines can be excellent tools for locating, comparing, and ordering fractions, but they are probably most effective when used in conjunction with benchmarks.

Another way to provide students with visual and symbolic experiences in comparing and ordering halves, thirds, fourths, sixths, and twelfths is to read aloud from the children's book *The Hershey's Milk Chocolate Fraction Book* (Pallotta 1999), which includes activities relating to the twelve pieces of a candy bar. The book also provides an additional explanation of the patterns and concepts related to ordering fractions.

"Making Fractions" is a little game that you can have your students play in pairs to review ways to compare fractions and use benchmarks. The only thing that two students need to play is a deck of cards, with all

In *The Hershey's Milk Chocolate Fraction Book* (Pallotta 1999), diminutive construction workers cut up gigantic chocolate bars, illustrating fraction concepts.

Largest fraction = $\dfrac{10}{2}$

Largest proper fraction = $\dfrac{2}{3}$

Smallest fraction = $\dfrac{2}{10}$

Smallest improper fraction = $\dfrac{3}{2}$

face cards removed, for a total of forty numbered cards. A player deals four cards to himself and four to his partner, and then both players make the largest fraction that they can by choosing a numerator and a denominator from the numbers on their cards (see the margin). The players compare their fractions, and the one with the larger fraction wins all the cards and becomes the dealer for the next round. If the players' fractions are equal, the round ends in a tie, and the players keep their cards. The game continues in this manner until the players have used all forty cards. At this point, the players count their cards, and the one with more cards wins. (You can also modify the game to require that players make only proper fractions—fractions that are less than 1—or change the object of the game to the formation of the smallest fraction possible.)

The comparing and ordering of fractions that this activity calls for will prepare students for the next activity, which turns their attention to a different representation of fractions—fractions as decimals. Understanding fractions as decimals and percentages is another major achievement for students in grades 3–5.

Fractions with a Point

Grades 4–5

Summary

Students expand their knowledge of the relationships between equivalent forms of fractions, decimals, and percentages.

Goals

- Represent fractions and terminating decimals by using visual models
- Determine fraction and decimal equivalents by using tenths and hundredths grids, parallel number lines, and calculators
- Understand relationships among fractions, decimals, and percentages

Prior Knowledge or Experience

- Experience in entering fraction and decimal numbers into a calculator
- Ability to simplify a fraction
- Skill in naming fractions and drawing models of fractions to represent tenths

Materials and Equipment

For each student—

- A copy of each of the following blackline masters:
  ○ "Decimal Grids—Tenths"
  ○ "Parallel Number Lines"
- Two copies of the blackline master "Decimal Grids—Hundredths"
- Two sheets of unlined paper
- A ruler
- A fraction calculator (optional)
- Access to the applet "Fraction Models" (optional)

pp. 163, 164, 165

For the teacher—

- A set of overhead decimal grids (cut from transparencies of the "Shaded Grids" templates on the CD-ROM)
- A transparency of the blackline master "Parallel Number Lines"
- An overhead projector
- A copy of the children's book *Piece = Part = Portion: Fractions = Decimals = Percents* (Gifford 2003)
- A copy of the children's book *Twizzlers Percentages Book* (Pallotta 2001; optional)
- An overhead fraction calculator (optional)

You can cut out overhead grids to show tenths from transparencies of the following templates:
• "Shaded Grids to Show 0.1, 0.2, 0.3, and 0.4"
• "Shaded Grids to Show 0.5, 0.6, 0.7, and 0.8"
• "Shaded Grids to Show 0.9, 1.0, 0.5, and 0.7"

To show hundredths, cut out overhead grids from transparencies of the following templates:
• "Shaded Grids to Show 0.03, 0.30, 0.51, and 0.13"
• "Shaded Grids to Show 0.30, 0.28, 0.17, and 0.41"

Activity

Engage

Review fractions that have a denominator of 10. Remind your students, "Any fraction with a denominator of 10 is related to a whole with ten equal parts. It takes ten of these parts, each called a tenth, to make the whole." Have the students name and draw models of fractions representing various numbers of tenths—for example, $\frac{1}{10}$, $\frac{3}{10}$, $\frac{5}{10}$, $\frac{7}{10}$, and $\frac{9}{10}$.

Give your students copies of the blackline master "Decimal Grids— Tenths." Work with them as a class to connect fractions with decimals and introduce decimal notation. On an overhead projector, show a ten-strip square with three strips shaded (from the "Shaded Grids" templates on the CD-ROM).

Have the students describe the characteristics of the shaded square. Ask—

* "How many strips divide the square?"
* "How many strips are shaded?"
* "Are all the strips the same size?"

Then have the students shade three strips in one of the squares on their activity page. Ask them to tell you the fraction name of the shaded part of the square. Write "$\frac{3}{10}$" on the board and have the students explain the meaning of the name.

Next, demonstrate how to write the fraction $\frac{3}{10}$ as the decimal number 0.3. Talk about differences between the expressions $\frac{3}{10}$ and 0.3, and discuss ways to read the decimal number ("zero point three," "zero and three-tenths," "three-tenths," "point three"). Gradually, as the activity unfolds, share the following facts about decimal notation with your students:

* A *decimal point* separates whole units from fractional parts of a unit in a number. The number 0.3 has zero whole units and $\frac{3}{10}$ of a unit.
* Whole units always appear to the left of the decimal point, and fractional parts of a unit always appear to the right.
* The digits to the right of the decimal point are the *numerator* of the fractional part of a unit. Thus, 3 is the numerator of the fractional part of the number 0.3.
* The *denominator* of a decimal fraction is not actually visible in the notation but is always 10, or 10 × 10, or 10 × 10 × 10, or the product of however many 10s will match the number of places in the numerator. The denominator of the fractional part of the number 0.3 is 10, since the numerator has only one place.

- The first place to the right of the decimal point is called the *tenths place* because a numerator that extends only to this place has a denominator of 10. The second place to the right of the decimal point is called the *hundredths place* because a numerator that extends to this place has a denominator of 100. The third place to the right of the decimal point is called the *thousandths place* because a numerator that extends to this place has a denominator of 1000. And so on.

- If we use decimal notation to write numbers that have no whole units but only fractional parts of a unit, we almost always write a zero to the left of the decimal point as a placeholder, as in 0.3. (By convention, a zero does not appear before a decimal fraction that cannot be greater than 1, such as a fraction that represents the probability of an event. However, this information may not be meaningful to students at this stage.)

Show a ten-strip square with a different number of strips—say, seven—shaded. Ask the students to shade a square on their sheet in the same way, and have them name the shaded part of the square as a fraction ($\frac{7}{10}$). Urge them to convert the fraction to a decimal equivalent (0.7). Show other fractions ($\frac{5}{10}$ and $\frac{9}{10}$, for example) with ten-strip squares and follow the same process until your students can reliably give the fraction and decimal names of the shaded portions of the squares.

Extend the students' understanding of decimals to hundredths. Show an overhead hundredths grid with 30 shaded squares (don't give the students copies of the blackline master "Decimal Grids—Hundredths" just yet). Ask the students, "What fractional part of the grid is shaded?" Accept both $\frac{30}{100}$ and $\frac{3}{10}$ as correct and write the fractions on the board. If the students suggest only one of these two fractions, write the other as well, and discuss why both answers are correct. Show the students how to write the fractions as decimals—0.30 and 0.3, respectively—and talk about similarities and differences between the two expressions. Use the overhead grid for 0.3 along with the grid for 0.30 to demonstrate the equivalence of the two.

On the overhead projector, show another hundredths grid, this time with just three squares shaded. Ask the students, "What fractional part of the grid is shaded?" Write the fraction $\frac{3}{100}$ and the decimal number 0.03 on the board. Then compare this number and its corresponding hundredths grid with the number 0.3 and its matching tenths grid. Discuss the importance of the placement of the digits in the numbers.

Continue showing the students hundredths grids with various numbers of squares shaded. Have the students tell you the fractions and decimals that name the number of squares shaded on each grid. Then have them explain the meaning of each name. If you wish, have the students make quick estimates of the fractional and decimal amounts and then determine the actual fraction and decimals represented. Discuss any differences between the estimates and the actual numbers.

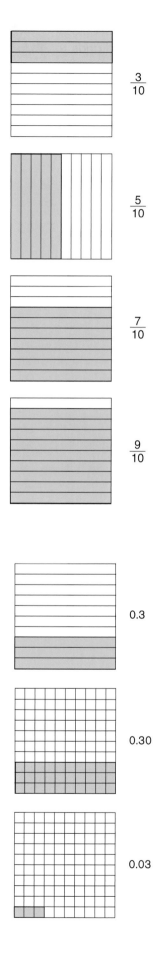

$\frac{3}{10}$

$\frac{5}{10}$

$\frac{7}{10}$

$\frac{9}{10}$

0.3

0.30

0.03

For additional practice, look back at the activity "Place Value in Whole Numbers and Decimals," which suggests using base-ten manipulatives to develop students' understanding of place-value names for decimals.

Explore

Now it is time to move the students from merely naming fraction and decimal equivalents to actually determining them. Limit your students' work at this stage to fractions that can be named as terminating decimals. The tasks suggested here focus on halves, fourths, fifths, and tenths.

Give each of your students two copies of the blackline master "Decimal Grids—Hundredths," and direct their attention to the first square grid on the sheet. Review ways to divide the grid into tenths (10 equal parts) and then into halves, fourths, and fifths. Set up a chart on the board or a transparency similar to that in figure 1.9, and write the fraction $\frac{1}{2}$ in column 1. Leave the other columns blank for now.

Tell the students that they are going to work with the grid to show $\frac{1}{2}$, and then they will convert it into a decimal. Walk them through the following four steps:

1. "Shade individual squares to represent one-half of the grid."

   (Remind the students that there are many ways to show $\frac{1}{2}$ with shaded squares on the grid.)

2. "Count the number of shaded squares. How many do you have?" (Enter 50 in column 2 in the chart.)

3. "Use that number as the numerator of a fraction. The denominator is 100, because you have one hundred squares in the grid."

   (Enter $\frac{50}{100}$ in column 3.)

4. "Write the fraction as a decimal. To do this, make a decimal point with a zero to the left, because you have no whole numbers. Then write 50, which is the numerator of your fraction, to the right of the decimal point. Now you have written the decimal number for $\frac{1}{2}$." (Enter 0.50, or 0.5, in column 4.)

Explain that although the students aren't writing the denominator explicitly, the decimal notation tells that the denominator is 100, because the numerator has two places—the tenths place and the hundredths place. Be sure that the students understand that the columns of the chart show the steps that they used to convert the fraction $\frac{1}{2}$ into the decimal 0.50, or 0.5. Tell them that they can use the same process to convert other fractions represented on hundredths grids into decimals.

Next, have the students fold a sheet of paper lengthwise to set up a four-column chart like the one in figure 1.9. Tell them to use the chart, along with other hundredths grids on their activity page, to convert the fractions $\frac{1}{4}$ and $\frac{4}{5}$ into decimal numbers. Talk the students through the process if necessary.

Once your students are using the process confidently, ask them to enter the following fractions in column 1 of their charts: $\frac{3}{4}$, $\frac{1}{5}$, $\frac{3}{5}$, and $\frac{9}{10}$. Have them change these fractions to decimals and complete the chart.

Fraction and Decimal Equivalents			
Simplified Fraction	Number of Shaded Squares (Numerator)	Numerator Written with a Denominator of 100	Fraction Written as a Decimal Number
1/2	50	50/100	0.50 (or 0.5)

As an additional challenge, you might ask the students to convert a number such as $\frac{1}{20}$ or $\frac{3}{25}$ into a decimal number.

To reinforce your students' thinking about fractions and their decimal equivalents, introduce the children's book *Piece = Part = Portion: Fractions = Decimals = Percents* (Gifford 2003). The book's brightly colored photographs show real-world examples of fractions, such as one shoe to represent $\frac{1}{2}$ as half of a pair of shoes. The illustrations give everyday representations of $\frac{1}{2}, \frac{1}{3}, \frac{1}{4}, ..., \frac{1}{12}$, as well as $\frac{2}{3}, \frac{3}{4}$, and $\frac{99}{100}$. Each photograph is accompanied by numerical expressions of the fraction and its decimal and percent equivalents. Cover the equivalent decimal numbers and percentages with sticky notes before sharing the book with your students, leaving only the fractions and the accompanying photographs for them to see. As you page through the book with the students, prompt them to determine each decimal equivalent, and then uncover the expression to verify their work. (Leave the percents for a later discussion; see the "Extend" section.) The decimal equivalents of some of the fractions ($\frac{1}{3}, \frac{1}{6}, \frac{1}{9}, \frac{1}{11}, \frac{1}{12}$, and $\frac{2}{3}$) do not terminate but have repeating digits; the book rounds them to the nearest hundredth or thousandth. You may want to save these more complex examples for later use (see "Extend").

Reflect

Discuss the various ways in which the students have determined equivalent fractions and decimals. Ask them, "What did you learn about the relationships between fractions and decimals?" Write a fraction such as $\frac{3}{5}$ on the board or an overhead transparency and have the students explain the various ways to change the fraction into a decimal.

Extend

To extend the students' work in determining equivalent fractions and decimals, you can have them work with parallel number lines. For fractions whose equivalent forms are repeating decimals, a number line is easier to use than a hundreds grid. Distribute copies of the blackline master "Parallel Number Lines," and make sure that every student has a ruler to use with it.

Fig. **1.9.**

A sample chart for determining fraction and decimal equivalents with a hundredths grid

Use the children's book *Piece = Part = Portion: Fraction = Decimal = Percent* (Gifford 2003) to reinforce students' skills in finding decimal equivalents for fractions.

Name a fraction—say, $\frac{3}{4}$. Have the students locate it on the appropriate number line. Then guide them in placing the ruler so that it makes a line that passes through $\frac{3}{4}$ and is parallel to the right edge of the activity sheet and intersects the number line that shows hundredths. (Figure 1.10 shows the process.) When the students have placed the ruler correctly, they can find the decimal equivalent of $\frac{3}{4}$ by inspecting the calibrations on the number line that shows hundredths. The numbers $\frac{3}{4}$ and 0.75 are equivalent because they are on the same line perpendicular to the parallel number lines.

Fig. **1.10.**

Using parallel number lines and a ruler to determine that 3/4 and 0.75 are equivalent

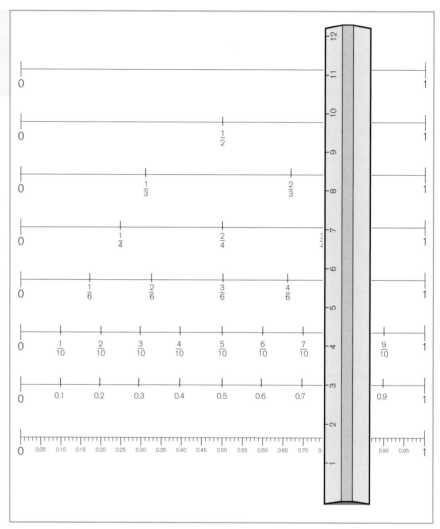

Fractions with denominators such as 3, 6, and 8 do not correspond to any calibrated number on the tenths or hundredths lines, and consequently they are difficult to locate exactly on such lines. Fractions with these denominators "fit" between hundredths calibrations. Remind the students to make sure that their ruler is as "straight" as possible—that is, that it makes right angles with the number lines—and then select the decimal number closest to the edge of their ruler.

Percent, written symbolically as "%," means "per hundred." When a whole is divided into a hundred parts, it is equal to 100%, which we can think of as 100 per hundred, or 100/100, or 1.

Navigating through Number and Operations in Grades 3–5

Thus, the students can determine that the decimal equivalent of $\frac{1}{3}$ is between 0.33 and 0.34 but closer to 0.33. Therefore, to the nearest hundredth, $\frac{1}{3}$ and 0.33 are equivalent.

Every fraction can be renamed as either a terminating or a repeating decimal. *Terminating decimals* can be represented with a finite number of nonzero digits. Fractions with terminating decimal representations have denominators whose only factors are 2, 5, or powers of 2 or 5—for example, 2, 4, 5, 8, 10, and so on. Most of the work in this activity has involved terminating decimals. *Repeating decimals* have a block of digits (called a *repetend*) that appear over and over in an unending sequence. Fractions with repeating decimal representations have denominators that have factors *other than* 2s or 5s—for example, 3, 6, 7, 9, and so on.

Students can begin work with terminating decimals by converting fractions with denominators of 2, 4, and 5. After working with these fractions, they could move on to repeating fractions with denominators of 3, 6, 7, and 9. Ask the students to round the resulting repeating decimal number to the nearest hundredth.

You can also easily extend your students' work from the decimal equivalents of fractions to equivalent percentages. Explain that *percent*, written symbolically as "%," means "per hundred." If we think of a whole as divided into a hundred parts, the whole itself is equal to 100%, or 100 per hundred, or $\frac{100}{100}$, or 1. A percentage (say, 75%) gives the number of parts (75) out of 100 that a particular fraction ($\frac{3}{4}$) represents. To extend the activity to percentages and relationships among fractions, decimals, and percentages, you can use hundredth grids to represent 100 percent. In addition, you can modify the activities that change fractions to decimals so that they require changing fractions to percentages.

As mentioned earlier, the book *Piece = Part = Portion: Fractions = Decimals = Percents* (Gifford 2003) includes representations of percentages. Introduce the book again, this time to extend your students' understanding of equivalents to include percentages. The children's book *Twizzlers Percentages Book* (Pallotta 2001) also shows ways of representing percentages with familiar real-world objects.

In addition, students can determine equivalent fractions, decimals, and percentages by using fraction calculators, if these tools are available. Calculators do not give students a conceptual grasp of the relationships among fraction, decimal, and percentage equivalents, but they do allow students to determine equivalent expressions of these numbers very quickly. Thus, in appropriate contexts, they can be very useful for finding equivalent decimals for repeating fractions. The Casio FX-55, Sharp EL-500L, and Texas Instruments Math Explorer (TI-12, TI-73) and Math Explorer Plus (TI-15) fraction calculators are all suitable for this purpose.

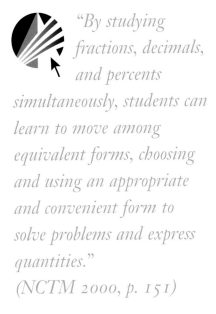

"By studying fractions, decimals, and percents simultaneously, students can learn to move among equivalent forms, choosing and using an appropriate and convenient form to solve problems and express quantities." (NCTM 2000, p. 151)

Share the children's book *Twizzlers Percentages Book* (Pallotta 2001) with your students to show ways of representing percentages with familiar real-world objects.

To pursue work with equivalent fractions, decimals, and percentages, distribute sheets of paper for your students to use to set up a three-column chart similar to that in figure 1.11. Then name fractions for the students to enter in the chart and rename as decimals and percentages.

Fig. **1.11.**

A sample chart displaying decimal and percent equivalents of given fractions

Equivalent Fractions, Decimals, and Percents		
Fraction	Decimal	Percent
1/2	0.5	50%
1/3	0.33	33%

The applet Fraction Models on the accompanying CD-ROM lets students select numerators and denominators to make different fractions, choose models to see visual representations of their fractions, and inspect the equivalent fraction, decimal, and percentage names for the each fraction represented by a model.

For additional practice with equivalent fractions, decimals, and percentages, have the students bring in examples of all three types of expressions from newspapers, magazines, or other printed matter. Ask them to tell how each is used, and then ask them to rename each in another form. Discuss possible reasons for the original choice—fraction, decimal, or percentage—and ask whether or not another name would have been better.

Conclusion

This chapter has presented activities designed to expand students' understanding of numbers and their skill in representing them. Individual activities have addressed concepts related to place value (whole numbers and decimals), classes of numbers (primes, composites, and squares), the meanings of fractions (wholes, collections, and locations on a number line), comparing and ordering fractions, and the relationships among equivalent fractions, decimals, and percentages. The activities in chapter 2 are intended to expand the students' skills with the four basic arithmetic operations—addition, subtraction, multiplication, and division.

Students can also work with the applet Fraction Models (on the CD-ROM) to consolidate their learning about equivalent factions, decimals, and percentages. The applet features sliders that allow students to select a numerator and denominator and name a fraction. They then select the area, set, or length model, and the applet gives a visual representation of the fraction. The applet also names the fraction shown both as a decimal number and as a percentage.

NAVIGATIONS SERIES

GRADES 3–5

NAVIGATING *through* NUMBER *and* OPERATIONS

Chapter 2
Understanding Operations

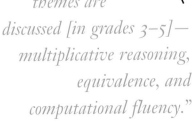

"Three central mathematical themes are discussed [in grades 3–5]— multiplicative reasoning, equivalence, and computational fluency."
(NCTM 2000, p. 144)

Principles and Standards for School Mathematics (NCTM 2000) highlights three central themes for students in grades 3–5: multiplicative reasoning, equivalence, and computational fluency. In the area of number and operations, students at this level should focus on the meanings of multiplication and division, relationships between the two operations on whole numbers, and basic understandings of fractions and decimals. In multiplying and dividing whole numbers, students must understand what each number represents. When they multiply 46 by 8, for example, they could be trying to find the total number of objects in 46 boxes with each box containing 8 objects, or they could be trying to find the total number of objects in 8 boxes with each containing 46 objects.

Students need practice in multiplying and dividing. Using diagrams and concrete materials in multiplying helps them see—literally—what each factor and each product represents. Students in grades 3–5 begin to understand how multiplication works by examining area models or rectangular arrays that show a product like 34×8 as 30×8 plus 4×8. Similarly, when students use diagrams or other materials to show division, they see that $272 \div 8$ can represent either an equitable sharing of 272 among 8 groups or a repeated subtraction of groups of 8 from 272. In the sharing model, the number of groups is known, but the size of each group is unknown. In a subtracting model, by contrast, the size of each group is known, but the number of groups is unknown. Both models of division are conceptually important.

Students can
work with the
applet Splitting
Arrays to Solve
Multiplication in connection
with the third activity,
Splitting Arrays.

This chapter presents five activities that focus on helping students gain an understanding of the meanings of operations. The first two activities develop students' understanding of the multiplication and division of whole numbers. In the third activity, students use arrays to solve multiplication problems. The fourth activity invites them to explore addition and subtraction of fractions. The fifth activity brings the chapter to a close with an investigation of multiplication and division by numbers close to 1. All the activities give students hands-on opportunities to see how and why operations with whole and rational numbers work.

The first activity, "Two Types of Multiplication Problems," helps students understand that they can model multiplication in two ways—by using equal groups or by comparing, using multiples. This insight allows students to meet the expectation in *Principles and Standards for School Mathematics* (NCTM 2000) that students in grades 3–5 will "understand various meanings of multiplication" (p. 148).

In the second activity, "Two Types of Division Problems," students solve different types of division problems. They learn to represent division with the sharing (or *partitioning*), model, as well as with the subtractive (or *measurement*) model. In addition, they complete tasks designed to investigate the relationship between multiplication and division as they focus on the meanings of division.

In "Splitting Arrays," the third activity, the students use arrays to "break up" multiplication problems with several combinations of factors—1 digit × 1 digit, 1 digit × 2 digits, and 2 digits × 2 digits—into easy-to-recall partial products. This lesson focuses on the importance of the distributive property of multiplication over addition. This property is not only a structural tool that defines the multiplication algorithm but also a helpful guide for mental mathematics. (Subsequent chapters also address splitting arrays.)

Where to situate fractions in the mathematics curriculum for grades 3–8 is often a perplexing issue. *Principles and Standards for School Mathematics* (NCTM 2000) recommends instruction at all levels that enables students to "compute fluently and make reasonable estimates" (p. 148) and encourages teachers of grades 3–5 to guide their students in using "visual models, benchmarks, and equivalent forms to add and subtract commonly used fractions" (p. 148). The fourth activity, "Adding and Subtracting Common Fractions," encourages students to use fraction models to develop their understanding of the addition and subtraction of fractions. This activity, which may take more than one day, emphasizes the use of fraction models to represent and compare fractions and perform addition and subtraction on them.

In the fifth activity, "Multiplying and Dividing by Numbers Close to 1," students multiply and divide by 1 and numbers that are slightly greater than or less than 1. They generalize about what happens to the product or quotient when the multiplier or divisor is a little greater than 1 or a little less than 1. This activity is aimed at students in grade 4 or 5 and focuses on estimation as well as beginning work with multiplication and division of decimals. As students extend their sense of number to decimals, the calculator can be a useful tool, because students at this level are not be expected to multiply or divide by decimals. This activity devotes more attention to what happens when certain numbers are multipliers or divisors than to the actual computations with such numbers. Students can use the applet "Splitting Arrays to Solve Multiplication Problems," which appears on the accompanying CD-ROM, to extend their learning from this final activity.

You may find it beneficial to extend some, if not all, of the activities in the chapter to occupy more than one day in your mathematics schedule. Or you might decide to use parts of activities as extensions to instruction or as tasks of the day. The activities can serve as guides as you help your students understand what happens when they multiply and divide whole numbers, add and subtract fractions, and multiply and divide decimals.

Two Types of Multiplication Problems

Grades 3 and 4

Summary

Students extend their thinking about multiplication by differentiating two types of multiplication problems, one based on the concept of equal groups and the other based on the concept of comparison.

Goals

- Solve two types of multiplication problems—one involving equal groups and the other involving comparison
- Classify multiplication word problems according to type—"equal groups" or "comparison"
- Create multiplication word problems of a specified type and match a specified number sentence with an appropriate problem

Prior Knowledge or Experience

- Skill in adding and subtracting whole numbers
- Experience with manipulative materials to explore beginning concepts in multiplication

Materials and Equipment

For each pair of students—
- A copy of the blackline master "Multiplication Work Mat"
- Four copies of the blackline master "Multiplication Recording Sheet"
- About 70 centimeter cubes, kidney beans, or other small objects to use as counters on the work mat
- Pencils
- A copy of the blackline master "Can You Solve It with Multiplication?"

For the teacher—
- A copy of the children's book *Amanda Bean's Amazing Dream: A Mathematical Story* (Neuschwander 1998)
- Play money (seven one-dollar bills or one five-dollar bill and two one-dollar bills; optional)
- A transparency of the blackline master "Can You Solve It with Multiplication?" (optional)
- An overhead projector (optional)

pp. 166, 167, 168

Activity

Engage

There are many real-life situations in which multiplication provides useful information. In this activity, your students learn about two types of multiplication problems. Prepare them to encounter the first type—problems involving a given number of groups of equal size—by turning their attention to a variety of everyday contexts in which someone might confront a problem of this type. Say, "Sometimes we are in a situation with a number of groups of people or objects, and we need to determine the total number of people or objects. If all the groups are equal and we know both how many are in a group and how many groups we have, we can find the total number of people or objects by multiplying the number of groups by the number in each." Give examples:

- If we have 6 cans with 3 tennis balls in each can, how many tennis balls do we have in all?
- If ice cream sandwiches are packed 12 to a box, and we have 9 boxes, how many ice cream sandwiches do we have?
- If 15 cars are traveling to the carnival, and each car is carrying 5 passengers, how many people are traveling to the carnival?"

Ask your students, "Can you think of other real-life example of this kind of multiplication problem?"

After the students have given their own everyday examples, tell them that you are going to help them explore this kind of multiplication problem by reading aloud the children's book *Amanda Bean's Amazing Dream* (Neuschwander 1998). Show them the illustrations as you read. Ask them to be on the lookout for things that come in groups with the same number in each group. After reading the book, have the students explain why Amanda Bean needs to learn her multiplication facts. (It's faster to multiply than to count, even if someone can count as fast as Amanda Bean can!)

Group your students in pairs, and distribute to each pair a copy of the blackline master "Multiplication Work Mat" along with a copy of the "Multiplication Recording Sheet." (Students can reuse the mats to represent all the problems in the activity, but they can show only up to four problems on any one recording sheet. For each part of the activity—"Engage," "Explore," "Reflect," and "Extend"—they will need a clean copy of the recording sheet to document their work. For clarity, you can have the students label the sheets "Sheet 1," "Sheet 2," etc., as they receive them.) Each pair of students will also need about 70 small counters, such as centimeter cubes, dried beans, or similar items.

Open *Amanda Bean's Amazing Dream* to the illustration that shows eight sheep riding on bicycles, with Amanda Bean asking, "How many wheels is that?" Hold up the picture for your students to see, and say, "Let's make Amanda Bean's question problem 1 on the 'Multiplication Recording Sheet.' But first let's use counters to represent the problem on the 'Multiplication Work Mat.' How do you suppose you could do that?"

Walk the students through the process (see fig. 2.1). Say, "Each bicycle has 2 wheels. Put 2 counters, to show the wheels on a bicycle, in one of the rectangles in the column on the left side of the work mat." Give the students time to do this, and then say, "There are 8 bicycles in all. What should we do to show the 8 bicycles?" If no one comes up with the idea of putting 2 counters in 7 more rectangles, lead the students to

In *Amanda Bean's Amazing Dream* (Neuschwander 1998), Amanda Bean can't see why she should learn to multiply. After all, she can count by ones, twos, fives, and tens very quickly. A fast-paced dream, with bicycling sheep delivering balls of yarn to grandmothers who rapidly knit the yarn into sweaters, overwhelms Amanda Bean's counting skills and shows her the usefulness of multiplication.

it. (Explain that the single rectangle on the lower right of the mat will come in handy later in the activity, but they should ignore it for now.)

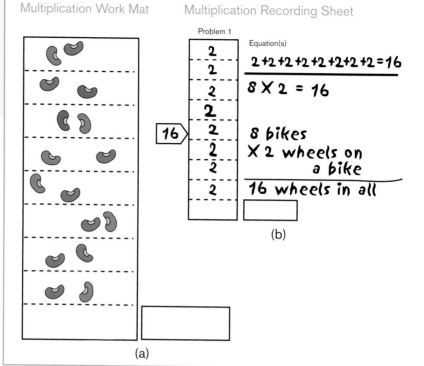

Next, guide the students in transferring the data displayed on the mat to the recording sheet, where they will make a numerical record of the problem. Say, "For problem 1, enter 2s in 8 of the rectangles on your 'Multiplication Recording Sheet.'" Remind the students that Amanda Bean wants to know how many wheels there are in all. Ask, "How can your work help you find the answer to Amanda Bean's question?" Have the students add 2s, count the counters on the mat, or multiply 2 by 8, and then record the total, 16, in the large "tag" to the left of the rectangles on the recording sheet. Ask, "What equation (or equations) can you write on your recording sheet to obtain this total number of wheels?" Wait while they enter $8 \times 2 = 16$, and perhaps $2 + 2 + 2 + 2 + 2 + 2 + 2 + 2 = 16$, in the space provided on the recording sheet.

Summarize the multiplication problem for the students: "There are 8 groups of 2 wheels, making a total of 16 wheels." If you wish, you can have the students express the multiplication problem and its product, with appropriate labels, in the space to the right of the rectangles on the recording sheet. (Figure 2.1 shows all the data for problem 1 on the recording sheet.) Point out that the students are not using the single rectangular boxes at the lower right for now.

Again hold up *Amanda Bean's Amazing Dream*, open now to the illustration in which each of the 8 sheep has 5 balls of yarn and Amanda Bean says, "Now I must count the yarn, too!" Have the students treat this situation as problem 2 on their recording sheets. Go through the same process as before, guiding them in framing the situation as a problem that they can represent with counters on their mats. Emphasize that here too they have 8 equal groups, with 5 balls of yarn in each group, so they can put 5 counters in each of 8 rectangles on the mat.

Then they should enter the data numerically on their recording sheet and solve Amanda Bean's problem either by multiplying 8 × 5, or by adding 5 + 5 + 5 + 5 + 5 + 5 + 5 + 5, to get 40 balls of yarn. (See the mat and recorded data for problem 2 below at the left.)

Present the following number sentence to the students as problem 3:

$$4 \times 6 = \square.$$

Guide them in writing an "equal groups" word problem that matches the number sentence. Use the following sample problems if necessary:

- A tailor is sewing 4 identical coats with 6 buttons on each. How many buttons does he need for the coats?
- Each of 4 cats has 6 kittens. How many kittens are there in all?

Have the students use their mats to show the problem that they have created for the number sentence. Direct them to record their data numerically on their recording sheets and solve the problem. (The mat and recorded data for the sample problem about kittens appears below at the right.)

For problem 4, write the following number sentences on the board:

$$3 \times 8 = \square$$
$$6 \times 5 = \square$$
$$7 \times 4 = \square$$

Have each pair of students choose a sentence and use it to write a matching word problem involving equal groups. Brainstorm with your

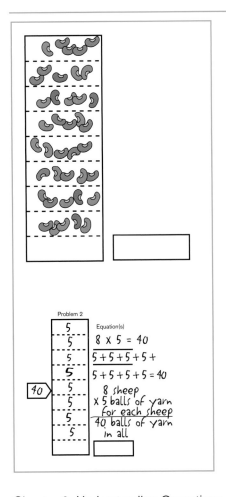

Problem 2

	5	Equation(s)
40	5	8 x 5 = 40
	5	5 + 5 + 5 + 5 +
	5	5 + 5 + 5 + 5 = 40
	5	8 sheep
	5	x 5 balls of yarn
	5	for each sheep
	5	40 balls of yarn
	5	in all

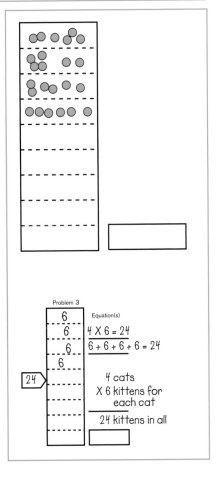

Problem 3

	6	Equation(s)
24	6	4 X 6 = 24
	6	6 + 6 + 6 + 6 = 24
	6	
		4 cats
		X 6 kittens for each cat
		24 kittens in all

Amanda Bean's Amazing Dream includes an illustration that shows baked items on a cart. For additional practice with different numbers of groups besides 8, give your students a "Multiplication Recording Sheet" and have them use it and their "Multiplication Work Mat" to solve the embedded multiplication problems (or their reverses):

$$2 \times 7 = 14$$
$$6 \times 3 = 18$$
$$4 \times 3 = 12$$
$$7 \times 4 = 28$$

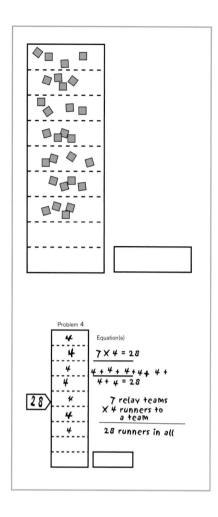

Problem 4

	Equation(s)
4	
4	7 × 4 = 28
4	4 + 4 + 4 + 4 + 4 +
4	4 + 4 = 28
4	7 relay teams
4	× 4 runners to
4	a team
	28 runners in all

28

students to come up with possible topics and situations for the word problems. A sample problem follows for each number sentence:

- $3 \times 8 = \square$: Three pizzas are cut into 8 slices each. How many slices of pizza are there in all?
- $6 \times 5 = \square$: Six children will pay $5 apiece to take the bus to the zoo and back. How much will their outing cost altogether?
- $7 \times 4 = \square$: Seven teams are participating in the annual relay race. Each team has 4 runners. How many runners are participating in the race?

When all the student pairs have come up with word problems, have them represent the problems on their mats and display their work as problem 4 on the reording sheets. (See the sample problem about relay runners represented in the margin.)

When all the pairs of students have finished working, have them share their work with the class. All pairs selecting the same number sentence should have the same arrangements of counters on their mats and should have entered the same data, but with different labels, on their recording sheets.

Conclude the students' work in this part of the activity by emphasizing that each of the word problems with which they have been working involves a given number of equal groups. When the students know how many groups they have and that all the groups are equal, they can solve the problem easily by multiplication.

Explore

After the students have a good understanding of multiplication problems that involve equal groups, turn their attention to a different type of multiplication problem—a problem involving a *comparison*. Say, "Let's create a new problem for Amanda Bean to solve." Then state the following problem:

Suppose that Amanda Bean made 3 caramel apples yesterday for a party. Then today she and her mom made 5 times as many. How many caramel apples did they make today?

Have your students continue to work in pairs, using the same "Multiplication Work Mat" as before. Distribute a clean copy of the "Multiplication Recording Sheet" to each pair of students.

Turn the students' attention to the new problem. Ask, "Is this the same type of problem as the ones that you have been solving?" (No; the problem does not give a particular number of equal groups or ask for the total number of people or objects in all the groups.)

Guide the students in representing this new type of problem on their work mats. Say, "This problem tells us that Amanda Bean made three caramel apples yesterday. Let's put that information in the rectangle that is off by itself at the lower right on the mat." Wait while your students correctly place three counters to represent the three apples. Then say, "The problem also tells us that Amanda Bean and her mother made five times as many caramel apples today. How can we use the main part of the mat to show today's apples?" Help the students understand that they can show "five times as many" by making a matching group of 3 apples five times. Have them place these groups in the main column of rectangles.

Navigating through Number and Operations in Grades 3–5

Then have your students use numbers and record the data as problem 1 on the new recording sheet. Be sure that they record the number for yesterday (3), all the numbers for today (3, 3, 3, 3, 3), the total (15), and the equations—the multiplication equation (5 × 3 = 15 and the addition equation (3 + 3 + 3 + 3 + 3 = 15). As before, you can have them show their work with labels in the space at the right on the recording sheet. Figure 2.2 shows a mat and a recording sheet for the problem.

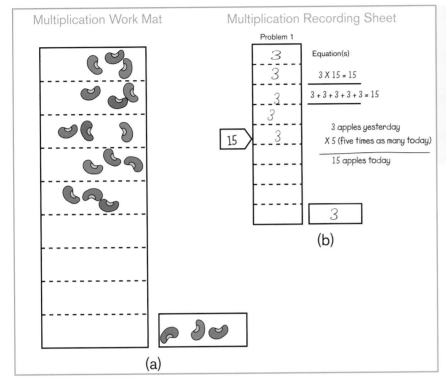

Fig. 2.2.

Using (a) the "Multiplication Work Mat" and (b) the "Multiplication Recording Sheet" to solve a comparison problem, "Suppose that Amanda Bean made 3 caramel apples yesterday for a party. Then today she and her mom made 5 times as many. How many caramel apples did they make today?"

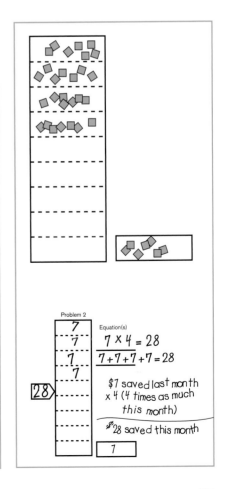

Build your students' skill in using the mat and recording sheet to solve comparison problems by giving them a new problem:

Suppose that Amanda Bean saved 4 times as much money this month as she did last month. Last month she saved $7. How much did she save this month?

Challenge the student pairs to represent this problem on the work mat and record their results as problem 2 on the recording sheet. (If you have play money available, you might show your students $7 with either seven one-dollar bills or one five-dollar bill and two ones and help them see that four times this amount would be $7 + $7 + $7 + $7, or $28.) When all the pairs have finished, ask them to share their methods. (The margin shows a completed mat and recording sheet.)

Summarize comparison problems, making sure that your students understand the following main ideas:

- These problems always *compare* two groups that have the same type of people or objects, but the groups are *unequal*.
- The size of one group is always a *multiple* of the other group.
- In representing these problems on the work mat, the students should place the smaller group in the single rectangle at the lower right and make multiple copies of this group in an appropriate number of rectangles in the main column on the left.

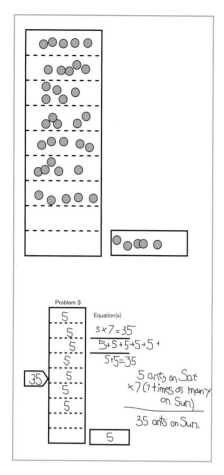

Remind the students that an "equal groups" problem always involves a given number of groups that are the same size, and problem solvers must find the total number in all the groups. By contrast, a comparison problem always deals with two groups of unequal size. The problem gives the size of the smaller group and the information that the other, larger group is a particular multiple of the smaller group. Problem solvers must find the size of the larger group.

On the board, write the following number sentence: $5 \times 7 = \square$. Have each pair of student create a comparison story problem to match the number sentence. If necessary, brainstorm about possible topics and situations for the students' problems. Use the following sample problems if doing so is useful:

- This year, Carrie had 5 candles on her birthday cake. Her father's cake had 7 times as many. How many candles did Carrie's father have on his cake?
- On Saturday, Mrs. Wilson saw 5 ants on her kitchen table and frowned. On Sunday, she counted 7 times as many. How many ants were now on Mrs. Wilson's table?

Ask the students to show their problem on the work mats and record it numerically as problem 3 on the recording sheet. (The margin at the top left shows the completed mat and numerical data for the sample problem about ants.) When all the pairs have finished, invite the students to share their stories. Point out the wide variety of the stories that match the given number sentence.

Write the following number sentences on the board:

$$3 \times 9 = \square$$
$$2 \times 4 = \square$$
$$6 \times 6 = \square$$

Ask your students to chose one of these number sentences, create a comparison story problem to match it, show it on their mats, and record it as problem 4 on their recording sheets. A sample problem follows for each number sentence:

- $3 \times 9 = \square$: Ursula needs \$3 to buy balloons for Susie's surprise party. Susie's mother needs 9 times that much to buy sodas, cake, and ice cream for the party. How much money does Susie's mother need?
- $2 \times 4 = \square$: Yesterday, Tim walked 2 blocks from his house to Fred's house. Today, he walked 4 times as far to get to Don's house. How many blocks did Tim walk to Don's house?
- $6 \times 6 = \square$: Scott's dog is afraid of Martha's cat even though the cat weighs only 6 lbs. Scott's dog weighs 6 times that much. How many pounds does Scott's dog weigh?

(The margin at the bottom left shows the completed mat and recorded data for the sample problem about Scott's dog.)

When all the students have finished, again have them share their work. Those who selected the same number sentence should have the same arrangements of counters on their mats and the same numerical data, with different labels, on their recording sheets.

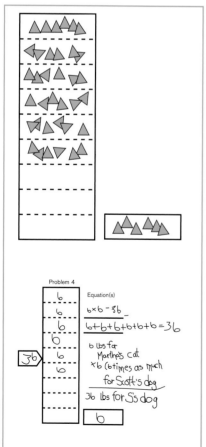

Reflect

Have the students reflect on their work by classifying a small set of multiplication problems by type. With the students continuing to work in pairs, distribute clean copies of the "Multiplication Recording Sheet" to each pair, along with a copy of the blackline master "Can You Solve It with Multiplication?" This sheet provides four word problems for the students to discuss and classify by type, in each case explaining their thinking. Then the students can solve the problems, using counters on the mats and entering their work on their recording sheets. The problems follow:

1. James and his dad made cupcakes as a birthday surprise for James's sister, who just turned 8. They decided to put 8 gumdrops on the top of each of the 6 cupcakes that they made. How many gumdrops did they put on the cupcakes in all? (Equal groups; problem tells how many equal groups of objects there are and the number of objects in each group [6 cupcakes with 8 gumdrops on each cupcake] and asks how many objects [gumdrops] there are in all [$6 \times 8 = 48$].)

2. Ankara and Simone sorted all the mystery books out of their book collections. Ankara had only 4 mysteries. Simone said, "I've got 9 times as many as you have." How many mystery books did Simone have? (Comparison; problem gives the size of a smaller group of objects of a particular type [4 mystery books for Ankara] and asks for the size of a larger group of objects of the same type [Simone's mystery books], which is a given multiple [9] of the smaller group [$4 \times 9 = 36$].)

3. Renaldo and Benny are picking apples to earn some extra money. Renaldo has picked 7 apples, but Benny has picked 6 times as many as Renaldo. How many apples has Benny picked? (Comparison; problem gives the size of a smaller group of objects of a particular type [7 apples for Renaldo] and asks for the size of a larger group of objects of the same type [Benny's apples], which is a given multiple [6] of the smaller group [$7 \times 6 = 42$].)

4. One summer, Tracy helped her dad plant flowers in their garden. Altogether, they planted 4 rows of flowers. Each row produced 8 flowers. How many flowers did the garden have in all? (Equal groups; problem tells how many equal groups of objects there are and the number of objects in each group [4 rows with 8 flowers in each row] and asks how many objects [flowers] there are in all [$4 \times 8 = 32$].)

Figure 2.3 shows a completed recording sheet for the four problems.

The task of sorting the problems will help cement the students' understanding of what they have learned. Invite them to share their solution methods when everyone has finished working. If you wish, you can make a transparency from the blackline master "Can you Solve It with Multiplication? to display on an overhead projector as an aid in discussing the problems.

Extend

To extend the students' work in this activity and give them a preview of division, distribute one final copy of the "Multiplication Recording

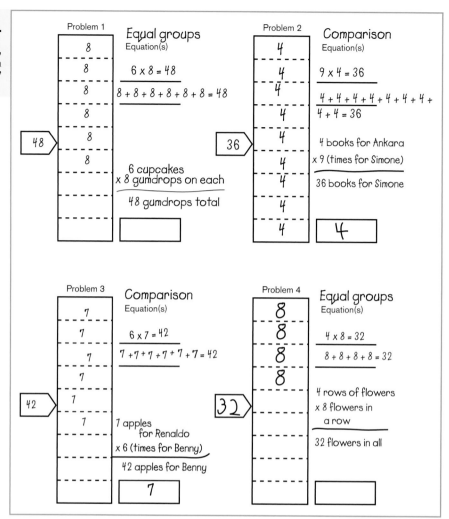

Sheet" to each pair of students, and challenge them to solve the following two problems:

1. Sandra and Monroe searched their classroom to find extra pencils. Monroe found 7 pencils, and Sandra found 28. How many times more pencils did Sandra find than Monroe?

2. Mrs. Abrams passed out 63 stickers to her 7 piano students. Each student got the same number of stickers. How many stickers did each student receive?

Have successful problem solvers explain their solution methods. Figures 2.4 and 2.5 show work mats and recording sheets for problem 1 and problem 2, respectively. Students should be able to solve both problems nicely by using the work mats and recording sheets. They can treat problem 1 as a comparison problem, although here they have the size of the smaller group and the size of the larger group, and they must find the multiple that describes the relationship between the two groups. This problem foreshadows division that involves "taking away" groups of a given size from a total. The students can solve problem 2 as an "equal groups" problem, although here they are actually finding the size of the group. They know how many groups there are in all, and they know the total number of objects in all the groups. This problem foreshadows division that involves "sharing" a total.

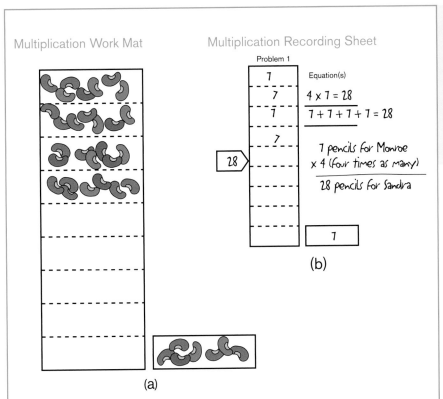

Fig. **2.4.**

Using (a) the "Multiplication Work Mat" and (b) the "Multiplication Recording Sheet" to solve "Extend" problem 1 (a comparison): "Sandra and Monroe searched their classroom to find extra pencils. Monroe found 7 pencils, and Sandra found 28. How many times more pencils did Sandra find than Monroe?"

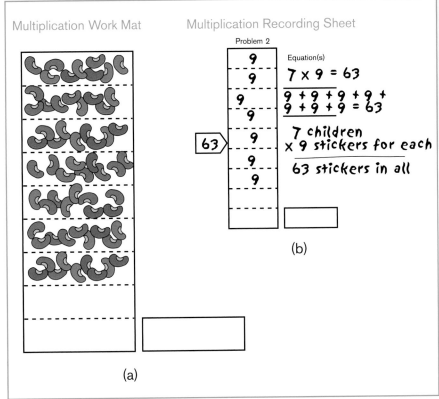

Fig. **2.5.**

Using (a) the "Multiplication Work Mat" and (b) the "Multiplication Recording Sheet" to solve "Extend" problem 2 (equal groups): "Mrs. Abrams passed out 63 stickers to her 7 piano students. Each student got the same number of stickers. How many stickers did each student receive?"

The purpose of this activity has been to use representation to develop an understanding of how multiplication works. The students have used work mats and recording sheets to differentiate models of multiplication based on equal groups and comparison. This work has prepared them to apply the ideas that they have encountered to division.

pp. 169, 170, 171

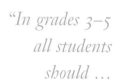

"The conceptual bases for operations with numbers and how those operations relate to real situations should be a major focus of the curriculum."
(Kilpatrick, Swafford, and Findell 2001, p. 413)

"In grades 3–5 all students should … identify and use relationships between operations, such as division as the inverse of multiplication, to solve problems."
(NCTM 2000, p. 148)

Two Types of Division Problems

Grades 3– 5

Summary

Students expand their understanding of division in ways that support the expectation of the Number and Operations Standard that all students in grades 3–5 will "identify and use relationships between operations, such as division as the inverse of multiplication, to solve problems" (NCTM 2000, p. 148).

Goals

- Solve two types of division word problems—"partitioning" (or "sharing") and "subtractive" (or "measurement") problems
- Solve division word problems
- Investigate the relationship between multiplication and division

Prior Knowledge or Experience

- Some knowledge of basic multiplication facts
- Beginning experiences with division

Materials or Equipment

For each pair of students—

- A copy of the blackline master "Division Work Mat"
- Four copies of the blackline master "Division Recording Sheet"
- A copy of the blackline master "Can You Solve It with Division?"
- About 70 centimeter cubes, kidney beans, or other small counters for use with the work mat
- Pencils

For the teacher—

- A copy of *Amanda Bean's Amazing Dream: A Mathematical Story* (Neuschwander 1998)
- A transparency of the blackline master "Can You Solve It with Division?" (optional)
- An overhead projector (optional)

Activity

Engage

Begin by reading the children's book *Amanda Bean's Amazing Dream* (Neuswander 1998) aloud to your students unless they are already very familiar with it from the preceding activity. The story will set problem solving in a concrete context. Pair each student with a partner, and give each pair a copy of the blackline master "Division Work Mat" and a copy of the "Division Recording Sheet." (Students can reuse the mats to represent all the problems in the activity, but they can show only up to four problems on any one recording sheet. As they move through the activity, they will need clean copies of the recording sheet to continue to document their work. For clarity, you can have the students label the sheets "Sheet 1," "Sheet 2," etc., as they receive them.)

Also give each pair of students about seventy counters, such as centimeter cubes, dried beans, or similar items, to use with the mat. Explain that they will use the work mat over and over to represent division problems in the activity, and they will use the recording sheet to keep track of their work.

Ask the students to listen carefully as you present the following invented problem for the fictional Amanda Bean:

> Suppose that Amanda Bean's mother baked 24 muffins by filling 4 muffin pans with batter to make the same number of muffins in each pan. How many muffins did she bake in each pan?

Say to the students, "Treat this problem as problem 1 on your 'Division Recording Sheet.' But first, how would you use counters to represent the problem on your 'Division Work Mat'?" The students should see that they can use the counters to represent the muffins, but where should they put the counters on the mat? Ask, "Are the 24 muffins the groups, or are they the total?" The students should recognize that the 24 muffins are the total. Guide them in putting 24 counters in the large oval on the mat to show the total.

Then ask, "How many groups are the 24 muffins separated into in the problem?" When the students understand that the four muffin pans make four groups, guide them in separating the "muffins" evenly into four of the smaller ovals. Tell the students, "When we separate a total into groups that are the same size, the process that we use is called *division.*"

Call the students' attention to the arrows on both the work mat and the recording sheet. Say, "See that the arrows point *away* from the large oval to the small, congruent ovals. In division, we move from a total to smaller, equal groups that together add up to the total."

For problem 1 (see figure 2.6), have the students write 24 in the long, horizontal rectangle on the recording sheet and a 6 in each of four squares in the row above. On the equation line, have them record the equation for this division problem: $24 \div 4 = 6$. Note that the students can use the extra space on the recording sheet to express the division and its quotient with appropriate labels.

Give the students a second problem, and ask them to represent it on their mats and enter their work as problem 2 on their recording sheets. Say, "Let's make another problem for Amanda Bean to solve":

> Suppose that Amanda Bean has 21 lollipops to share evenly among 7 sheep. How many lollipops will each of the sheep get?

Again, emphasize that the students should ask themselves, "What is the total?" (21) and, "Into how many equal groups is the total being separated?" (7). Watch while the students count out 21 counters for the lollipops and put them in the large oval on the mat. Make sure that they understand that they will be separating these counters into 7 equal

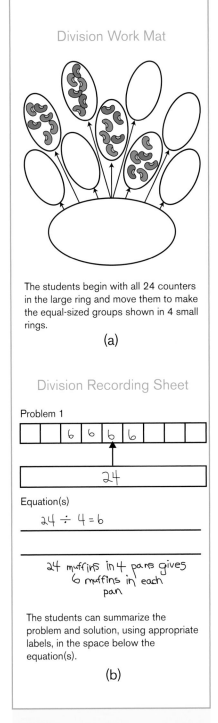

Division Work Mat

The students begin with all 24 counters in the large ring and move them to make the equal-sized groups shown in 4 small rings.

(a)

Division Recording Sheet

Problem 1

| | | 6 | 6 | 6 | 6 | | | |

24

Equation(s)

$24 \div 4 = 6$

24 muffins in 4 pans gives 6 muffins in each pan

The students can summarize the problem and solution, using appropriate labels, in the space below the equation(s).

(b)

Fig. **2.6.**

Using (a) the "Division Work Mat" (with beans as counters) and (b) the "Division Recording Sheet" to solve a partitioning problem, "Suppose that Amanda Bean's mother baked 24 muffins by filling 4 muffin pans with batter to make the same number of muffins in each pan. How many muffins did she make in each pan?"

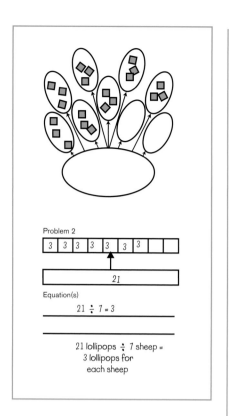

Problem 2

| 3 | 3 | 3 | 3 | 3 | 3 | 3 | | | |

21

Equation(s)

21 ÷ 7 = 3

_____

21 lollipops ÷ 7 sheep =
3 lollipops for
each sheep

groups in small ovals. Check to see how successful the students are in partitioning the 21 counters into seven groups of 3 and recording their work (see the margin).

Explain that the process here, as in the muffin problem, is *division*. Have the students write the equation for this division problem: $21 \div 7 = 3$. The lollipop problem and the muffin problem are similar in that each one gives a total and a particular number of groups. To solve such problems, the students must determine the size of each group.

Division problems like these two are called *partitioning* problems. To make the term concrete, explain to your students that light interior walls in office buildings are often called *partitions*. Office managers hire builders to put up partitions to divide a large space into smaller component spaces. In division, *partitioning* involves dividing a number into a specified number of equal parts.

Have your students use their mats to solve two more partitioning problems, and ask them to record these as problems 3 and 4 on their recording sheets:

- Clara read 14 pages in her storybook in 2 days. If she read the same number of pages on both days, how many pages did she read on each day?
- Ronnie baked 35 cookies to give to his 5 cousins. Each cousin got the same number of cookies. How many cookies did each cousin get?

Figure 2.7 shows both problems on the recording sheet.

Fig. **2.7.**

Two partitioning problems ("Engage" problems 3 and 4) entered on the "Division Recording Sheet"

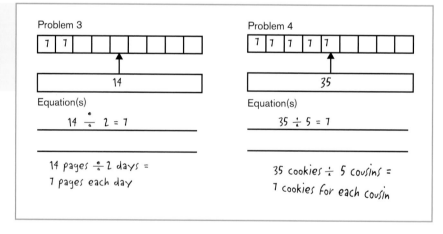

Problem 3

| 7 | 7 | | | | | | | | |

14

Equation(s)

14 ÷ 2 = 7

_____

14 pages ÷ 2 days =
7 pages each day

Problem 4

| 7 | 7 | 7 | 7 | 7 | | | | | |

35

Equation(s)

35 ÷ 5 = 7

_____

35 cookies ÷ 5 cousins =
7 cookies for each cousin

Explore

When you think that your students have a good grasp of division as partitioning, move on to another type of division problem—problems that are often called *subtractive*, or *measurement*, division. A subtractive division problem gives the solver a total number of people or objects and the size of the groups into which the total is separated but not how many groups there are in all.

Give each pair of students a clean copy of the "Division Recording Sheet" and introduce the following problem:

Jenny worked 3 hours at the movie theater each day after school until she had worked 18 hours in all. How many days did she work at the movie theater?

Ask the students, "How can you use the work mat and the counters to solve this problem?" Guide them in determining that 18 hours is the total. Wait while they count out 18 counters and place them in the large oval on their work mats. Then say, "Jenny's work schedule divided this total into groups of 3 hours, since that is how long she worked each day. But we need to know how many days she worked in all."

See if your students can discover on their own that they can subtract 3 hours repeatedly from the total of 18 hours, each time moving 3 counters from the large oval into a different small one, to determine that 6 groups of 3 hours make up the total of 18 hours. For number 1 on the recording sheet, have them record 18 in the long, horizontal rectangle and a 3 in each of 6 small squares above. On the equation line, have them write the division equation for this problem: $18 \div 3 = 6$. Figure 2.8 shows the problem on a "Division Work Mat" and a "Division Recording Sheet."

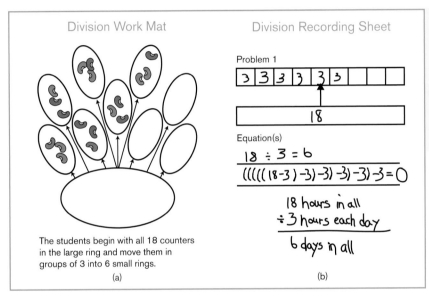

Division Work Mat   Division Recording Sheet

Problem 1

| 3 | 3 | 3 | 3 | 3 | 3 | | | |

| 18 |

Equation(s)

$18 \div 3 = 6$

$(((((18-3)-3)-3)-3)-3)-3 = 0$

18 hours in all
÷ 3 hours each day
6 days in all

The students begin with all 18 counters in the large ring and move them in groups of 3 into 6 small rings.

(a)   (b)

Fig. 2.8.

Using (a) the "Division Work Mat" (with beans as counters) and (b) the "Division Recording Sheet" to solve a subtractive problem, "Jenny worked 3 hours at the movie theater each day after school until she had worked 18 hours in all. How many days did she work at the movie theater?"

Give your students three more subtractive division problems to solve by using their work mats and recording sheets. Have them show these as problems 2, 3, and 4 on their "Division Recording Sheets." Use the following problems or ones of your own choosing.

- Jeremy had 36 books to put on his shelves. He put 9 books on each shelf. How many shelves did he use for these books? (See the mat and recording sheet in the margin.)
- Selena has 28 treats to share with her friends. She decides to give each friend 4 treats. With how many friends can Selena share treats? (See the recorded data in fig. 2.9.)
- A loaf of bread has 18 slices. Mike's mom uses 6 slices each time she packs lunches for the family. How many times will she be able to make lunches from one loaf of bread? (See the recorded data in fig. 2.9.)

Reflect

Guide the students in reflecting on what they have learned about partitioning and subtractive division problems. Remind them that they have solved some division problems that tell how many equal groups

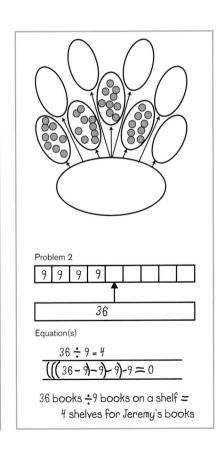

Problem 2

| 9 | 9 | 9 | 9 | | | | | |

| 36 |

Equation(s)

$36 \div 9 = 4$

$(((36-9)-9)-9)-9 = 0$

36 books ÷ 9 books on a shelf = 4 shelves for Jeremy's books

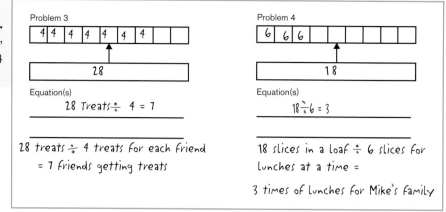

"partition," or "share," a total number of people or objects. These problems ask how many people or objects are in each group. Point out that the students have also solved division problems that tell how many people or objects are in each equal group of people or objects that is being "taken away," or "subtracted," from the total number of people or objects. These problems ask how many such groups are in the total.

At this point, the students do not need to learn the names of the two types of division problems, but they should be able to analyze them and describe how they are alike and unlike. To help your students internalize the similarities and differences, distribute a clean copy of the recording sheet to each pair of students for use with their work mat. Also give each pair a copy of the blackline master "Can You Solve It with Division?" This activity sheet displays the following problems, which, as indicated in parentheses, are of both types:

1. Sonya was sorting her pencils. She had 30 pencils, which she put into 6 equal piles. How many pencils did she put in each pile? (Partitioning; problem tells how many equal groups of pencils [6] "partition," or "share," the total [30 pencils], and asks problem solvers to find the size of each group [5, or 5 pencils in each pile].)

2. Mrs. Smith is arranging transportation for a class trip. She plans to drive, and some parents will, too. Mrs. Smith has 24 students in her class, and she plans to assign 4 children to each car. How many cars will Mrs. Smith need for the trip? (Subtractive; problem tells how many children [4] are in each equal group that is being "taken away" or "subtracted" from the total [24], and asks problem solvers to find how many such groups there are [6, or 6 cars for the trip].)

3. Kevin has $15.00 to use to buy balls that cost $3.00 apiece. How many balls can Kevin buy? (Subtractive; problem tells how many dollars [$3] are in each equal group that is taken away from the total [$15]; problem solvers must find the number of such groups [5, or 5 balls].)

4. Katy is decorating goody bags for her birthday party. She has 5 goody bags that she must decorate in the next 35 minutes. How many minutes should she spend on each bag? (Partitioning; problem tells how many equal groups [5 goody bags] partition, or "share," the total [35 minutes], and asks problem solvers to find the size of each group [7, or 7 minutes for each goody bag].)

Have the students work in pairs and use their work mats and recording sheets to solve all four problems. To facilitate discussion of the problems, you can make a transparency of the blackline master and display it on an overhead projector. (Fig. 2.10 shows the data from the problems entered on a recording sheet.)

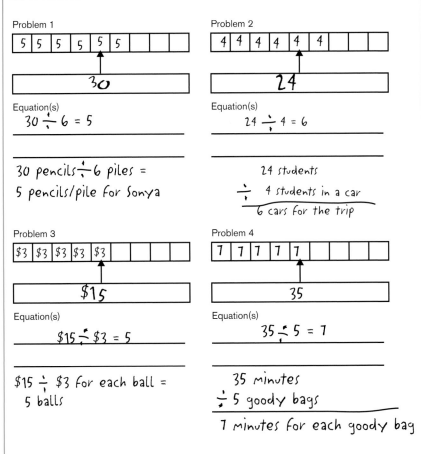

Fig. **2.10**

"Reflect" problems 1–4 shown on the "Division Recording Sheet"

When the students have finished working, say, "How are these problems alike? How are they are different?" Help the students see that both kinds of division problems give the total number to be divided. However, a partitioning problem gives the number of equal groups and asks problem solvers to determine the size of each group. The process is just the opposite in a subtractive problem. The problem gives the size of each group, and problem solvers must determine the number of groups.

Extend

The students have now learned how to use the "Division Work Mat" and the "Division Recording Sheet" to solve two types of division problems. To extend the activity, help them discover that they can use these tools to solve multiplication problems as well as division problems. In so doing, they will make important discoveries about the relationship between multiplication and division.

Begin by giving your students the following problem:

Alice bought 5 cartons of eggs. Each carton has 6 eggs in it. How many eggs did Alice buy?

Ask the students, "Can you use the 'Division Work Mat' to solve this problem?" The problem is of course actually a multiplication problem, but do not say so.

Seat the students again in pairs with the same work mats, and distribute new recording sheets. Guide the whole class through the problem. Say, "Alice has 5 cartons of eggs, and each carton has 6 eggs in it. Let's think about the 6 eggs. Is '6 eggs' the total number of eggs that Alice bought?" (No) "Is it the number of groups of eggs that she bought?" (No) "Is '6 eggs' the size of a group?" (Yes)

Direct your students' attention to their division mats. Say, "If each group has 6 eggs, where should we put 6 counters on our mats to show 6 eggs in a group?" (In one of the small ovals; see the margin) When all pairs of students have placed 6 counters correctly, say, "Now, how many groups of this size did Alice buy?" (5, because she bought 5 cartons, with 6 eggs in each) Tell your students to look at their mats again, and ask, "What should we do now to show the 5 cartons?" (Put 6 counters in each of 4 more small ovals, for a total of 5 ovals with 6 beans apiece.) Watch while your students make 5 groups of 6 on their mats.

Direct your students' attention back to the problem. Say, "What does the problem ask us to find out?" (How many eggs Alice bought) Make sure your students understand that the problem is asking for a total by saying, "The problem asks 'how many?' Does this mean 'how many eggs in a group?'" (No) "Does it mean how many groups of eggs?" (No) "Does it mean how many eggs in all?" (Yes) Emphasize the word *total*: "To solve the problem, we need to find out how many eggs in all Alice bought—the *total* number of eggs in all the cartons."

Ask the students, "Where can we show a total on our mats?" (In the large ring) Say, "How can we show Alice's total?" (By moving all the counters to the large ring) Be sure that your students understand why they are moving all the counters and combining them. They should now be set for the question, "How many eggs did Alice buy?" Watch to see how your students arrive at 30. Do they count by 1s (or 2s, or 3s, etc.) without thinking in terms of 5 groups of 6? Or do they count five 6s or—better yet—simply multiply 5 × 6?

Now ask the most important question: "What equation matches this problem?" Help them see that the best equation is 5 × 6 = 30, because it clearly and directly gives the information that we begin with and yields the information that we need to find out: 5 cartons of eggs × 6 eggs in each carton = 30 eggs in all. Say, "We start with 5 groups, each of which has 6 items. The problem asks us to combine these to make a *product*, which we get by multiplying. Our product is 30—Alice bought 30 eggs in all."

On the "Division Recording Sheet," have the students write a 6 in each of 5 small squares and 30 in the longer rectangle for problem 1 (see the margin). Then on the equation line have them write the multiplication equation: 5 × 6 = 30. Connect this activity to earlier multiplication problems in which they also combined equal groups to make a total.

Next, have the students solve the following problem by using counters on their division mats and entering data on their recording sheets. Again, do not indicate the type of problem:

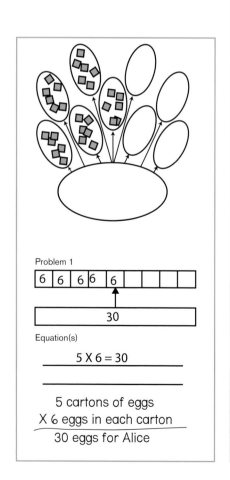

Problem 1

6	6	6	6	6					

30

Equation(s)

_____ 5 X 6 = 30 _____

_____

5 cartons of eggs
X 6 eggs in each carton
_____
30 eggs for Alice

Francisco worked 30 mathematics problems. He worked 6 problems on each sheet of paper. How many sheets of paper did he use?

If necessary, ask the students, "Do the 30 mathematics problems represent the total or the groups?" (The total) Watch to be sure that the students place 30 counters in the large oval on the mat to show the total and then subtract groups of 6, moving each group to a small oval. In this way, they will determine that Francisco used 5 sheets of paper. Have them record their work as problem 2 on the recording sheet, entering 30 in the large rectangle, 6s in 5 small squares, and the equation that matches this problem ($30 \div 6 = 5$) on the appropriate line. (The work mat and recording sheet are shown in the margin.)

Now have the students compare the problems about Alice and Francisco and the solutions on the recording sheets. Ask the students, "How are these two problems alike?" (They use the same numbers—30, 5, and 6. Both can be solved on the "Division Work Mat" and entered on the "Division Recording Sheet." Both involve making 5 groups of 6 counters. The total in both problems is 30.) Then ask, "How are these two problems different?" (The equation for the first one is $5 \times 6 = 30$, but the equation for the second one is $30 \div 6 = 5$. One starts with the groups, but the other one starts with the total. One is multiplication, but the other is division.)

Gather the students around a table, and make 5 groups of 6 counters on a "Division Work Mat" for all the students to see. Emphasize the central idea that both problems involve 5 groups of 6 counters, for a total of 30 altogether. However, the multiplication problem presents (or starts with) the groups, and the division problem presents (or starts with) the total.

Have the students review their work on the recording sheet for these two problems. They should note that both records show 5 groups of 6, but one record has the multiplication equation ($5 \times 6 = 30$), and the other has the division equation ($30 \div 6 = 5$). For the multiplication problem (problem 1), have the students cross out the arrow pointing up and replace it with an arrow pointing down. Emphasize that in multiplication problems, groups are combined to create a total.

Give your students the following two problems to solve on the "Division Work Mat" and record as problems 3 and 4 on their copies of the "Division Recording Sheet":

• Priscilla planted 6 rows of flowers, with the same number of flowers in each row. If Priscilla planted 42 flowers altogether, how many flowers did she plant in each row?

• Alex delivered 7 newspapers a day for 6 days. How many newspapers did he deliver altogether?

After the students have finished working, discuss both problems. (Figure 2.11 shows solutions on mats and entries on recording sheets.) Ask the students to identify one of the problems as a multiplication problem and the other as a division problem. Then have them discuss how the two problems are alike and different.

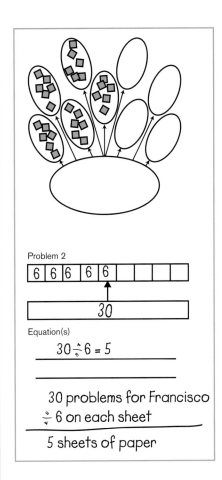

Problem 2

6	6	6	6	6				

30

Equation(s)

$30 \div 6 = 5$

_____

30 problems for Francisco
$\div$ 6 on each sheet
_____
5 sheets of paper

Fig. **2.11.**

Using the "Division Work Mat" and
"Division Recording Sheet" to solve (a)
a division problem ("Extend" problem 3)
and (b) a multiplication problem
("Extend" problem 4)

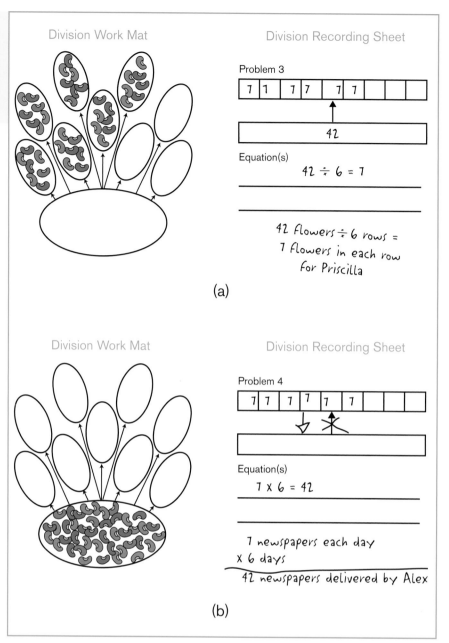

(a)

(b)

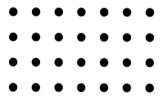

As a summarizing activity, draw on the board an array consisting of 4 rows of 7 dots (see the margin). Have the students write both a multiplication equation ($4 \times 7 = 28$ or $7 \times 4 = 28$) and a division equation ($28 \div 4 = 7$ or $28 \div 7 = 4$) to describe the array. Emphasize that multiplication and division are both appropriate ways of describing and representing 4 groups of 7 items or 7 groups of 4 items. Then have the students write a word problem to match each equation. Sample problems follow:

- Mr. Brown has asked Pete to walk his dog every day for 4 weeks. Pete wants to know how many days he'll be walking the dog. How can Pete figure out the number of days? ("Equal groups" multiplication problem; $4 \times 7 = 28$)

- Arthur and his family are going to Canada for a 28-day vacation. They plan to visit 7 provinces and spend equal time in all of them.

How many days will they spend in each one? (Partitioning division problem; 28 ÷ 7 = 4)

- Felicity planted 7 tomato plants in her garden yesterday. Today she planted 4 times as many tomato plants in the garden. How many tomato plants did she plant today? (Comparison multiplication problem; 7 × 4 = 28)

- Rhonda baked 28 cookies. She gave 4 cookies apiece to her friends. How many friends received cookies from Rhonda? (Subtractive division problem; 28 ÷ 4 = 7)

This activity of using an array to represent multiplication and division can serve as a useful transition to the following activity, "Splitting Arrays."

Splitting Arrays

Grades 3–5

Summary

Students find products for multiplication problems by using dot arrays and splitting them into parts. This activity supports the expectation of the Number and Operations Standard that all students in grades 3–5 "should … understand and use properties of operations, such as the distributivity of multiplication over addition" (NCTM 2000, p. 148).

Goals

- Find the product of a one-digit factor and a one-digit factor
- Find the product of a one-digit factor and a two-digit factor
- Find the product of a two-digit factor and a two-digit factor
- Relate the distributive property of multiplication over addition to splitting arrays to determine the products of one- and two-digit numbers

*"All students
should …
understand
and use properties of
operations, such as the
distributivity of
multiplication over
addition."
(NCTM 2000, p. 148)*

Prior Knowledge or Experience

- Experience with counting patterns and skip counting
- Preliminary work with basic multiplication facts

Materials and Equipment

For each student—

- A copy of the blackline master "10 × 10 Dot Array"
- A copy of the blackline master "30 × 36 Dot Array"
- A new, full-length pencil
- One or two pieces of dark-colored string, about 10 inches long (or pipe cleaners, straight uncooked spaghetti, or "pick-up sticks")
- Two half-sheets of unlined paper (colored or white)
- One or two sheets of regular lined paper (for recording problems and solutions; optional)
- Access to the applet Splitting Arrays to Solve Multiplication (on the CD-ROM; optional)

pp. 172, 173

Activity

Engage

Ask your students to solve the following problem mentally:

At the school fair, four boys look into their pockets and discover that each of them has a nickel and two pennies. They decide to combine their coins to buy a cone of cotton candy that costs 25 cents. Do they have enough money to buy the cotton candy?

After giving the students a minute or two to consider the problem, have them share their ideas and solution methods. Focus on the key idea of putting all the boys' nickels together (to make 4 nickels) and all their pennies together (for 8 pennies in all) to determine the total. The equation for this problem is 20 + 8 = 28. The boys have 28 cents, which is enough to buy the cotton candy.

Give each student or pair of students a copy of the blackline master "10 × 10 Dot Array," a new pencil or other object to use as a divider, and two half-sheets of unlined paper. Discuss how the students can use the dot array to show the problem as a 4 × 7 array—that is, 4 horizontal rows of 7 dots each. Demonstrate how to use the two half-sheets of paper to cover the rest of the dots in the 10 × 10 array so that only 4 rows of 7 dots are visible in the upper left-hand corner. Have the students place the pencil (or other divider) vertically between the fifth and sixth columns of dots to create a 4 × 5 array to the left of the pencil and a 4 × 2 array to the right. Figure 2.12 shows the arrangement of the pencil and half-sheets of paper to split the 4 × 7 array.

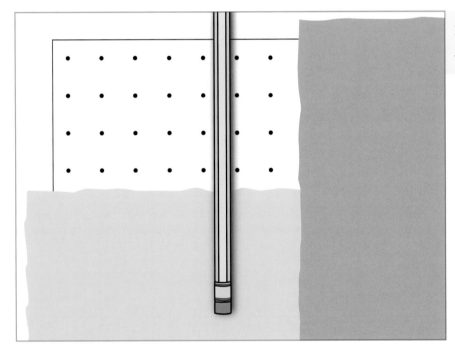

Fig. **2.12.**

A split array for 4 × 7

Point out that the 4 × 5 array can represent the four boys' nickels, for a total of 20 cents, and the 4 × 2 array can represent their pennies, for a total of 8 cents. By merging the arrays into one 4 × 7 array, your students can see that the boys in the problem have 28 cents, which is more than enough to buy the cotton candy.

Depending on your students' experience with multiplication, you may want to give them one or both of the following problems instead of or along with the first one:

• Four girls saw a strip of unusual stickers for 45 cents at the school store. Each girl had a dime and two pennies left over from buying lunch. The girls combined their coins on the counter of the store. Did they have enough to buy the strip of stickers?

• Four children saw a used kite in the window of the thrift shop. Each child had a quarter and three pennies. The price marked on the kite was $1.15. Can the children combine their coins to buy the kite?

Let your students tell how they would approach these problems. Try to get them to focus on the idea of putting like coins together. In the first problem, putting the 4 dimes together gives 40 cents, and putting all the pennies together gives 8 pennies. Thus, the girls had 48 cents—more than enough to buy the strip of stickers for 45 cents. In the second problem, putting all the quarters together gives $1.00, and putting the pennies together gives 12 cents. The children had $1.12, or 3 cents less than they needed to buy the kite for $1.15—maybe the thrift shop owner let them purchase it at a slight discount!

After your students have shared their mental solution methods, distribute copies of the blackline master "30 × 36 Dot Array," and show them how to use it, along with the half-sheets of paper and a string or other slender divider, to solve these two problems (see fig. 2.13).

Fig. **2.13.**

Using the blackline master "30 × 36 Dot Array," together with two half-sheets of paper and a string, to create arrays and split them to solve two problems

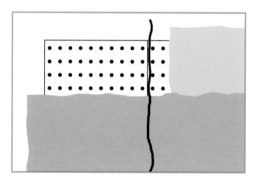

Four girls saw a strip of unusual stickers for 45 cents at the school store. Each girl had a dime and two pennies left over from buying lunch. The girls combined their coins on the counter of the store. Did they have enough to buy the strip of stickers?

(a)

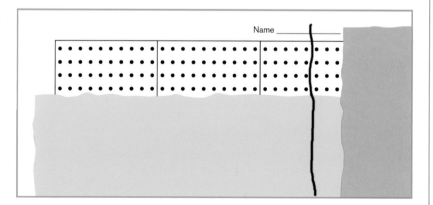

Four children saw a used kite in the window of the thrift shop. Each child had a quarter and three pennies. The price marked on the kite was $1.15. Can the children combine their coins to buy the kite?

(b)

Explain that they should use the same procedure as for solving the earlier problem. The students can represent the problem about the stickers at the school store by the equation $(4 \times 10) + (4 \times 2) = 48$, or 48 cents, and the problem about the kite at the thrift shop by the equation $(4 \times 25) + (4 \times 3) = 100 + 12 = 112$, or 112 cents, or \$1.12.

Explore

Depending on your students' prior knowledge or experience with one- and two-digit factors, you can give them a variety of multiplication problems to solve by using one of the dot arrays, two half-sheets of paper, and a pencil, string, or other divider. To provide additional experience in using the 10×10 array to find the product of two one-digit factors, you can offer such problems as the following:

- Spiders have 8 legs. How many legs would 3 spiders have?
- Six baseball teams are out on the playground. Each team has 9 players. How many baseball players are on the playground?
- $6 \times 4 = ?$
- $3 \times 8 = ?$
- $4 \times 9 = ?$
- $7 \times 6 = ?$

To provide additional experience in using the 30×36 array to find the product of a one-digit factor and a two-digit factor, you can give such problems as the following:

- Adults usually have 32 teeth. How many teeth would 4 adults have if each one has a full set of 32 teeth?
- The average foot of a twelve-year-old is about 18 centimeters long. If you found three twelve-year-olds whose feet were of average length, what distance would their feet measure if you placed them all heel to toe? (*Hint*: Remember that each twelve-year-old has more than one foot!)
- A team of four girls ran in a relay race. Each girl ran her segment of the race in exactly 12 seconds. The winning time in the race was 45 seconds. Do you think the girls won the race? Why, or why not?
- $4 \times 24 = ?$
- $7 \times 33 = ?$
- $5 \times 17 = ?$
- $8 \times 28 = ?$

For each problem that you give, have the students use the half-sheets of paper to outline the array representing the original multiplication problem on the appropriate blackline dot array. Then have them use a divider to split the array into two parts that they can use to find the product mentally. For problems involving two-digit numbers, the students may use pencil and paper to record two partial products and then add the two parts together. For example, for the problem 8×28, students might think of 8×20 and 8×8, writing both partial products, 160 and 64, and adding them together to find a single product for the original problem.

Challenge the students to find three different ways to split the array and find the product. For each problem, have the students identify the way of splitting the array that makes it easiest to determine the product mentally. Have them justify their selections. Also have them identify ways of splitting the arrays that they used frequently and tell why they used these ways.

You may have some students who are ready for problems calling for the product of a two two-digit factors. Have these students use the 30×36 array and the same techniques as before, outlining arrays with two half-sheets of colored paper and using string to split them. First, present some easy problems, in which both factors are multiples of 10 (such as 10×10, 10×20, 20×20, 10×30, and 20×30). The students will not need to split their outlined arrays with a string to solve these problems.

Next, have them solve problems in which only one factor is a multiple of ten (such as 10×13, 10×34, 20×23, and 30×27). Now they will need to use a string to split the array that they display on the blackline dot array. Have the students explain how they found the products and how they split their dot arrays. In particular, focus on rows or columns of ten dots and the "blocks" of one hundred dots within the arrays that represent the multiplication problems. (Students can also use the applet Splitting Arrays to Solve Multiplication to work on these types of problems.)

Challenge the students by asking, "If you know the factors of the problem, can you predict how many squares of one hundred and how many rows or columns of ten will be in an array?" Students who can answer this question are well on their way to understanding the distributive property of multiplication over addition, expressed symbolically as $a \times (b + c) = (a \times b) + (a \times c)$. For example, students' split arrays can help them see that $30 \times 35 = 30 \times (30 + 5) = (30 \times 30) + (30 \times 5)$. (See fig. 2.14.)

Fig. 2.14.
A split array for 30×35

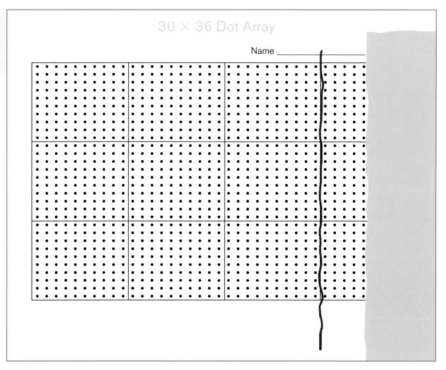

Reflect

Help your students reflect on their work by asking them to determine some simple products mentally (one factor × one factor) with only the 10 × 10 array in front of them—no colored paper or pencil, string, or other divider. This will also give them an opportunity to practice their multiplication facts up to 10 × 10. Say, "See if you can make a mental picture of the array for each fact and determine how to split it without using a pencil or divider." Use a similar procedure to have the students multiply one-digit factors by two-digit factors mentally while looking only at the 30 × 36 array.

To deepen reflection in another way, have the students solve some problems without any array at hand as a visual aid. Encourage them to visualize the arrays and split them mentally into smaller arrays that involve products that they can calculate easily.

Also help your students reflect on the distributive property and its symbolic expression $a \times (b + c) = (a \times b) + (a \times c)$. Present the multiplication problem $7 \times 26 = \square$. Have the students use half-sheets of colored paper and the 30 × 36 array to outline an array representing 7×26 (7 rows of 26 dots). Then have them place a string or other divider vertically between the 20th and 21st dots in each row (see fig. 2.15).

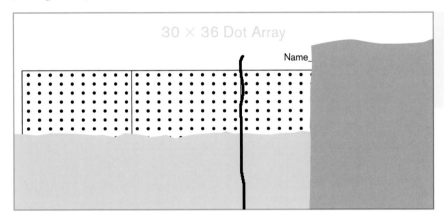

30 × 36 Dot Array

Name_

Fig. **2.15.**

An outlined 7 × 26 array,
split by a string to show that
$7 \times 26 = 7 \times (20 + 6) = (7 \times 20) + (7 \times 6)$

Ask the students, "What multiplication problem and product does the array to the left of the divider represent?" ($7 \times 20 = 140$) Then ask, "What multiplication problem and product does the array to the right of the divider represent?" ($7 \times 6 = 42$) Finally, show that the entire array (7×26) is composed of the two smaller arrays, showing that $7 \times 26 = 7 \times (20 + 6) = (7 \times 20) + (7 \times 6)$.

Repeat the process for a similar problem, such as 9×34 (see fig. 2.16). Then challenge the students to use the same method to show that $30 \times 24 = (30 \times 20) + (30 \times 4)$ (see fig. 2.17).

Extend

Depending on your students' interest and skill, you may want to extend the activity by giving them two-digit multiplication problems in which neither factor is a multiple of 10. If you think your students are ready for this work, demonstrate to them how they can adapt the techniques that they have been using to solve these more challenging problems. Again, they will work with the 30 × 36 array and their two half-sheets of colored paper, but this time they should use two strings or other dividers.

Fig. **2.16.**

An outlined 9 × 34 array,
split by a string to show that
9 × 34 = 9 × (30 + 4) = (9 × 30) + (9 × 4)

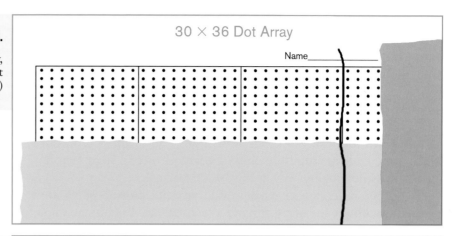

Fig. **2.17.**

An outlined 30 × 24 array,
split by a string to show that 30 × 24 =
30 × (20 + 4) = (30 × 20) + (30 × 4)

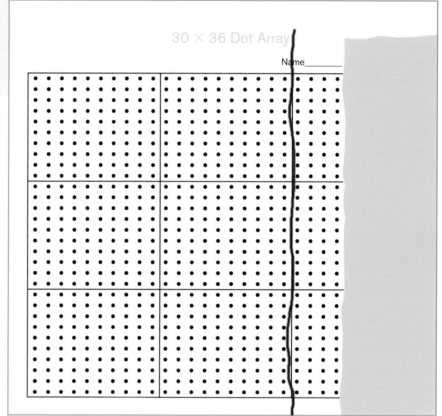

Consider a problem such as 17 × 23, for example. With neither factor a multiple of 10, the students can outline a 17 × 23 array that they then split into four conceptually simpler arrays that allow them to handle the problem without difficulty.

They should begin by outlining a 17 × 23 array in the usual way, with the two half-sheets of colored paper. (See fig. 2.18.) Then they will place one string between the twentieth and twenty-first columns and the other string between the tenth and eleventh rows. In this way, they will partition the 17 × 23 array into four arrays that represent partial products that they can easily obtain: 10 × 20, 7 × 20, 10 × 3, and 7 × 3. Adding these partial products will give them the product 17 × 23. Help your students see that the four arrays illustrate repeated use of the distributive property:

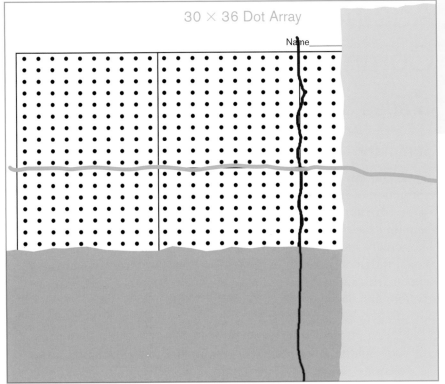
30 × 36 Dot Array

Name_____

Fig. **2.18**

An outlined 17 × 23 array, split by two strings to show that

$$17 \times 23 = (10 \times 20) + (10 \times 3) + (7 \times 20) + (7 \times 3)$$
$$= 200 + 30 + 140 + 21$$
$$= 391$$

If your students understand this process, let them use the 30 × 36 array, the two dividers, and two strings to solve such problems as 21 × 23, 13 × 32, 18 × 14, and 23 × 27. This experience will lay a useful foundation for expanding polynomials in algebra.

This activity has helped students understand—

- the meaning of multiplication;
- how to use the products of certain multiplication problems mentally to determine the answer to related multiplication problems; and
- how multidigit multiplication rests on basic multiplication facts relating to the products of one-digit factors.

This work lays the groundwork for understanding the distributive property. The following activity gives the students an opportunity to explore the addition and subtraction of fractions.

"The area model [for multiplication] is important because it helps students develop an understanding of multiplication properties." (Graeber 1993)

Adding and Subtracting Common Fractions

Grades 3–5

Summary

Students apply their understanding of operations to the addition and subtraction of fractions. They experience the subtraction of fractions as a process of comparing two fractions to find the difference between them (but they can also interpret it as a process of "taking away"). The activity supports the expectation of the Number and Operations Standard that all students in grades 3–5 "should … use visual models, benchmarks, and equivalent forms to add and subtract commonly used fractions and decimals" (NCTM 2000, p. 148).

Goals

- Write addition and subtraction equations and inequalities with fractions
- Develop "operation sense" relating to adding and subtracting common fractions

Prior Knowledge or Experience

- Experience in representing fractions
- Preliminary experience in comparing fractions

Materials and Equipment

For each student or pair of students—

- A manipulative fraction model (for example, fraction circles, fractions strips, or pattern blocks; templates available on the CD-ROM) with several copies of most or all of the following numbers:

$$1, \frac{1}{2}, \frac{1}{3}, \frac{1}{4}, \frac{1}{6}, \frac{1}{8}$$

For the teacher—

- A variety of manipulative fraction models (for example, fraction circles, fraction strips, and pattern blocks; templates available on the CD-ROM)
- An overhead projector
- Overhead fraction models

Activity

Engage

Distribute manipulative fraction models, such as fraction circles, fraction strips, or pattern blocks, to pairs of students. Ask them to use these to solve the following problem:

*"All students
should … use
visual models,
benchmarks, and equivalent
forms to add and subtract
commonly used fractions
and decimals."
(NCTM 2000, p. 148)*

Navigating through Number and Operations in Grades 3–5

If you add a fraction to itself and the sum is more than 1, what must always be true about your fraction?

Discuss the students' conclusions. Do they see that the fraction they start with must be greater than $\frac{1}{2}$? Even though this fact may not be clear to them at this point, have them try the following two problems:

- If you add a fraction to itself and the sum is more than $\frac{1}{2}$, what must always be true of your fraction?
- If you add a fraction to itself and the sum is more than $1\frac{1}{2}$, what must always be true of your fraction?

Because these problems do not seek exact answers, some students may find them difficult. Instead, the problems ask for characteristics of the fractions that meet the given requirement. Have the pairs of students share their ideas about solutions with the whole class. Try to elicit a variety of explanations involving different models or contexts, such as sections of circles (or pizzas), fraction strips, number lines, measuring cups, or pattern blocks. Focus on the key idea of putting parts together to make the whole. Make sure that your students understand that a fraction added to itself is greater than a given number—such as 1, $\frac{1}{2}$, or $1\frac{1}{2}$—when the fraction is more than half of the number. For example, because $\frac{1}{3}$ is more than half of $\frac{1}{2}$, $\frac{1}{3}+\frac{1}{3}$ must be more than $\frac{1}{2}$.

In the following parts of the activity, the students continue to put fractional parts together as well as separate a fraction or a whole number into parts. The goal is to develop a sense of the meaning of adding and subtracting fractions—not to use common denominators or the standard numerical procedures for adding or subtracting fractions symbolically.

Explore

Write the following seven numbers on the board: $\frac{1}{2}, \frac{2}{3}, \frac{3}{4}, 1, 1\frac{1}{4}, 1\frac{1}{3}, 1\frac{1}{2}$. Have each student or pair of students choose a number that is less than 1 from this set. Ask them to use the fraction models to represent their number with fraction sections. Then have them find two other fraction sections that add up to the number they chose and write the matching addition sentence. For example, if the students chose the number $\frac{3}{4}$, they might combine $\frac{1}{2}$ and $\frac{1}{4}$ to equal $\frac{3}{4}$ and write $\frac{1}{2}+\frac{1}{4}=\frac{3}{4}$.

When the students can easily find and combine two fraction sections, have them find and combine three, and then four, fraction sections. Afterward, have them find and combine two (then three, and then four) *identical* fraction sections that add up to the number they chose and write the matching addition sentences. Note that all parts of this last task may not be possible. The students' ability to complete the task will depend on the fraction that they chose and the fraction sections available to them.

You can use commercial fraction models if they are available.

 The CD-ROM includes templates that you can reproduce on cardstock to make fraction circles, fraction strips, and pattern blocks for your students to work with in the activity. (See pp. 27–28 for instructions.)

 If commercially produced overhead fraction models are unavailable, you can make transparencies from the "Fraction Circles," "Fraction Strips," and "Pattern Blocks" templates on the CD-ROM, color the fraction pieces with markers, and cut out the pieces for use on the overhead projector.

"The curriculum should provide opportunities for students to develop a thorough understanding of rational numbers [and] their various representations including common fractions."
(Kilpatrick, Swafford, and Findell 2001, p. 416)

Next, have the students choose a number that is *greater* than 1 from the same set of seven numbers. Direct the students to repeat the same steps as before:

1. Find two fraction sections that add up to the number and write the matching addition sentence.

2. Repeat the process, using first three and then four fraction sections.

3. Find two (and later three or four) *identical* fraction sections that add up to the number and write the matching addition sentences.

The next task involves inequalities rather than equalities, but the idea is similar. Have the students find three fractions whose sum is *less* than 1 (a whole) and then write the matching addition sentence for the inequality. For example, $\frac{1}{3} + \frac{1}{4} + \frac{1}{6} < 1$. Afterward, have the students find four fractions that have a sum *greater* than 1 and ask them to write the resulting statement of inequality.

Reflect

Have the students reflect on their work so far by focusing again on the characteristics of numbers that fit a certain requirement, as they did in the "Engage" section of the activity. Let the students continue to work in pairs on each of the following problems:

- If two fractions are both less than 1, what must be true of their sum? (It must be less than 2.) What if the two fractions are both less than $\frac{1}{2}$? (Their sum must be less than 1.)

- If two fractions are both greater than 1, what must be true of their sum? (It must be greater than 2.) What if the two fractions are each greater than $\frac{1}{2}$? (Their sum must be greater than 1.)

- If a fraction is added to itself, what must be true of the fraction if the sum is less than $\frac{1}{2}$? (The fraction must be less than $\frac{1}{4}$.) What if the sum is less than $1\frac{1}{2}$? (The fraction must be less than $\frac{3}{4}$.)

Give the students a few minutes to work, and then have them share their results and solution methods. Be sure that they are focusing on the ideas involved and not the computational mechanics of the task. For example, in the first problem, the "big idea" for the students to grasp is that if each of two fractions is less than 1, their sum must be less than 2.

Extend

When your students can add as many as four fractions with ease, move on to subtracting fractions. Introduce subtraction as a process of finding the difference between two fractions. Have the students start with a section representing $\frac{1}{2}$ in a set of fraction manipulatives. Guide them in representing the subtraction of $\frac{1}{3}$ from $\frac{1}{2}$ by using a $\frac{1}{3}$ section from the manipulatives to cover as much of the $\frac{1}{2}$ section as possible. To find the amount left uncovered—the *difference*—have the students find the fraction section that fits the empty space exactly $\left(\dfrac{1}{6}\right)$ and write the matching subtraction sentence, $\dfrac{1}{2} - \dfrac{1}{3} = \dfrac{1}{6}$.

In the same manner, have the students find the difference between $\dfrac{2}{3}$ and $\dfrac{1}{6}$ and write the matching subtraction sentence, $\dfrac{2}{3} - \dfrac{1}{6} = \dfrac{1}{2}$. Direct the students to repeat the process with 1 and $\dfrac{3}{4}$.

Give your students the following tasks, which involve finding pairs of fractions that differ by *more than* or *less than* a specified amount:

- Find two fractions that differ by more than $\dfrac{1}{2}$. (For example, $\dfrac{7}{8}$ and $\dfrac{1}{4}$: $\dfrac{7}{8} - \dfrac{1}{4} = \dfrac{5}{8} > \dfrac{1}{2}$.) Two fractions that differ by less than $\dfrac{1}{2}$. (For example, $\dfrac{3}{4}$ and $\dfrac{1}{2}$: $\dfrac{3}{4} - \dfrac{1}{2} = \dfrac{1}{4} < \dfrac{1}{2}$.)

- Find two fractions that differ by more than $\dfrac{1}{3}$. (For example, $\dfrac{7}{8}$ and $\dfrac{1}{2}$: $\dfrac{7}{8} - \dfrac{1}{2} = \dfrac{3}{8} > \dfrac{1}{3}$.) Two fractions that differ by less than $\dfrac{1}{3}$. (For example, $\dfrac{7}{8}$ and $\dfrac{3}{4}$: $\dfrac{7}{8} - \dfrac{3}{4} = \dfrac{1}{8} < \dfrac{1}{3}$.)

- Find two fractions that differ by more than $\dfrac{3}{4}$. (For example, $\dfrac{9}{10}$ and $\dfrac{1}{10}$: $\dfrac{9}{10} - \dfrac{1}{10} = \dfrac{8}{10} > \dfrac{3}{4}$.) Two fractions that differ by less than $\dfrac{3}{4}$. (For example, $\dfrac{7}{8} - \dfrac{1}{2}$, $\dfrac{7}{8} - \dfrac{1}{2} = \dfrac{3}{8} < \dfrac{3}{4}$.)

- Some numbers, such as $1\dfrac{1}{4}$ and $2\dfrac{1}{2}$ combine whole numbers and fractions in a single expression. These numbers are called *mixed numbers*. Find two mixed numbers that differ by more than 1. (For example, $3\dfrac{2}{3}$ and $2\dfrac{1}{2}$: $3\dfrac{2}{3} - 2\dfrac{1}{2} = \dfrac{7}{6} > 1$.) Two mixed numbers that differ by less than 1. (For example, $3\dfrac{1}{3}$ and $2\dfrac{1}{2}$: $3\dfrac{1}{3} - 2\dfrac{1}{2} = \dfrac{5}{6} < 1$.

Problems such as these can help students develop number sense about common fractions by determining their differences. Some students will be able to solve these problems by visualizing fraction sections for the given quantities. Others will need to use the fraction sections from the manipulative sets. Be sure to have the students explain their thinking about the problems.

A good way to extend your students' understanding of the addition of fractions and the use of equivalent fractions is to have them work with the Fraction Game Tool on the Web at http://illuminations.nctm.org/tools/fraction/fraction.asp. Figure 2.19 shows the screen of the applet for a game. A player clicks on the pile of cards in the upper right corner of the screen to turn over a card showing a fraction (for example, $\frac{2}{5}$, as shown in fig. 2.19).

Fig. **2.19.**

A screen from the Fraction Game Tool on the Illuminations Web site, displaying the first card and the first move of a game

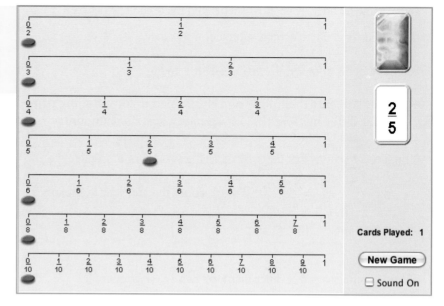

The player then slides a marker in one of the number lines ("tracks"; the game is sometimes called "Fraction Track") to a "stopping position" that represents a move that is less than or equal to that fraction.

For $\frac{2}{5}$, the player need not slide the marker in row 4 to $\frac{2}{5}$ as in the figure.

He or she could slide markers in any row except row 1, which offers no possibility of a move that represents a fraction that is less than or equal to $\frac{2}{5}$.

The player continues to turn over cards and move markers in this way until he or she has succeeded in moving all the markers in all the rows all the way to the right. (The markers change color when they reach 1 at the right end of a row.) The object is to get all the markers to the right side of the screen while turning over the fewest cards. Note that players may turn over cards for which they can make no moves.

For example, in figure 2.20, the player has just turned over $\frac{1}{10}$. But the marker in the "tenths" row is already all the way to the right, and the available stopping positions in all the other rows represent moves that are greater than $\frac{1}{10}$, so the player can do nothing with this card but must turn over another and try again.

The activity Adding and Subtracting Common Fractions has given students some opportunities to think about characteristics and equivalences of fractions in the context of addition and subtraction. The next activity, Multiplying and Dividing by Numbers Close to 1, concludes chapter 2 by extending some of this work to multiplication and division.

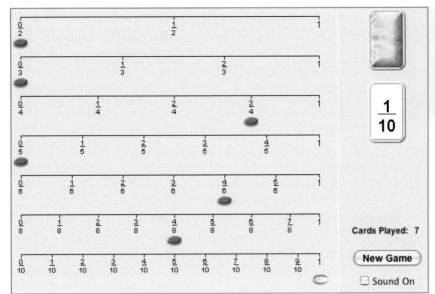

Cards Played: 7

New Game

☐ Sound On

Fig. **2.20.**

A player has turned over $\frac{1}{10}$ when he or she cannot use it, since all available "stopping positions" and moves represent fractions that are greater than $\frac{1}{10}$

Let your students work with the Fraction Game Tool on the Illuminations Web site (http://illuminations.nctm.org/tools/fraction/fraction.asp) to extend their understanding of addition of fractions and fraction equivalents.

Multiplying and Dividing by Numbers Close to 1

Grades 4–5

Summary

This activity focuses on the effects of multiplying and dividing numbers by quantities that are slightly greater than or less than 1. The activity supports the expectation of the Number and Operations Standard that all students in grades 3–5 should "understand the effects of multiplying and dividing whole numbers" (NCTM 2000, p. 148). It also embodies the idea that students in grades 3–5 "should explore the effects of operating on numbers with particular numbers" (NCTM 2000, p. 149).

Goal

- Understand the effects of multiplying or dividing by numbers close to 1

Prior Knowledge or Experience

- A basic understanding of decimals
- Preliminary work in comparing decimals

Materials and Equipment

For each student or pair of students—

- A copy of each of the following blackline masters:
  - "Multiplying by Special Numbers"
  - "Dividing by Special Numbers"
- A calculator
- Pencils

pp. 174–76, 177–79

Activity

Engage

Write the following problem on the board for all students to see:

$$1\frac{1}{2} \times 12 = \square.$$

Say, "Tell the class as much about this product as you can." Explain that the goal is not to determine the exact answer but to think about the magnitude, or size, of the product and why it has that magnitude. Focus on the meaning of the multiplication: "What does 'one and one-fourth times a quantity' mean?" Ask the students to think of a word problem to match the multiplication. (For example, "Lucy took 12 photos on the class trip. Tom took one and one quarter times as many. How many photos did Tom take?" [15 photos]) Have the students use their problem to reinforce the idea that the product is definitely greater than 12.

Next, write the following problem on the board:

$$\frac{3}{4} \times 12 = \square.$$

Again say, "Tell the class as much about the product as you can." Have the students focus again on the magnitude of the product:

- "How large is the product?"
- "Is the product less than 12, or is it greater than 12?"
- "Why is the product that size?"

As the students consider this last question, be sure that they are thinking about the meaning of the multiplication: "What does 'three fourths times a quantity' mean?" Again, ask them to come up with a word problem to match the multiplication. (For example, "We all know that there are 12 eggs in a dozen. If we cooked $\frac{3}{4}$ of a dozen eggs, how many would we cook?" [9 eggs])

When your students are certain of the magnitudes of these products, move on to the next section of the activity.

Explore

Distribute to each student or pair of students a copy of the activity sheet "Multiplying by Special Numbers," a calculator, and one or two pencils. Tell them that first they are going to explore the effect of multiplying by numbers that are slightly greater than 1, such as one and one tenth ($1\frac{1}{10}$, or 1.1) and one and fifteen hundredths ($1\frac{15}{100}$, or 1.15).

Use a number line to show your students 1, 1.1, and 1.5 in relation to one another. Say, "On your activity sheet, look at the bottom row of table 1, and find "$A =$ _____" in column 1. Choose a number A that is just slightly greater than 1 and enter it in the table."

Next, direct your students' attention to row 1, column 4, in the table. Say, "Choose a number B that is greater than 50, and enter it here in the table." Then let the students follow the steps on the activity sheet to complete the table. In so doing, they will multiply 8, 26, and the number they chose for B by 1, 1.1, 1.15, and the number they chose for A. This work will show them the effect of multiplying by numbers close to 1.

Guide the students in using their calculators to complete steps 3–6 on the work sheet. Using calculators to multiply numbers by decimal values near 1 allows students to focus on the ideas involved, as *Principles and Standards* recommends, rather than becoming mired in complex and tedious computations.

Discuss the students' results. Ask, "What do you notice about the products in the column 2 (under the number 8)?" (All the products are greater than 8 except the product that results from multiplying by 1.) Then ask, "What do you notice about the products in column 3 (under the number 26)?" (All the products are greater than 26 except the product that results from multiplying by 1.) Focus on the idea that the product of a number n and 1 is n (since 1 is the multiplicative identity), but the product of n ($n > 0$) and a number m that is slightly greater than 1 is greater than n.

"With calculators and computers students can examine more examples or representation forms than are feasible by hand, so they can make and explore conjectures easily." (NCTM 2000, p. 25)

Use examples to show your students why this is so. You might say, for instance, "Of course, $1 \times 8 = 8$. But what if I have 1.2×8? My product will be made up of one group of 8 plus part (two tenths) of another group of 8, so it will be greater than 8." Similarly, the students should see that 1.15×26 must be slightly greater than 26.

Ask the students to complete steps 7–9 on the activity sheet. Here they make a prediction about the products of the number B that they selected and numbers that are slightly greater than 1. Then they verify their prediction by using their calculators and finding the products. Discuss the students' results.

Guide the students through the remainder of the activity page. Now they choose a number C that is slightly less than 1 and enter it in column 1 of table 2. This time they should notice that using C to multiply 8, 26, and a number D that is greater than 60 results in products that are less than 8, 26, and D. They should see that the product of n ($n > 0$) and a number m that is slightly less than 1 is always less than n.

Reflect

To help the students consolidate their learning about multiplication by a number that is slightly greater than or less than 1, write the following two multiplication statements on the board:

- $0.9 \times 21 = \square$.

- $1.02 \times 57 = \square$.

As before, ask the students, "What can you tell me about these products?" Make sure that they give reasons for their responses. Then have the students complete the following sentences:

- "Whenever a number that is greater than 0 is multiplied by another number that is *less* than 1, then the product is always _____." (The students should recognize that the product is always less than the original number.)

- "Whenever a number that is greater than 0 is multiplied by another number that is *greater* than 1, then the product is always _____." (The students should recognize that the product is always greater than the original number.)

The students should now be ready to extend their thinking to division by numbers that are slightly greater than and slightly less than 1.

Extend

Distribute to the students copies of the activity sheet "Dividing by Special Numbers." The activity sheet merely translates the format of "Multiplying by Special Numbers" to division, so leading the students through its steps should not be difficult. Note that depending on the numbers in a division, the quotient could have more than two decimal places. For example, $4 \div 1.1 = 3.6363636$. Students should ignore the decimal digits beyond the hundredths place in a quotient.

The divisions that the activity sheet calls on the students to make with their calculators are straightforward. Nevertheless, students often find it difficult to understand why dividing by a divisor that is slightly greater than 1 yields a quotient that is less than the dividend. One way to demonstrate this fact is with an example.

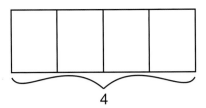

4

Ask the students to think about $4 \div 1\frac{1}{2} = \square$. Another way to state the problem is, "How many groups of $1\frac{1}{2}$ can you find in a group of 4?" Draw a row of four squares on the board (see the upper right margin). Then ask a student to come to the board and show how many groups of $1\frac{1}{2}$ are in the row. The student's division of the row should show that there are $2\frac{2}{3}$ groups of $1\frac{1}{2}$ in the row of 4.

Thus, $4 \div 1\frac{1}{2} = 2\frac{2}{3}$. Emphasize that the quotient is smaller than the dividend because the divisor is greater than 1.

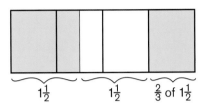

$1\frac{1}{2}$ $1\frac{1}{2}$ $\frac{2}{3}$ of $1\frac{1}{2}$

$4 \div 1\frac{1}{2} = \square$

How many groups of $1\frac{1}{2}$ are in 4?

$4 \div 1\frac{1}{2} = 2\frac{2}{3}$

Likewise, students often find it difficult to understand why dividing by divisors slightly less than 1 yields a quotient that is greater than the dividend. You can demonstrate this fact with another example.

Say to your students, "Think about the problem $20 \div 5 = \square$. Another way to state this problem is, 'How many 5s are in 20?'" The students should readily see that there are four 5s in 20. Say, "Now think about the problem $4 \div \frac{4}{5} = \square$. Here we are dividing by a number that is slightly less than 1. We can restate this problem in the same way that we did before: 'How many $\frac{4}{5}$s are in 4?'" Use fraction circles or other manipulatives to show that it takes five $\frac{4}{5}$s to make 4, so $4 \div \frac{4}{5} = 5$ (See the lower right margin.) In other words, when 4 is divided by a divisor less than 1 (for example, $\frac{4}{5}$), the quotient is greater than 4.

Conclusion

This chapter has focused on developing students' understanding of operations: multiplication and division of whole numbers, the use of arrays to solve multiplication problems, addition and subtraction of fractions, and multiplication and division by numbers close to 1. Chapter 3 expands the students' fluency and flexibility in using basic number combinations, or *facts*, and thinking strategies that can help students learn them.

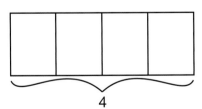

4

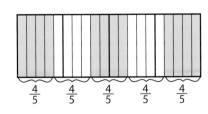

$\frac{4}{5}$ $\frac{4}{5}$ $\frac{4}{5}$ $\frac{4}{5}$ $\frac{4}{5}$

$4 \div \frac{4}{5} = \square$

How many $\frac{4}{5}$s are in 4?

$4 \div \frac{4}{5} = 5$

NAVIGATING *through* NUMBER *and* OPERATIONS

Chapter 3
Fluency with Basic Facts

Basic facts are combinations of two one-digit numbers under the operations addition, subtraction, multiplication, and division. Examples of basic facts are

$6 + 3 = 9, 6 - 3 = 3,$
$6 \times 3 = 18, 6 \div 3 = 2.$

An important goal of the Number and Operations Standard is for students to develop fluency and flexibility with basic number facts—combinations (such as $7 \times 8 = 56$) of two one-digit numbers under the basic operations of addition, subtraction, multiplication, and division. The students' skill with basic facts should grow naturally out of their development of thinking strategies that help them learn the facts as they solve problems.

Thinking strategies equip students with tools that they can use to solve a host of problems, including those that involve unknown basic facts, mental mathematics, and estimation with larger numbers. Fostering students' facility with basic facts in the context of problem solving can support the larger goal of developing students' number sense, as outlined in *Curriculum and Evaluation Standards for School Mathematics* (NCTM 1989) and *Principles and Standards for School Mathematics* (NCTM 2000). A problem-centered approach to basic facts can help students to—

- invent and make sense of their own solutions to problems that call for basic facts;
- sharpen their thinking as they explain their methods to other students;
- listen and try to make sense of other students' thinking;
- attempt to use and make sense of new thinking strategies; and
- begin to develop an ability to make strategic choices about when to use different thinking strategies.

Research has demonstrated that a problem-centered approach that focuses on efficient thinking strategies can be effective in five ways:

1. Students can memorize the facts more quickly with a problem-centered approach than with drill and practice. Many teachers believe students memorize facts more rapidly with extra practice and drill than through problem solving. However, research has repeatedly indicated a different result (Isaac and Carroll 1999; Kilpatrick, Swafford, and Findell 2001). Despite the fact that the process of helping students learn efficient thinking strategies appears to take more time initially, it actually helps students memorize the basic facts sooner than they do through an approach of practice and drill (Thornton and Smith 1988). In fact, for some students, practice and drill do not seem to help with long-term memorization of the facts. Even with extra drill, probably more than one-third of all students have significant retention difficulties, and many never memorize the basic facts (Brownell and Chazal 1935).

2. The responses of students who have efficient thinking strategies are much more accurate and just as quick, if not quicker, than those of students who have had a great deal of drill and practice. These differences reflect in part the fact that students of lower ability are capable of learning efficient thinking strategies, though they may initially need extra time to do so. However, after they have succeeded and have had even a relatively small amount of practice, their performance nearly matches that of average students (Gabriele, Rathmell, and Leutzinger 1998).

3. Students who have efficient thinking strategies demonstrate a much better retention of facts than students who have learned them through drill and practice. Not only do students with thinking strategies nearly maintain their speed and accuracy over summer vacation, but they also continue to use these strategies spontaneously. Moreover, they are able to apply these same strategies to mental computation with larger numbers, even after summer vacation (Leutzinger 1998).

4. Students with efficient thinking strategies do not have to resort to less effective methods to solve problems involving basic facts. For example, they rarely count on their fingers. On timed tests they do not skip around on the page looking for "easy" problems. They have no need for these immature behaviors, because they have more productive ways to think.

5. Perhaps most important, students with efficient thinking strategies come to believe that they can make sense of mathematics. The drill-and-practice technique, which provides no way to figure out the more difficult facts without simply remembering them, can lead to repeated failures on timed tests for students with retention problems. These impasses, in turn, lead to a lack of perseverance on many other mathematical tasks and a belief on the part of students that they cannot succeed at mathematics.

Although some practice is necessary to ensure mastery of basic facts, thinking strategies that allow students to develop fluency and flexibility

Research has shown that efficient thinking strategies can be more effective than drill and practice in helping students retain basic facts.

with the facts can enhance learning, retention, and application. The evidence strongly supports an instructional decision to emphasize such strategies.

Students can extend their thinking strategies to work with larger numbers. The reasoning process that helps students learn the basic facts is also a core component of the thinking that helps them succeed at mental computation with larger numbers. In some instances, using larger numbers increases the probability that students will try a new thinking strategy. If they can still easily count their way through a problem, why risk something new? Larger numbers make these inefficient strategies ineffective, so the use of larger numbers encourages new thinking.

The activities in chapter 3 are designed to help students learn, use, and make sense of a variety of thinking strategies involving basic facts. The first activity focuses on learning basic facts through problem solving. The second activity gives students a new strategy—"make 10 to add"—when they are using repeated addition to solve problems involving multiplication facts. The third activity shows students how they can solve problems involving multiplication facts by splitting arrays in ways that allow them to work with two or more known facts. The fourth activity uses multiplication "concept cards" as a tool to help students practice their basic facts and relate multiplication to division. The fifth activity lets students practice basic multiplication facts by finding two single-digit factors for specific products as well as finding "mystery" products and associated factors from sets of clues.

A Problem-Solving Approach to Basic Facts

Grades 3–5

Summary

In this two-part activity, students develop thinking strategies for learning basic facts by focusing first on addition and subtraction word problems and then on multiplication and division word problems.

Goals

- Recognize when to use each of the four basic operations in problem solving
- Review or learn multiple thinking strategies for each operation and become fluent and flexible in their use, both with basic facts and with mental computation

Prior Knowledge or Experience

- Understand various meanings of addition, subtraction, multiplication, and division
- Understand how addition, subtraction, multiplication, and division relate to one another in all their different meanings

Materials and Equipment

For each student—

- A copy of each of the following blackline masters:
  - "Addition and Subtraction Word Problems"
  - "Multiplication and Division Word Problems"

pp. 180, 181

Activity

The following activity is in two parts. The first part focuses on learning addition and subtraction facts through problem solving, and the second part focuses on learning multiplication and division facts through the same approach.

Part 1—Addition and Subtraction

Engage

Giving students daily word problems is one way to teach them new thinking strategies related to basic facts while at the same time developing their understanding of when to use a particular operation in a problem context. Teachers should attempt to extend each student's thinking every day (Fraivillig 2001). A five-minute session involving a simple word problem can be a catalyst for a very interesting class discussion. Moreover, such sessions help students learn thinking strategies that develop their number sense as well as their fluency and flexibility with basic facts.

You can follow a very simple format in each five-minute session:

- Pose a simple word problem.
- Give your students about a minute to solve the problem with their own strategies.
- Have two or three students share their solution strategies with the class.
- Discuss the different strategies that the students suggest.

A transcript of a five-minute session follows:

Teacher: Look at the problem on the board: "Robert had an orchard with 6 rows of trees. Each row had 8 apple trees in it. How many apple trees did Robert have in his orchard?" Take about a minute to solve the problem. Think about how you would explain your answer.

Tom: I got 48. I added 8 up 6 times.

Teacher: Good. Did anyone solve the problem a different way?

Alisha: I thought, "Three 8s are 24, and 24 + 24 = 48."

Teacher: That's interesting. So you split the problem in half and then doubled the first answer. Instead of thinking "six 8s," you thought "three 8s" and then doubled the product. Did anyone else do the problem in a different way?

Scott: I thought, "Five 8s are 40, and 8 more makes 48."

Teacher: Another good idea. You split off five rows of 8 and then added one more 8… Well, we've just heard three good ways to solve this problem. Today, I'd like us all to focus on what Alisha did. Who can remember what that was?

Mari: She split the 6 in half and figured out three 8s. Then she doubled that.

Teacher: That's right. Let's all try to use that thinking in solving a new problem: "Suppose Jo had 12 nickels. How much money did she have in cents?"

Jim: Well, 6 nickels make 30 cents. So 12 nickels make twice that much, or 60 cents.

Teacher: How many of you think that Jim used the same thinking as Alisha?… That's right! Sometimes splitting a problem in half is a good way to think about it. Try to remember that strategy when you're solving a problem like this.

Notice that the teacher enhanced the students' learning by highlighting the strategy suggested by Alisha and asking the students to try this strategy in solving a new problem. By highlighting an efficient strategy, you can create opportunities to extend your students' thinking. Begin by asking the student who explained the problem to repeat the strategy. Then ask another student to explain the same thinking. Summarize the thinking, and demonstrate it concretely as a student explains it.

"Children should learn single-digit number combinations [facts] with understanding." (Kilpatrick, Swafford, and Findell 2001, p. 413)

By highlighting an efficient strategy, you can extend your students' thinking.

The strategy that you highlight should be one that will allow students to determine the answer quickly and accurately. Furthermore, it should be a strategy that is conceptually accessible to most students in the class. Be prepared for the fact that not every student will be able to apply the strategy correctly after the first, second, or even third explanation or demonstration of it.

You might give your students additional practice in using the new strategy to help them become sure of when to use it and how to use it effectively. Encourage the students to try the new thinking in new situations, perhaps with larger numbers. Such an approach to problem solving not only helps students learn new thinking strategies but also develops their confidence and flexibility in using the strategies. If you regularly repeat this procedure, many—if not all—of your students will soon be using the strategy spontaneously.

Explore

Distribute to each student a copy of the blackline master "Addition and Subtraction Word Problems." (The problems and solutions appear in fig. 3.1.) Ask the students to approach these problems in the same way that they approached the problem in the five-minute session. Have the students read the problems and then solve them. Encourage them to create their own solutions to each problem by drawing diagrams, solving the problem mentally, using counters, or working in other ways.

Fig. **3.1.**

Problems on the blackline master "Addition and Subtraction Word Problems"

1. Jefferson Elementary School has 231 students. On Monday, only 228 students were present in the school. How many students were absent? (3 students)

2. The Bobcats scored 31 points in the first half of the basketball game. They scored 29 points in the second half. How many points did the Bobcats score in all? (60 points)

3. Mrs. Wilson had $63 in her wallet. She went to the store and bought a few groceries. Later she looked in her wallet and found that she had only $56. How much money did she spend at the store? ($7)

4. So far during the basketball season, Jo has made 38 consecutive free throws. If she makes 3 more free throws without missing any, how many consecutive free throws will she have made? (41)

5. Jamie is saving money to buy a DVD player. She has already saved $68. On Saturday she will earn $8 more. How much money will she then have? ($76)

6. Mr. and Mrs. Johnson are writing thank-you notes for their wedding gifts. They bought a box of 72 note cards. On Monday, they used 3 cards to write 3 notes. How many thank-you cards are left in the box? (69)

Walk among your students as they work and note their different solution strategies. For each problem, ask two or three students to explain their strategies to the class.

Extend

Select a thinking strategy suggested by one of your students in the discussion of the solutions to the problems on the activity sheet "Addition and Subtraction Word Problems." Focus your students' attention on this strategy, and ask them to try it on another problem. Figure 3.2 shows a number of useful strategies for addition and subtraction, paired with sample problems for your use in extending the activity. If necessary, provide other problems that match the strategy. Encourage the students to create word problems that they can easily solve with a particular strategy.

Fig. **3.2.**

Thinking strategies and sample problems for learning basic addition and subtraction facts

- **Count up to subtract.** Begin with the number that you need to subtract and count up to the number that you are subtracting from, keeping track of how many numbers you name as you count.

  Sample problem: "Mark weighs 88 pounds. James weighs 91 pounds. How much more does James weigh than Mark?"

  To apply the strategy: Begin with 88 and count up to 91, naming three additional numbers (89, 90, 91) to get to 91. Thus, James weighs 3 pounds more than Mark.

Problem 1 on the activity sheet also lends itself to the use of this strategy.

- **Use a double to add.** Look at the two numbers that you need to add, and if they are close to each other, see if doubling one of them, or a number that is close to both of them, can help you solve the problem. Double the number (by adding it to itself), and then add on or take away any number(s) that you must to solve the problem.

  Sample problem: "Elm Street Elementary School has 51 fourth graders and 50 fifth graders. How many fourth and fifth graders does the school have altogether?"

  To apply the strategy: Inspect the numbers 50 and 51, and double 50 to get 100. Then add 1 to account for the fact that one of the original numbers was 51 instead of 50. Thus, the school has 101 fourth and fifth graders altogether.

Problem 2 on the activity sheet also lends itself to the use of this strategy.

- **Make a ten to subtract.** Round up the number that you are subtracting to the next multiple of 10. Make the subtraction, and then add to your answer the number that you added to your original number when you rounded up to make it a multiple of 10.

Fig. **3.2**. (continued)

Sample problem: "Amos has 37 feet of wire fencing to go around his garden. His garden measures 45 feet around. How many more feet of wire fencing does Amos need?"

To apply the strategy: Round up 37 to 40, which is the nearest multiple of 10. Then subtract 40 from 45, obtaining 5. But now you must add 3 to your answer, since you added 3 to your original number, 37, when you rounded up. This made your original number larger before you subtracted from 45. So now you must add 3 back into your answer to make it the right size: $45 - 37 = (45 - 40) + 3 = 8$; Amos needs 8 more feet of wire fencing for his garden.

Problem 3 on the activity sheet also lends itself to the use of this strategy.

- **Count on to add.** Take the larger of the two numbers that you are adding (your larger addend), and "count on" as many numbers as your smaller addend tells you to add.

Sample problem: "Walt is collecting aluminum cans to raise money for his class. He had 85 cans at the end of last week. On Monday, he found 3 more cans. How many aluminum cans does he have in all?"

To apply the strategy: This problem asks you to add 85 and 3. Start with the larger number, 85, and count on 3 more numbers (86, 87, 88). The last number that you count on, 88, is your total. Walt has 88 cans in all.

Problem 4 on the activity sheet also lends itself to the use of this strategy.

Look on the CD-ROM for the applet Make Ten to Add, which provides opportunities for students to develop their skill in using this important strategy.

- **Make a ten to add.** If two numbers are difficult to add, round one of them up or down to make a multiple of 10. Add the multiple of 10 and the other number. If you rounded up, then subtract from your answer the number that you added to your original number when you made it a multiple of 10. If you rounded down, then add to your answer the number that you subtracted to make your original number a multiple of ten.

Sample problem: "Brian's birthday is 91 days away. Then Freda's birthday is just 13 days after Brian's. How many days away is Freda's birthday?"

To apply the strategy: Round 91 down to 90, the nearest multiple of 10. Add 13 to 90, obtaining 103. But you subtracted 1 from 91 when you rounded down, so your answer (103) is too small, and you need to add 1 to make it the right

Fig. **3.2**. (continued)

size: 91 + 13 = (90 + 13) + 1 = 104;
Freda's birthday is 104 days away.

Problem 5 on the activity sheet also lends itself to the use of this strategy.

- **Count back to subtract.** Start with the number that you are subtracting from (your minuend), and count backward by ones, naming as many numbers as the other number (the subtrahend) tells you to take away.

  Sample problem: "The school has 48 third graders. On Tuesday, 3 of them were ill. How many third graders were in school on Tuesday?"

  To apply the strategy: Start with 48 (the minuend), and count backward to "take away" three numbers: 47, 46, 45. On Tuesday, 45 third graders were in school.

Problem 6 on the activity sheet also lends itself to the use of this strategy

For each problem that the students consider, discuss thinking strategies they might use for an efficient solution. For example, the "use a double to add" strategy works well for problems such as $50 + 51 = \square$, or $39 + 41 = \square$, whose addends are close to each other, but is less efficient for other problems, such as $64 + 37 = \square$. After the students complete a problem, ask them to explain and summarize their work.

Part 2—Multiplication and Division

Engage
Lead the students in another five-minute session, this time focusing on a simple multiplication or division word problem. Again, follow the format that you used before:

- Pose a simple word problem (for example, "Angela did 35 sit-ups on Monday and the same number on Tuesday, Wednesday, Thursday, and Friday. How many sit-ups did Angela do from Monday through Friday?").

- Give your students about a minute to solve the problem with their own strategies.

- Have two or three students share their solution strategies with the class.

- Discuss the different strategies that the students suggest.

Once again, highlight one student's strategy, and ask the students to use it to solve a new problem.

Explore
Distribute to each student a copy of the blackline master "Multiplication and Division Word Problems." (The problems and solutions appear in fig. 3.3.) Ask the students to approach these problems just as they approached the problem in the five-minute session. Have the students read the problems and then solve them. Encourage them to create their own solutions by drawing diagrams, solving the problems mentally, using counters, or working in other ways.

Fig. **3.3.**

Problems on the blackline master "Multiplication and Division Word Problems"

1. Marci has 14 nickels. How much money does Marci have in dollars and cents? ($0.70)
2. Four girls earned $280 by painting rooms in a house. If they divide the money equally, how much money will each girl receive? ($70)
3. Tom's uncle said, "I have 120 pounds of mulch in the trunk of my car. Will you help me unload it?" The mulch was in 40-pound bags. How many bags did Tom and his uncle unload from the car? (3 bags)
4. Kayla bought 4 shirts that cost $15 each. How much money did she spend? ($60)
5. Kim is reading a book with 80 pages. She plans to read the same number of pages each day for 5 days. How many pages should she read each day to finish in 5 days? (16 pages a day)
6. Steve loaded bags of cement onto his truck for a small construction job. He made 3 trips, carrying one 50-pound bag each time. How many pounds of cement did Steve put on his truck? (150 pounds)

Walk among the students as they work and note their solution strategies. For each problem, have two or three students explain their solutions.

Extend

Select a thinking strategy suggested by one of your students in the discussion of the solutions to the problems on the activity sheet "Multiplication and Division Word Problems." Focus your students' attention on this new strategy, and ask them to try it on another problem. Figure 3.4 shows a number of useful strategies for multiplication and division, paired with sample problems for your use in extending the activity. If necessary, provide other problems that match the strategy. Encourage the students to create word problems that they can easily solve with a particular strategy.

Fig. **3.4.**

Thinking strategies and sample problems for learning basic multiplication and division facts

- **Use patterns to multiply.** Use skip-counting patterns (2s, 5s, 9s, etc.), to multiply efficiently.

  Sample problem: "Samantha has 34 nickels. How much money does she have in dollars and cents?"

  To apply the strategy: This problem lends itself to a variety of approaches that combine skip-counting patterns and known facts:

  1. If you know that 20 nickels equal $1.00, you might count fourteen 5s to get 70 cents and then add: $1.00 + $0.70 = $1.70.

Fig. **3.4.** (continued)

2. You might reason that 10 nickels equal 10 × 5, or 50, cents, so 30 nickels equal $1.50, and then count four 5s to get 20 cents more, or $1.70 in all.

3. If you know that 20 nickels equal $1.00, you might reason that 40 nickels equal $2.00 and then take away six 5s to get the value for 34 nickels: $2.00 – $0.30 = $1.70.

Problem 1 on the activity sheet also lends itself to the use of this strategy.

• **Use multiplication to divide.** Solve a division problem by setting up the related multiplication problem and finding the missing factor.

Sample problem: "Five boys earn $400 by mowing lawns. If they share the money equally, how much will each boy get?"

To apply the strategy: If solving 400 ÷ 5 = □ is more challenging than solving 5 × □ = 400, then find the missing factor in the related multiplication. Since 5 × 80 = 400, each boy will get $80.

Problem 2 on the activity sheet also lends itself to the use of this strategy.

• **Use repeated subtraction to divide.** Let the divisor tell you "how many" to take away repeatedly from the dividend until it is entirely gone (or is smaller than your divisor). Keep track of how many times you subtract before the dividend is "used up" in this way. Your total number of subtractions is the quotient of the original division problem.

Sample problem: "Jenny is making bookshelves. Each shelf is 3 feet long. How many shelves can Jenny cut from a board that is 14 feet long?"

To apply the strategy: If 14 ÷ 3 = □ does not give you a solution efficiently, take the divisor, 3, and subtract it repeatedly from the dividend, 14, until 14 is "used up":

$$14 - 3 = 11$$
$$11 - 3 = 8$$
$$8 - 3 = 5$$
$$5 - 3 = 2$$

Note that your last difference, 2, is smaller than your divisor, 3. So you must stop taking away 3 after a total of 4 subtractions. Thus, Jenny can make 4 shelves, with 2 feet of board left over.

Problem 3 on the activity sheet also lends itself to the use of this strategy.

Fig. **3.4.** (continued)

- **Split a multiplication problem into two simpler multiplication problems.** Make a multiplication problem easier and quicker to solve by breaking it down into two multiplication problems whose products you can find efficiently and which you can add together to obtain the product of the original problem.

    Sample problem: "Jodi bought 6 CDs. Each CD cost $12. How much money did Jodi spend?"

    To apply the strategy: If $6 \times \$12 = \square$ does not give you a solution readily, break the problem into two products that are easier for you to handle. For example, $12 = 10 + 2$, and $6 \times (10 + 2) = (6 \times 10) + (6 \times 2) = 60 + 12 = 72$. So Jodi spent $72 on the 6 CDs.

Problem 4 on the activity sheet also lends itself to the use of this strategy.

- **Use patterns to divide.** Use skip-counting patterns (2s, 5s, 9s, etc.), to divide efficiently.

    Sample problem: "Mr. Hardin built a bookcase. He shared his design with the students in his woodworking class, and 5 students decided to build bookcases just like Mr. Hardin's. Altogether, the students' bookcases took 120 feet of wood shelving. How many feet of shelving did each student's bookcase take?"

    To apply the strategy: This problem lends itself to approaches that combine skip-counting patterns and known facts. For example, if you know that five 20s equal 100, you can say that each of the 5 bookcases took 20 feet of shelving (or 100 feet altogether) plus 1/5 of the 20 remaining feet of shelving. Then if you count by 5s to 20, you easily see that four 5s equal 20, so each bookcase will use $20 + 4$, or 24, feet of wood shelving.

Problem 5 on the activity sheet also lends itself to the use of this strategy.

- **Use repeated addition to multiply.** Select one of the factors in a multiplication problem, and continue adding it to itself as many times as the other factor tells you to.

    Sample problem: "Carrie printed 3 copies of a paper that was 15 pages long. How many pages did she print in all?"

    To apply the strategy: If solving $15 \times 3 = \square$ is challenging, then choose one of the two factors—say, 15—and add it to itself 3 times, as indicated by the other factor, 3: $15 + 15 + 15 = 45$. So Carrie printed 45 pages in all.

Problem 6 on the activity sheet also lends itself to the use of this strategy.

For each problem that the students consider, discuss which thinking strategies they might use to solve the problem efficiently. Let the students use any appropriate strategy for addition, subtraction, multiplication, or division. They may even invent their own strategies! After the students complete a problem, ask them to explain and summarize their work.

Be sure to highlight interesting strategies that students use to solve the problems instead of giving them a list of strategies to use. The strategies identified here will often emerge naturally from students' thinking.

In the next activity, the students explore the "make ten to add" strategy and apply it to multiplication.

"Make Ten" to Multiply

Grades 3 and 4

Summary

Students make sense of a new thinking strategy—"making ten"—by illustrating it concretely, explaining it in writing, discussing it orally, and considering how it can help with multiplication facts.

Goals

- Make ten to add
- Use the "make ten to add" strategy to help solve multiplication problems

Prior Knowledge or Experience

- Experience in working with base-ten blocks
- An understanding of the place-value structure of the base-ten system

Materials and Equipment

For each student—

- A copy of each of the following blackline masters:
  - "Make Ten to Add"
  - "'Make Ten' Work Mat"
- Base-ten blocks (at least 7 tens-blocks and 16 ones-blocks for each student)
- Access to the applet Make Ten to Add (optional; on the CD-ROM)

pp. 182, 183

Teaching multiplication as repeated addition makes multiplication accessible to students by building on what they already know.

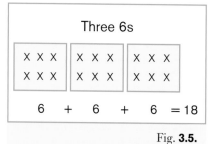

Three 6s		
x x x x x x	x x x x x x	x x x x x x
6 +	6 +	6 = 18

Fig. **3.5.**

Using repeated addition to multiply 3×6

Engage

Teachers commonly introduce multiplication as a process of repeated addition. This approach makes multiplication very accessible by building on what students already know. The students know how to add, so they find it very natural to use repeated addition to find the total number of people or objects in several groups of the same size (see fig. 3.5).

Students who approach multiplication as repeated addition may begin to experience difficulty, however, when they encounter problems that require them to regroup numbers. For example, a student might struggle to use repeated addition to solve $3 \times 8 = \square$ if he or she cannot efficiently add $16 + 8$. In general, multiplications that cause the most difficulty seem to be 3×7, 3×8, and 3×9. Adding $14 + 7$, $16 + 8$, or $18 + 9$, all of which have totals in the twenties, can stymie students.

Solving all these problems requires a "renaming" of ones as tens. Students who do not have an efficient strategy for adding beyond the next ten often end up counting by ones—frequently on their fingers—to find the sum. Many students who struggle with the harder multiplication facts use a combination of three strategies to solve such problems: They might start with a known fact, then use repeated addition, and finally count on their fingers to complete the solution. For example, to find the product 7×8, a student might think, "I know that five 8s are 40, so six 8s are $40 + 8$, or 48." But 48 plus 8 more may be beyond their reach without counting eight additional numbers (49, 50, 51, 52, 53, 54, 55, 56). So to keep track of their counting, they often use their fingers.

Some students do not even start with a known fact. They simply use repeated addition and count on their fingers. For example, to solve 7×8, they might add $8 + 8$ to get 16, count on their fingers to add 8 more, and then count on their fingers to add 8 again. They might know that $32 + 8$ is 40 and that $40 + 8$ is 48. But then they have to count on their fingers again to add $48 + 8$. This process takes a long time. Moreover, the probability of error in the process is high.

Learning to use addition strategies, such as "make ten" or "add with endings," can be extremely helpful to students who are struggling with the harder multiplication facts. To make ten, the students simply use *complements* of numbers that add to ten. For example, to solve $18 + 9 = \square$, a student can think, "I know that 18 plus 2 is 20. That leaves 7 more to add. And $20 + 7$ is 27." To add with endings, a student might think, "I know that $8 + 9$ is 17. So when I add $18 + 9$, the ones digit is going to be 7. And I know that the answer has to be in the 20s, so it must be 27."

Either of these strategies can provide students with an efficient way to use some known fact to establish an unknown basic multiplication fact. Figure 3.6 shows some common examples.

Problem	"Make ten" thinking strategy
$3 \times 7 = ?$ >	"Two 7s is 14. $14 + 6$ is 20, and 1 more is 21."
$3 \times 9 = ?$ >	"Two 9s is 18. $18 + 2$ is 20, and 7 more is 27."
$4 \times 8 = ?$ >	"Three 8s is 24. $24 + 6$ is 30, and 2 more is 32."
$6 \times 7 = ?$ >	"Five 7s is 35. $35 + 5$ is 40, and 2 more is 42."
$9 \times 8 = ?$ >	"Eight 8s is 64. $64 + 6$ is 70, and 2 more is 72."

Fig. **3.6.**

Using the "make ten" strategy to establish an unknown multiplication fact

Students who cannot rename ones efficiently as tens often end up counting by ones on their fingers to find a sum.

Students make a ten by using complements—numbers that together add to ten: 1 and 9, 2 and 8, 3 and 7, 4 and 6, and 5 and 5.

Distribute to each student a copy of the blackline masters "Make Ten to Add" and "'Make Ten' Work Mat," as well as a small group of base-ten blocks (see the Materials list). Engage the students in the "make ten" strategy by giving them a sample problem and helping them solve it with base-ten blocks on the work mat.

For example, write the problem $27 + 6 = \square$ on the board. Guide the students in representing the larger addend, 27, by placing two tens-blocks on the left side of the mat, under the heading "Tens," and seven ones-blocks in cells of the top ten-frame to the right, under the heading "Ones" (see fig. 3.7). Then have them show the smaller addend, 6, by placing six ones-blocks in cells of the lower ten-frame. Next, guide them in moving three ones-blocks from the lower frame to the remaining cells of the top frame (as indicated in the figure), filling the frame to "make ten."

Discuss with the students the fact that they can "trade" ten ones-blocks for one new tens-block, which they can then add to the collection of two tens-blocks on the left, making a total of three tens-blocks. (Be sure that the students remove all ten ones-blocks from the top frame in the exchange.) Then have the students solve $27 + 6 = \square$ by counting tens (3 tens, or 30) and ones (3 ones, or 3), for a total of 33.

Fig. **3.7.**

Preparing to move 3 ones to "make ten" to
solve 27 + 6 = ☐

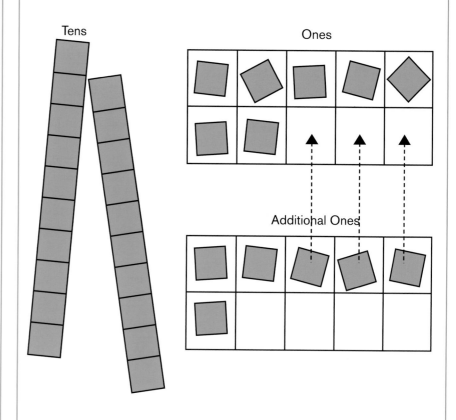

"Make Ten" Work Mat

Name _____

Tens

Ones

Additional Ones

$$27 + 6 = 2 \text{ tens} + 7 \text{ ones} + 6 \text{ ones}$$
$$= 2 \text{ tens} + (7 \text{ ones} + 3 \text{ ones}) + 3 \text{ ones}$$
$$= 2 \text{ tens} + 1 \text{ ten} + 3 \text{ ones}$$
$$= 3 \text{ tens} + 3 \text{ ones}$$
$$= 30 + 3$$
$$= 33$$

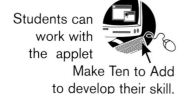

Students can
work with
the applet
Make Ten to Add
to develop their skill.

Explore

When you are sure that your students understand the process of
making a ten to add, have them work by themselves with base-ten
blocks on the work mat. Tell them to solve each problem on the activity
sheet "Make Ten to Add" by applying the "make ten" strategy. Circu-
late as the students work to be certain that they are using the strategy
efficiently and confidently. Note that the students must write a sentence
for each problem, explaining how they made a ten and then arrived at
the sum. For example, if the students had the problem 19 + 5 = ☐, they
might write, "19 + 1 is 20, and 4 more is 24."

Although the students may be able to solve the problems efficiently
without the "make ten" strategy, the focus of this activity is on learning

a strategy that can help them with particular addition problems that arise as they solve multiplication problems.

Extend

Help your students determine when the "make ten" strategy can help them solve multiplication problems. Ask them, "Can you identify a multiplication problem where you might use the 'make ten to add' strategy to help you solve the problem?" For example, for the problem $3 \times 9 = \square$, they might think: "Well, I know that two 9s are 18, so three 9s are equal to 18 + 9." Then they can apply the strategy of "making ten to add": $(18 + 2) + 7 = 20 + 7 = 27$. So, $18 + 9 = 3 \times 9 = 27$.

Have your students identify other multiplication problems where "making ten" helps them solve the problem. Ask them to give a full explanation of their thinking and solution processes.

Also extend your students' thinking by asking, "How might you use a similar thinking strategy to take away numbers? Could you use a similar strategy to find the difference between two numbers?"

In the next activity, the students again explore multiplication by splitting arrays (also see the activity Splitting Arrays in chapter 2), this time to help them represent and develop fluency with multiplication facts.

Help your students identify multiplication problems that they could solve efficiently by using the "make ten to add" strategy.

Learning Multiplication Facts with Arrays

Grades 3–5

Summary

Students learn multiplication facts by showing them graphically in arrays. They apply familiar multiplication facts to establish new ones by splitting the arrays and combining partial products to form whole products.

Goals

- Recognize patterns in multiplication facts
- Use arrays to represent multiplication facts
- Use thinking strategies to determine multiplication facts

Prior Knowledge or Experience

- An understanding of the meaning of multiplication

Materials and Equipment

pp. 184, 185–86, 187–88

For each student—
- A copy of each of the following blackline masters:
  - "Dime Array"
  - "Splitting Arrays"
  - "Splitting More Arrays"
- 70–80 counters (centimeter cubes, dried beans, buttons, or other small objects)
- Two half-sheets of unlined paper (colored or white)
- A new, full-length pencil (or other slender object long enough to "split" the array on the blackline master "Dime Array")
- One or two sheets of lined paper for recording work

For the teacher—
- Nine blank index cards
- An overhead projector
- A blank transparency
- A transparency of the blackline master "Dime Array"
- A transparency of the blackline master "16 × 25 Dot Array" (on the CD-ROM)

Activity

Engage

Research indicates that representing concepts can greatly enhance students' abilities to understand and solve problems. Furthermore, using facts that students know helps them learn facts that they do not know. For multiplication, students can both show concepts graphically and use familiar facts to establish new ones by working with arrays, which they can split and recombine to form the whole. They can then extend this technique to the multiplication of larger numbers and even rational numbers.

Distribute seventy to eighty counters to each student. Then hold up nine blank 3-by-5-inch index cards, and use a marker to write a single digit, 1–9, on each card. Make each digit large and bold for all the students to see. Turn the cards face down on a desk or table and shuffle them while the students watch.

Say, "Suppose we have a certain number of groups of people, and each group contains the same number of people as every other group. I'm going to draw two of our numbered cards. Let's let the first number tell us how many people are in each group, and the second number tell us how many groups we have in all."

Then draw two cards—say, a "5" and a "3"—and show them to your students. Write on the board, "5 people in each group," and, "3 groups." Then say, "Arrange counters on your desk to represent the multiplication fact that these two numbers give you." Check to see if the students have represented "3 groups of 5" in some manner with their counters (see fig. 3.8).

Ask the students to use pencil and paper and write the total number of counters (people) in their representation. Ask, "What multiplication fact do your counters show?" (5 × 3 = 15, or 3 × 5 = 15) Be sure to follow this question by another of equal importance: "How did you determine the answer?"

Listen to your students' strategies, and reinforce particular ways of determining the total, such as using patterns, adding on to known facts, or doubling known facts (if either of the numbers is even). For the problem 3 × 5 = □, students may have used the pattern learned from counting by 5s (5, 10, 15), or they may have known that 5 × 2 equals 10 and understood that adding on another 5 will give 15. Use a transparency on the overhead projector to demonstrate how to represent this multiplication fact.

Continue to draw pairs of numbered cards and have the students represent the corresponding multiplication facts. Always ask them to explain how they determined their answers.

Explore

Next, distribute copies of the blackline master "Dime Array" to each student, along with two half-sheets of paper for them to use to cover rows or columns to outline smaller arrays. (This process will be familiar to your students if they have already completed the activity Splitting Arrays in chapter 2.)

Pose a problem such as the following: "Kenneth took all the dimes out of his coin bank and arranged them in 4 groups, with 7 dimes in each group. How many dimes did Kenneth have in all?" (28) "How many cents?" (280) "How much money in dollars and cents?" ($2.80)

Guide your students in covering rows and columns of the 10-by-10 array on the blackline master to expose a 4-by-7 array (see fig. 3.9). Check to see if they have made the correct representation, and then have them use paper and pencil to record their answers.

"Instructional materials and classroom teaching should help students learn increasingly abbreviated procedures for producing number combinations rapidly and accurately without always having to refer to tables or other aids." *(Kilpatrick, Swafford, and Findell 2001, p. 413)*

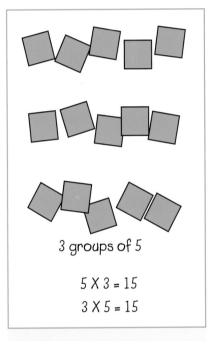

3 groups of 5

5 X 3 = 15

3 X 5 = 15

Fig. **3.8.**

Using counters to show 3 groups with 5 people in each group

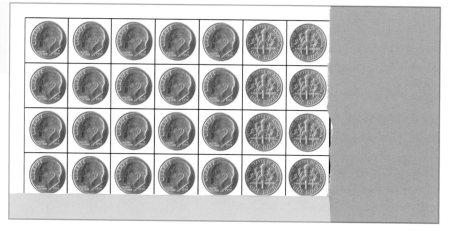

Fig. **3.9.**

Using sheets of paper to outline a 4-by-7 array to show Kenneth's dimes

Have students explain how they determined their answers. Encourage the students to use patterns, add on to known facts, or double known facts ($2 \times 7 = 14$ [known fact], and $2 \times 14 = 28$ [doubling known fact], so $4 \times 7 = 28$). Ask the students, "Is it easier to represent this multiplication situation as groups of objects or as an array?"

Pose additional problems of the same type. Two samples follow:

- Deborah sold lollipops for 10¢ apiece at the school fair. As children bought lollipops, Deborah stacked dimes on the table in front of her. She put 5 dimes in each stack. At the end of an hour, Deborah had 4 stacks of dimes. How many dimes did Deborah have in all? (20)

- Pete's grandmother sprained her ankle. Each day for an entire week, Pete picked up her newspaper and mail and brought them to her in her chair. Each day, his grandmother told him to take 8 dimes out of her coin jar. How many dimes did Pete have at the end of the week? (56) How much money was this in dollars and cents? ($5.60)

If "smaller" facts would be more appropriate for your students, you can decrease the numbers in these problems or use small numbers in other problems that you invent. Figure 3.10 shows the dime array for the problem about Pete's dimes.

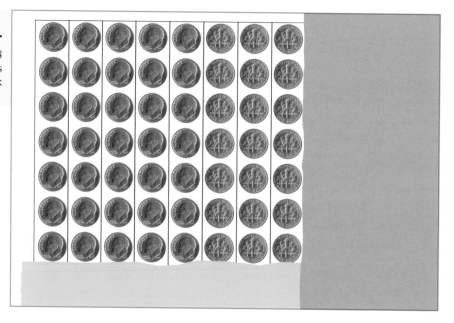

Fig. **3.10.**

Using sheets of paper to outline an 7-by-8 array to show Pete's dimes from his grandmother after a week

Next, pair each student with a partner. Have one student in each pair call for a multiplication fact and the other student use the dime array and two half-sheets of paper to represent the fact and state it completely (including the answer). Then have the first student state the total number of cents in the array and the equivalent amount in dollars and cents. Let the pairs of students repeat this exercise several times.

Have the students work by themselves with the dime array and two half-sheets of paper to determine the following multiplication facts:

$$3 \times 8 = \square$$
$$3 \times 9 = \square$$
$$4 \times 4 = \square$$
$$4 \times 6 = \square$$
$$5 \times 8 = \square$$

Tell the students to use a separate sheet of paper to record the facts that they establish.

When the students are finished, discuss their work on each problem. Ask, "How many dimes did you show in your outlined array? How much money does your array represent in cents? How much in dollars and cents?" Ask them to explain how they determined their answers.

Your students are likely to experience greater difficulty with some problems than with others. They may have already discovered that they can simplify these problems by splitting their outlined array into two component arrays that represent known multiplication facts that they can add together to yield the more challenging product.

Consider, for example, the sample problem about Pete's dimes from his grandmother, represented in figure 3.10. Depending on your students' experience with multiplication, they may have difficulty multiplying 7 by 8 (7 days times 8 dimes each day), or 8 by 7, to obtain 56—the total number of dimes.

However, by placing a pencil on their outlined 7-by-8 array as a divider, they may be able to split the array into two more accessible arrays—say, a 5-by-8 array and a 2-by-8 array. These two arrays might present them with facts that they know or can ascertain readily. Perhaps they are skillful in counting by 5s (5, 10, 15, 20, 25, 30, 35, 40) and know that $2 \times 8 = 8 + 8 = 16$. If so, they can easily add the products (40 and 16) of the arrays created by splitting the original array to determine that $7 \times 8 = 56$.

Have the students represent $8 \times 6 = \square$ on the "Dime Array" sheet. Instruct them to split the array into two parts, each of which represents a multiplication fact that they know. Then have them share how they split the array. Ask them, "How did you use facts that you already knew to determine the product 8×6?"

As students describe their thinking on this problem, show their process on a transparency of "Dime Array." Split the array as the students suggest, indicating which parts of the array they are using. Remember to ask the students to give the total number of cents (480), and the amount in dollars and cents ($4.80), as well as the number of dimes in each array. (See fig. 3.11.)

When your students thoroughly understand the idea of splitting an array into two arrays that represent known facts, distribute copies of the

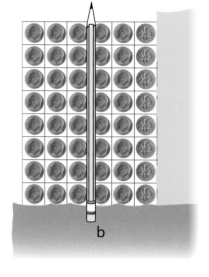

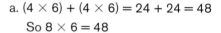

a. (4 × 6) + (4 × 6) = 24 + 24 = 48
   So 8 × 6 = 48

b. (8 × 3) + (8 × 3) = 24 + 24 = 48
   So 8 × 6 = 48

c. (5 × 6) + (3 × 6) = 30 + 18 = 48
   So 8 × 6 = 48

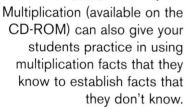

Working with the applet Splitting Arrays to Solve Multiplication (available on the CD-ROM) can also give your students practice in using multiplication facts that they know to establish facts that they don't know.

blackline master "Splitting Arrays." To complete this activity sheet, they must give a multiplication fact for each array of small circles. Then they must show how they could split the array to arrive at the fact if they didn't know it. Discuss the students' work.

Extend

Extend the concept of splitting arrays by showing a 16 × 25 array on the overhead projector (a template for a transparency is available on the CD-ROM). Have a student show how to split the array into two or more arrays, each of which represents a multiplication that the student knows (see fig. 3.12). Then ask another student to come forward and split the array in a different way.

Give each student a copy of the blackline master "Splitting More Arrays." Let the students discover ways of splitting an array that seem to help consistently. Give them some hints, such as the following:

1. If one of the factors is an even number, split that factor to divide the array in half, and then double the product for one half.

2. If one of the numbers is greater than 5, split off either 5 rows or 5 columns, and then add the product of the new 5-by-*n* or *n*-by-5 array to the product of the remaining array.

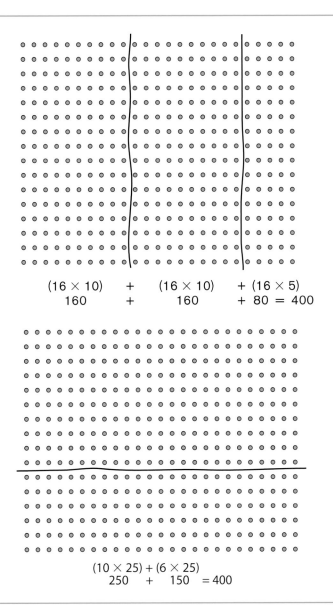

$(16 \times 10) \quad + \quad (16 \times 10) \quad + (16 \times 5)$
$160 \quad + \quad 160 \quad + \quad 80 = 400$

$(10 \times 25) + (6 \times 25)$
$250 \quad + \quad 150 \quad = 400$

These two ways of splitting an array into parts can help students with nearly all the harder multiplication facts. Be sure that your students see that if both factors are greater than 10, they can split off either 10 rows or 10 columns. Allow the students to experiment with this idea and discover that using tens makes multiplying easier.

Discuss other strategies that students may have used to split the various arrays. For example, a student may split an array in a different way, depending on the specific facts that he or she knows.

In the next activity, the students continue to learn multiplication facts—this time by using multiplication concept cards. Again, the activity helps them use facts that they know to learn new facts.

Building on Known Facts

Grades 3–5

The CD-ROM includes ten pages of paired templates for two-sided "concept cards," designed to reinforce multiplication facts for 5s, 6s, 7s, 8s, and 9s. Reproduce the cards on both sides of sheets of paper or cardstock, making sure that the fronts and backs align. Laminate the cards for greater durability, if you wish, before cutting them out.

Summary

Students use multiplication concept cards to help them see patterns in multiplication facts, find unknown facts from known facts, and relate multiplication to division.

Goals

- Recognize patterns of multiplication facts
- Establish relationships among families of facts
- Add on to or double known facts

Prior Knowledge or Experience

- Understand multiplication as repeated addition

Materials or Equipment

For each pair of students—

- A set of cards from the templates "Multiplication Concept Cards" (on the CD-ROM)

For the teacher—

- An analog clock, with the hours and minutes marked (optional)
- An overhead projector (optional)
- One or two transparencies (optional)
- An overhead calculator (optional)

Activity

Engage

Distribute to each pair of students a set of cards made from the "Multiplication Concept Cards" templates. Explain that one side of each card shows a small, raised number to the left of a large number in a circle. On the other side, the same raised number appears to the left of a large number inside a square. For example, one card has $\boxed{{}^5_6}$ on one side and $\boxed{{}^5_{30}}$ on the other. Together, the two sides of this card represent the multiplication fact "six 5s equal 30." Note that no operation symbols ("×" or "÷") appear on the cards. This deliberate omission is intended to help the students focus on the concepts rather than the symbols associated with the operations.

Have your students begin with the concept cards marked with small 5s (nine cards in all). A highly efficient way to determine the 5s facts is to count by 5s. However, students who are solving a problem by counting by 5s will almost always find that it is more efficient to start their count from a multiple of 5 that is greater than 5×1. To help your students develop this skill, have them lay out the 5s cards, "circle side"

up, in order from 1 to 9. Then ask the students to turn a particular card over, "square side" up. Ask questions that will help your students count by 5s, starting with the number revealed in the square.

For example, say that you ask the students to turn over the card that shows ⁵⃝6 , revealing ⁵⃞30 on the other side. This card represents the fact that six 5s equal 30, a fact that we can also express as 6 × 5 = 30, or 5 × 6 = 30. Say to the students, "You see that six 5s are 30. Look at your next card, which has a 7 in a circle. This card represents seven 5s (or 7 × 5, or 5 × 7). What number do you think is on the back of this card?" (35) "What multiplication fact does this card give you?" (7 × 5 = 35, or 5 × 7 = 35) "So if you were counting by 5s, beginning with 30, what number would you count next?" Have the students verify their answer by turning over the next card.

Tell the students to turn all the cards to the circle side again, and repeat this process of asking them to turn over a card. In addition to asking the students what number they think is on the back of the card that comes *after* the card that they have turned, ask what number they think is on the card *before* it. In this way, the students will practice the facts that they need to know to count backward as well as forward by 5s from any multiple of 5 up to 45.

Another efficient way to determine 5s facts is to relate the numerals on a clock to the time, in minutes, that has elapsed since the hour (for example, "1" on the clock stands for one group of 5 minutes "past the hour," "2" stands for two 5s, or 10 minutes, past the hour, and so on). Students can easily see that they can determine seven 5s, represented in the cards as ⁵⃝7 , by considering the minutes represented by "7" on a clock face. If you think the clock model might help your students with 5s facts, you can demonstrate this process to them by using an analog clock with the minutes marked (see fig. 3.13).

Explore

Have the students work with the cards to solidify multiplication facts for other "families"—6s, 7s, 8s, and 9s. Ask them to lay out the cards in order for one of these families and turn over the cards that represent facts that they know. Then have them use these known facts to determine any facts that they do not know.

For instance, in working with the cards for 6s, the students might turn over the card that shows ⁶⃝2 or two 6s, and use the fact that two 6s are 12 to help them find that four 6s are 24 (two 6s + two 6s = four 6s; 12 + 12 = 24). Or they might turn over the card that shows ⁶⃝5 , or five 6s, and use that to help them with find that six 6s are 36 ([five 6s] + 6 = 30 + 6 = 36), or that seven 6s are 42 (30 + 12 = 42).

Always ask the students to explain their thinking. Write several familiar facts on the board or an overhead transparency, and ask the students to indicate how they could use those facts to help determine facts they do not know.

Extend

Pair each student with a partner, and have each pair lay out the cards for a particular family of facts in the same way as before. One student

"Fluency with basic number combinations develops from well-understood meanings for the four operations and from a focus on thinking strategies."
(NCTM 2000, p. 152; referring to Thornton [1990] and Isaacs and Carroll [1999])

7 groups of 5 minutes, or 35 minutes past the hour

Fig. **3.13.**

Using the face of an analog clock to determine 5s multiplication facts

in each pair should remove all the cards that represent facts that he or she does not know. Then he or she should select a card representing a fact that he or she *does* know and place this card with the square side (product) up. Directly below this card, the student should place one of the cards for an "unknown" fact, with the circle side (factor) up. Then the student should share with his or her partner how he or she can use the known fact to help determine the unknown fact. After the student has worked through all his or her cards for unknown facts in the same way, the second student in each pair should go through the process.

Emphasize to the students the importance of using facts that they know to help them determine facts they do not know. Every day you might show a card containing a fact that all your students know quite well and then show a card containing a fact that some might not know. Ask the students to explain how they could use the card containing the fact that they know to help determine the unknown fact. Stress the idea of adding on to a known fact or doubling it. For example, if students know that five 7s are 35, they can easily complete the fact for six 7s by adding on another 7 to 35 to get 42. Or if they know that four 6s are 24, then they can double 24 to find that eight 6s are 48.

You can extend the students' work to division by having the pairs of students lay out the cards for a particular family with the square sides (products) up. Now they will let the number in the box represent the dividend and the small number above it stand for the divisor. The number inside the circle on the other side of the card will be the quotient. Have them turn over a card representing a division fact that they think they know (for example, the card with $\boxed{\overset{5}{30}}$ facing up and $\overset{5}{\textcircled{6}}$ facing down, representing the division fact "30 ÷ 5 = 6"), and ask them to speculate about the division facts represented by cards before and after the turned card.

If you have access to an overhead calculator, you might flash a few multiplication or division facts on the screen every day. Ask the students, "What other facts can you determine from these facts?" They can use doubling, halving, adding on, or subtracting to establish new facts. For instance, you might show the fact "5 × 8 = 40." By using the strategy of halving, the students can easily determine that 5 × 4 = 20. By starting again with the original fact (5 × 8 = 40) and using the strategy of adding on another 8, they can determine that 6 × 8 = 48. By taking the original fact again and adding on another 16, they can determine that 7 × 8 = 56. And by using the strategy of subtracting an 8 from both sides of the equals sign in the original fact, they can determine that 4 × 8 = 32.

The next activity builds on ideas in this activity, helping students learn the one-digit factors involved in basic multiplication facts and use them to establish related division facts.

To Divide, Think "Multiplication"

Grades 3–5

Summary

Students develop facts and skills for division by focusing on and exploring related multiplication facts.

Goals

- Relate multiplication facts to division facts
- Determine the one-digit factors of the products in basic multiplication facts
- Solve problems involving multiplication and division

Prior Knowledge or Experience

- An understanding of multiplication as repeated addition
- An understanding of division as repeated subtraction
- Concrete experience in partitioning (with objects)

Materials and Equipment

For each student—
- A copy of each of the following blackline masters:
  ○ "Facts and Factors"
  ○ "Mystery Multiplication Facts"
- One or two sheets of paper
- A four-function calculator (optional)

For the teacher—
- An overhead projector (optional)
- One or two transparencies (optional)

Activity

Engage

Multiplication facts that students know can help them solve division problems. For example, if they know that 4 times 5 equals 20, they can easily determine that 20 divided by 5 equals 4, and that 20 divided by 4 equals 5. The language that you use to explain division should be closely tied to the language that you use to explain multiplication. For example, for the division problem $20 \div 5 = \square$, you could phrase the question this way: "How many 5s are in 20?" (4) This language makes it clear that knowing the multiplication fact "$4 \times 5 = 20$" can help in solving $20 \div 5 = \square$.

The previous activity showed how working with multiplication concept cards can aid students in seeing such relationships and learning how to

"Finding and using patterns and other thinking strategies greatly simplifies the task of learning multiplication facts. Moreover, finding and describing patterns are a hallmark of mathematics." (Kilpatrick, Swafford, and Findell 2001, pp. 191–92)

pp. 189, 190–191

use multiplication in dividing. Recall that each card has a small, raised number that is repeated on both sides to designate the multiplication "family." A larger number in a circle on one side of the card is a factor of the product that appears in a square on the other side. When a student sees the side of a card with the square (the "product" side), he or she should think, "What number times the small number equals the number in the square?" As the student turns over the card to verify the answer, he or she reinforces an understanding of the inverse relationship between multiplication and division.

On the board or an overhead transparency, write a multiplication fact—for example, $4 \times 7 = 28$. Ask the students, "What two division facts can you find in this multiplication fact?" Students should recognize that they can treat the product of 4 and 7—28—as the dividend of a division problem. If they treat one factor as the divisor in this problem, the other factor becomes the quotient. Moreover, they can switch the roles (divisor and quotient) of the two factors in the division of 28, thus arriving at two division facts: $28 \div 7 = 4$, and $28 \div 4 = 7$.

Ask the students to give you other multiplication facts that they know. Write them on the board or a transparency, and have the students then state division facts involving the same factors and product.

Explore

Although the focus of the tasks that follow is explicitly on multiplication facts, the ability to take these facts apart and put them back together, as students do here, helps in establishing basic division facts. Begin by telling your students that you are going to think of a multiplication fact that they are all know well. Say, "I'm not going to tell you the whole fact. Instead, I'll give you only the product of two 'mystery' factors." Then write on the board or an overhead transparency,

"_____ $\times$ _____ = 14."

Ask the students, "What multiplication fact has 14 as a product?" Students might suggest the following multiplication statements:

$$2 \times 7 = 14$$
$$7 \times 2 = 14$$
$$1 \times 14 = 14$$
$$14 \times 1 = 14$$

Explain that basic facts are always combinations of two *one-digit* numbers under the operations addition, subtraction, multiplication and division. So $1 \times 14 = 14$ and $14 \times 1 = 14$ do not qualify as *basic* multiplication facts.

Present other multiplication facts in the same way—by giving the product of two unknown one-digit factors, which the students must identify. Select only facts that you are confident that most of your students know. Students find it difficult to relate the product to factors if they do not know the associated multiplication fact.

Show another product from a basic multiplication fact and vary the process described above by saying, "I'm thinking of one of the factors of this product. Can you guess what number I have in mind?" For example, show your students "_____ $\times$ _____ = 21." Have the students

The ability to take multiplication facts apart and put them back together helps in establishing basic division facts.

write their guess on a sheet of paper. If the factor you are thinking of is 3, tell the students who wrote "3" on their paper to give themselves two points—one for the correct selection of a factor and one for the lucky selection of the particular factor that you had in mind. The students who selected the other factor, 7, should give themselves one point for the correct selection of a factor. Repeat this process at least five times, using products from multiplication facts that the students know well. Have the students keep track of their scores.

Extend

Once your students have developed some skill in working with basic multiplication facts in this way, select a range of numbers—say, 30–40. Write the range on the board or a transparency. Then ask your students to help you write all the numbers in that range that are products in basic multiplication facts. For example, in the 30–40 range, the numbers 30, 32, 35, 36, and 40 are all products of two one-digit factors. Elicit the students' help in stating all the basic multiplication facts that have these products:

$$5 \times 6 = 30, \text{ and } 6 \times 5 = 30$$
$$8 \times 4 = 32, \text{ and } 4 \times 8 = 32$$
$$5 \times 7 = 35, \text{ and } 7 \times 5 = 35$$
$$6 \times 6 = 36$$
$$8 \times 5 = 40, \text{ and } 5 \times 8 = 40$$

Identify a new range of numbers—say, 45–55—and have the students again work as a class to list all the facts whose products fall in that range. (You might also have the students list all the multiplication facts whose products have a specific digit in the ones place, such as 0.) To give ample opportunities to students who find the work very challenging, you might invite these students to make guesses and check their ideas with a calculator. For example, a student who guesses that the product of 7 times 7 falls in the 40–50 range can test his or her conjecture by entering "7 × 7" in a calculator and getting a product of 49.

Next, write on the board or a transparency a two-digit number with a digit missing from either the tens or the ones place. Suppose that you write "__2." This expression could represent any of the following two-digit numbers: 12, 22, 32, 42, 52, 62, 72, 82, or 92. Say to your students, "Suppose '__2' is the product in a basic multiplication fact. What number—or numbers—might '__2' be?" The students should test the possibilities:

- $12 = 2 \times 6$ (or 3×4, or 4×3, or 6×2)
- 22 is not the product of any combination of one-digit factors
- $32 = 4 \times 8$ (or 8×4)
- $42 = 6 \times 7$ (or 7×6)
- 52 is not the product of any combination of one-digit factors
- 62 is not the product of any combination of one-digit factors
- $72 = 8 \times 9$ (or 9×8)
- 82 is not the product of any combination of one-digit factors
- 92 is not the product of any combination of one-digit factors

There are seven multiplication facts whose products fall in the range 45–55:

$$5 \times 9 = 45, \text{ and } 9 \times 5 = 45$$
$$6 \times 8 = 48, \text{ and } 8 \times 6 = 48$$
$$7 \times 7 = 49$$
$$6 \times 9 = 54, \text{ and } 9 \times 6 = 54$$

Focusing on the products in multiplication facts can help students gain skill with division facts.

On the basis of their testing, the students should conclude that "__2" can represent 12, 32, 42, or 72.

Distribute copies of the blackline master "Facts and Factors," and have the students complete the problems by applying the strategies that they have used in class. After they have finished working, call on students to explain their solutions.

Next, distribute copies of the blackline master "Mystery Multiplication Facts." This time, the students may benefit from working in pairs so that they can discuss their ideas with a partner as they work. When the students have completed the activity sheet, ask for volunteers to present their solutions and explain their thinking.

Focusing on the products in multiplication facts can help students gain skill with division facts. When students are presented with a division problem such as $32 \div 4 = \square$, they often find it much easier to think, "What times 4 equals 32?" If they know that 8 times 4 equals 32, they have an efficient way of determining that 32 divided by 4 equals 8. Attempting to count by 4s to 32 would involve them in a longer process with a greater chance of error.

When you relate division to multiplication, allow counting initially, but later encourage more sophisticated methods of solving problems. The sequence of tasks suggested in this activity can help your students develop important strategies for relating multiplication to division, making them more proficient with division facts.

Conclusion

This chapter has presented activities designed to help students gain flexibility with basic facts. The activities have reinforced a strong understanding of the four operations as well as the development of thinking strategies that promote fluency with basic facts. Such fluency is essential as students progress to multidigit computation.

NAVIGATING *through* NUMBER *and* OPERATIONS

Chapter 4
Fluency with Algorithms

The computational methods that students develop for working with multidigit numbers should be grounded in an understanding of relationships among numbers and operations. Instructional emphasis on mathematical ideas—such as the structure of the base-ten number system and the properties of the operations—provides students with a meaningful learning environment. Such an environment can support the students' development of *computational fluency*, which comprises—

- an understanding of several computational methods for solving problems;
- an ability to choose flexibly among these methods;
- an ability to explain and justify particular approaches to particular problems; and
- skill in solving problems and producing accurate answers efficiently (NCTM 2000; Russell 2000).

In the past, the customary goal of classroom teaching was to develop the students' ability to recall and use a single algorithm for each operation. Teaching today places a much higher value than teaching in the past on the students' acquisition of a variety of appropriate methods and tools for computing with whole numbers. Today's instruction aims at developing the students' ability to choose among these tools and methods—such as mental computation, estimation, calculators, and paper and pencil—according to the context and nature of the task.

Instructional emphasis on mathematical ideas provides students with a meaningful learning environment.

For example, if three friends are trying to determine whether they have enough money to see a movie, an estimate may be adequate to provide the information they need. However, when they are at the point of purchasing the three tickets at the window of the theater, they will be dealing with an exact amount, and a calculator-based cash register will determine precisely how much they must pay.

The Number and Operations Standard emphasizes students' broad computational needs and their development of understanding and flexibility in approaching problems in a variety of contexts, in and out of school. This flexibility depends on the students' access to a range of strategies that they can deploy appropriately to solve problems involving each operation. Students who are so equipped are in the very advantageous position of choosing the strategy that best fits the numbers in a particular problem. For example, such students might solve $28 \times 4 = \square$ by reasoning that $(25 \times 4) + (3 \times 4)$ equals $100 + 12$, or 112. They might solve $537 - 98 = \square$ by reasoning that $537 - 100$ equals 437, but since $537 - 100$ takes 2 more away than $537 - 98$, they would add the 2 back in: $437 + 2 = 439$.

As students progress from grade 3 through grade 5, they should consolidate their repertoires of computational methods for working with whole numbers. This process involves mastering a few strategies that they understand well and can use efficiently and accurately for each operation. These methods include both student-generated strategies and conventional algorithms, such as the procedures that are widely taught in the United States. The standard algorithms taught in countries around the world vary (Phillipp 1996; Ron 1998), and algorithms taught in the United States today are different from those taught in the past (Ross and Pratt-Cotter 2000). No matter what algorithm students use, they should understand and be able to explain their method.

Students in grades 3–5 also begin to develop approaches for adding and subtracting common fractions and decimals. Like their strategies for working with whole numbers, the students' strategies for handling fractions should be grounded in their understanding of the relationships among numbers and operations. Instruction in these grades should not emphasize the development of generalized algorithms to solve all decimal and fraction problems. Instead, students should have opportunities to explore ways of combining, separating, and comparing fractions and decimals. Classroom approaches should stress developing the students' conceptual understanding by using visual models, finding connections among representations, establishing relationships between and among the operations, and exploring the properties of the operations.

This chapter's five activities are designed to develop students' computational fluency. The first three activities focus on building flexibility in computing with multidigit numbers. In Adding Up to Subtract, students use an open number line to develop "adding up" strategies for subtraction. Summing Partial Products to Multiply guides students in applying the distributive property to find partial products. In Using Mental Mathematics to Divide, students solve division problems by decomposing the whole amount. The remaining two activities focus on other aspects of computation. Going Over or Under to Estimate gives students practice in estimating products for multiplication problems. Taking an Hour for Clock Fractions explores the use of models, benchmarks, and equivalent forms in adding common fractions.

Adding Up to Subtract

Grades 3–4

Summary

Students use "open" number lines to solve subtraction problems by figuring out a sequence of efficient "jumps" that can take them from the part they are taking away to the whole from which they are taking the part. The jumps use benchmarks, such as 5s, 10s, 25s, and 100s, to produce easy solutions to the problems. (For an explanation of the strategy of "adding up" to subtract, see also part 1 of the activity A Problem-Solving Approach to Basic Facts in chapter 3.)

Goals

- Use the strategy of "adding up" to solve subtraction problems
- Use addition and subtraction relationships that the students know, especially those involving benchmarks such as multiples of 10 and 100
- Use open number lines to represent solution strategies for subtraction problems
- Develop flexibility and greater efficiency in solving subtraction problems with larger numbers

Prior Knowledge or Experience

- Work with benchmarks
- Work with semistructured and open number lines

Materials and Equipment

For each pair of students—

- One or two sheets of paper
- One or two pencils
- A copy of each of the following blackline masters:
  - "Traveling in the City—Spinners"
  - "Traveling in the City—Open Number Lines"
- A large paper clip

Activity

Engage

Number lines are visual representations that help students think about the relationships among numbers. An "open" number line can aid students in thinking about and finding the distance, or *difference*, between two numbers. Number lines often show every whole number over the visible length of the line. By contrast, an open line shows only the numbers that result from a particular action (Fosnot and Dolk 2001).

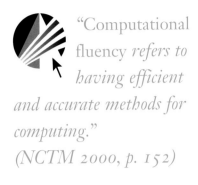

"Computational fluency *refers to having efficient and accurate methods for computing.*" (*NCTM 2000, p. 152*)

pp. 192, 193

Tell your students that they are going to work together as a class to solve the subtraction problem 54 – 25 = □. Write the problem on the board and draw an open number line. Then mark your line to show 25 and 54 (leaving ample space between the two numbers). Ask the students to suggest ways to "jump" from 25 to 54. Mark your line to show a student's suggestions, and then erase those marks and redraw your line or make a new one to show another student's ideas.

A student may suggest jumping five places, from 25 to 30, and then 10 more places, to 40, and then another 10 places, to 50, and then four more places, to 54. This suggestion breaks the distance (or difference) between 25 and 54 into four jumps: 5 places + 10 places + 10 places + 4 places, or 29 places in all. An even simpler method would consist of three jumps: five places, to 30, and then twenty places, to 50, and then four places, to 54. Figure 4.1 shows these three jumps: 5 places + 20 places + 4 places = 29 places in all.

Fig. 4.1.

An open number line representing the equation 54 – 25 = □

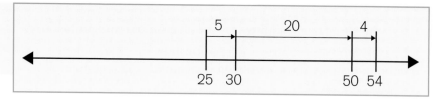

If your students do not propose either of these ways of jumping, introduce them yourself. Explain that these ways make the jumps easy to think about and keep track of, because they make use of multiples of ten—numbers that we commonly think about and use as benchmarks.

Students who have not previously used numbers as benchmarks might find it easier to start with a semistructured, rather than an open, number line. Such a number line would have multiples of 10 marked and labeled. If your students are working with two-digit numbers, give them semistructured lines showing the numbers 0, 10, 20, 30, 40, 50, 60, 70, 80, 90, and 100. Later, have them extend the lines and mark the numbers 110, 120, 130, and so on, up to 200.

As an intermediate step before moving to an open number line, introduce semistructured number lines marked by 25s, 50s, or even just 100s, depending on the sizes of the numbers that your students are using. After they become accustomed to using the labeled benchmarks on the semistructured number lines, you can introduce an open number line and have them supply their own benchmarks.

Use of an open number line not only encourages students to work with benchmarks but also supports an understanding of place-value concepts. The students consider place value as they make jumps of 5, 10, 100, and other multiples of 5. Furthermore, as students decide which points to mark on their open number lines, they see what part of a computation they have completed and what part they still must do. Moreover, the visual representations that open number lines provide make it easy for students to compare strategies with one another.

To solve the problem 54 – 25 = □ on an open number line, some students will probably find it very efficient to jump directly from 25 to 50. In fact, as students learn to construct a mental map of an open number line, they may no longer need to draw a number line but instead will be able to visualize the jumps for many problems as they

A benchmark is a point of reference or a standard against which we can make measurements for comparison and assessment.

reason mentally or jot down numbers to keep track of their intermediate steps. In these ways, an open number line serves as a visual prop as students build more efficient mental strategies.

This activity encourages students to use open number lines to represent and solve problems about traveling in a city. Present the following problem to the students:

Thomas lives at the corner of 48th Street and King Drive. His friend Bernard lives on the corner of 73rd Street and King Drive. Thomas's mother says it is too far for Thomas to walk to Bernard's house. How many blocks would Thomas have to walk to get to his friend's house? Do you think this distance is too far to walk?

Ask the students to summarize the problem and then have them represent it symbolically. Emphasize that they need to find the distance from Thomas's house to Bernard's house—that is, the number of blocks between 48th and 73rd Streets. Equations might include the following:

$$73 \text{ blocks} - 48 \text{ blocks} = \square \text{ blocks}$$
$$48 \text{ blocks} + \square \text{ blocks} = 73 \text{ blocks}$$

Have the students set up this problem on an open number line as shown in figure 4.2.

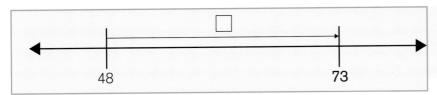

Fig. **4.2.**

An open number line representing the equation 73 blocks – 48 blocks = □ blocks

Say to the students, "We need to figure out how many blocks there are from 48th Street to 73rd Street. The number is too large to count by ones. How might we make some bigger jumps along the line to figure out that distance?" As before, sketch some of the students' solutions on the board, emphasizing the use of benchmarks such as multiples of 10. Figures 4.3 and 4.4 show two students' solutions.

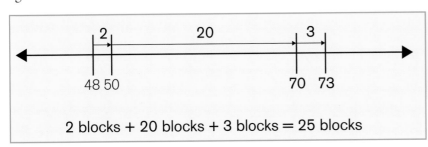

Fig. **4.3.**

An open number line representing a solution to the equation 73 blocks – 48 blocks = □ blocks, in three jumps

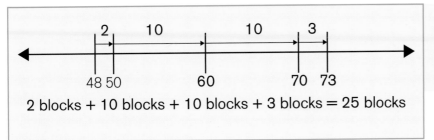

Fig. **4.4.**

An open number line representing a solution to the equation 73 blocks – 48 blocks = □ blocks, in four jumps

Be sure that your students understand the convenience of using 10s as benchmarks in making a sequence of jumps from 48 blocks to 73 blocks to determine efficiently that there are 25 blocks between the two. Explain that other numbers can serve as benchmarks too. In solving other problems, they may want to use 5s, 25s, 100s, or even larger numbers as benchmarks.

Arrange your students in pairs and present a new problem—with larger numbers—for the students to explore with their partners:

> Carol plans to ride the Wisconsin Avenue bus to the zoo. The bus will pick her up at 144th Street, and she will ride it all the way to the zoo, getting off at 352nd Street. How many blocks will Carol ride the bus to get to the zoo?

Have each pair draw an open number line on a sheet of paper, and tell the students to mark the relevant numbers (144 and 352) on their lines, leaving ample space between them. Figures 4.5 shows an open number line for the problem. Direct the students to represent the problem symbolically in an equation (such as 352 – 144 = □) before thinking about a sequence of jumps that would give them an easy solution.

Fig. **4.5.**

An open number line representing the equation 352 blocks – 144 blocks = □ blocks

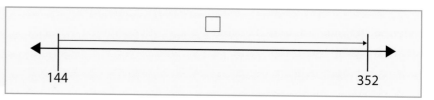

Ask, "Can you suggest some benchmarks for jumps along the line?" Students might identify 150, 175, 200, and 300 as a sequence of possible benchmarks on the line. They might also suggest jumping by 10s or 20s or even jumping 200 blocks, from 144 to 344.

Have the students work with their partners to show a sequence of efficient jumps from 144 to 252 on their open number lines. After these jumps, they can make a single jump of 100 blocks to complete the problem. See what patterns of jumps they create and whether they use benchmarks and record numbers at reasonable points on the line.

Ask a few students to draw and label their representations on the board and explain their reasoning. Have the other students see if they can follow those students' reasoning and compare their own solutions with those on the board. Figure 4.6 shows one possible set of jumps.

Fig. **4.6.**

Two jumps to move from 144 to 252 on an open number line, followed by a jump of 100 to reach 352

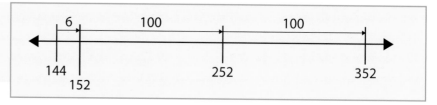

Explore

Distribute to each pair of students a copy of the blackline master "Traveling in the City—Spinners," which shows a "start" and a "stop" spinner. Also give each pair a large paper clip, as well as a copy of the blackline master "Traveling in the City—Open Number Lines." Tell the students, "Today, you are going to use open number lines to help you solve subtraction problems about traveling in the city. You and your partner will work together to identify benchmarks and decide on the size of your jumps."

Have the students use a pencil to anchor the end of a paper clip in the center of the "start" spinner (see the margin; your students can straighten an end of the paper clip as shown, if they wish). Tell them, "Spin to find the number of the street at which you will start your trip. Then anchor the paper clip in the center of the 'stop' spinner and spin to find the numbered street of your destination."

The students can take turns recording their work on one of the open number lines on the activity sheet, marking the "start" and "stop" streets, along with the benchmarks that they used, and the size of each jump. They should also record an equation and the answer for each problem produced by their spins of the start and stop spinners.

To adjust the activity to suit a wide range of learners in your class, including those of lower ability, you could change the numbers on the spinners to multiples of 5, 10, or 100. For example, the second spinner might have only multiples of 100 and the first spinner might include numbers that end in 5 that are less than 100.

Extend

Review your students' work, and select several solutions that they recorded for problems produced by spins of the spinners. Share the students' work with the whole class. You might select a problem that has a two-digit "start" number and another that has three-digit "start" number. Ask several pairs of students to solve these problems in different ways on the board. Analyze and compare the various solutions.

Figure 4.7 shows a student's work to find the distance from 168th Street to 347th Street without a number line. Present this sample of work, and have your students analyze the reasoning behind it. Ask them to discuss how this work is similar to their work with an open number line.

Your students can also use open number lines for adding. Ask them to think about the problem $76 + 27 = \square$. Talk through the following two solutions:

- "You could start with a number close to 76—say, 75. Then you could move 30 places, or three jumps of 10. Where would this put you? But look at your problem—you would need to drop back 3 places to make a total of 27 places instead of 30. Then you would have to add 1, since your starting number was actually 76, not 75. So what would your "stop" number be?" (103)

- "You could start at 76 and jump 4 to 80, then 20, to 100, then 3 more to 103."

Give your students another addition problem to solve by the same method. Say, "What if you had to solve the problem $246 + 178 = \square$? What benchmarks would work? How big would your jumps be? Where would you end?"

In this activity, the students have gained experience with the use of open number lines and benchmarks to add up to subtract. In the next activity, they explore the distributive property of multiplication over addition by working with multiplication "chains."

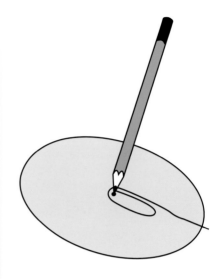

168	+	(2)	= 170	2
170	+	(30)	= 200	30
200	+	(140)	= 340	140
340	+	(7)	= 347	7
				179

Fig. 4.7.

A sample of work by a student to show the distance from 168th Street to 347th Street ($347 - 168 = \square$)

Summing Partial Products to Multiply

Grades 3–5

Summary

By applying the distributive property in the creation of multiplication "chains"—sequences of simple multiplication problems that make complex multiplication problems more approachable—students become more efficient in using both mental and paper-and-pencil computations to solve multiplication problems.

Goals

- Solve multiplication problems by "breaking," or *decomposing*, a factor, emphasizing use of the distributive property
- Use rectangles to represent partial products
- Develop greater fluency in solving multiplication problems

Prior Knowledge or Experience

- Experience in decomposing numbers
- An understanding of the meaning of multiplication

Materials and Equipment

For each pair of students—
- A copy of each of the following blackline masters:
  ◦ "Multiplication Chains—Sheet A"
  ◦ "Multiplication Chains—Sheet B"
- Paper and pencils, including a blank sheet of paper to use as a cover sheet

For the teacher—

- An overhead projector (optional)
- One or two overhead transparencies (optional)

pp. 194, 195

Activity

Engage

Problem solvers often break complex problems into sequences of simpler, related problems to help obtain solutions. The use of groups of smaller problems, sometimes called mathematical "chains," is an important problem-solving strategy. Such chains highlight and apply fundamental relationships among numbers and operations.

A multiplication chain can help students think about how to begin work on a problem, how to decompose numbers, and how to combine information to find a solution. Working with a chain helps students consider how to use what they know to turn a difficult problem into one that is easier to solve.

For example, the problems $2 \times 7 = \square$ and $50 \times 7 = \square$ can be a chain that uses the distributive property of multiplication over addition to make the problem $52 \times 7 = \square$ easier to solve. On the board (or an overhead projector), display the first problem in this multiplication chain:

$$2 \times 7 = \square$$

Ask the students to solve this problem and explain their reasoning. Write in 14 when the students supply the answer.

Below this multiplication, write the second problem in the chain:

$$50 \times 7 = \square$$

Have the students solve this problem. Say, "See if you can find the answer without using paper." Enter 350 when the students come up with the answer. Again, have the students explain their reasoning.

Next, write the more challenging problem that these two equations can aid in solving:

$$52 \times 7 = \square$$

Ask your students, "Can the two equations that we already had on the board help us solve this multiplication problem? If so, how?" Guide your students in seeing that the sum of these products, or 14 + 350, is 364, which is also the product of 52 and 7. If necessary, have the students use paper and pencil to multiply 52 times 7 to obtain 364 as the product.

When the students clearly understand that the product of 52 and 7 is equal to the product of 2 and 7 plus the product of 50 and 7, tell them, "We saw that it's fairly easy to multiply 2 times 7 and 50 times 7. Why are those multiplications easier than multiplying 52 times 7?" ($2 \times 7 = 14$ is a basic multiplication fact, and 50 is a multiple of ten) Emphasize the purpose of making the simpler multiplications: "By adding up the products of these easy problems, we can get the product of the harder problem."

Say, "Let's think of $52 \times 7 = \square$ as a multiplication problem about equal groups: if we have 52 groups of objects, with 7 objects in each group, how many objects do we have in all?" Illustrate this situation by drawing a very "tall" rectangle on the board with the height labeled "52 groups" and the width labeled "7 objects" (see fig. 4.8).

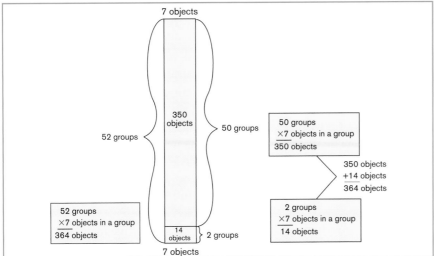

Fig **4.8.**

A representation of 52 groups with 7 objects in each group:
$52 \times 7 = (2 + 50) \times 7 = (2 \times 7) + (50 \times 7)$

Say, "We can break our 52 groups into 50 groups of 7 objects and 2 groups of 7 objects." Draw a line across the width of your rectangle to show this splitting of the 52 groups. Continue by saying, "You can see that doing this doesn't change the problem, but it gives us numbers that are easier to use in multiplying. Now we have $(2 \times 7) + (50 \times 7) = 52 \times 7$."

Explain that this process of thinking about a problem like $52 \times 7 = \square$ uses the distributive property of multiplication over addition: the multiplication ($\times 7$) is distributed, or spread, over the two parts that 52 is broken into, 50 and 2. Thus, $(50 + 2) \times 7$ is equal to $(50 \times 7) + (2 \times 7)$ by the distributive property. The partial products, 350 and 14, must then be added together to give the whole product.

The following multiplication chain also uses the distributive property:

$$3 \times 12 = \square$$
$$20 \times 12 = \square$$
$$40 \times 12 = \square$$
$$\text{-----}$$
$$63 \times 12 = \square$$

Write the problems one at a time on the board for your students to solve and discuss as before. When the students understand that the problems $3 \times 12 = \square$, $20 \times 12 = \square$, and $40 \times 12 = \square$ compose a chain for $63 \times 12 = \square$, assign each student a partner and have each pair of students draw a rectangle that shows this breaking of 63 groups of 12, along with the resulting partial products.

Prompt the students to think about the relationships among the problems as they work their way along the chain. Select a few pairs of students to draw their rectangle on the board for discussion. Their drawings should look similar to that in figure 4.9.

Check to see if your students are grasping the concepts and are secure with the reasoning. If not, you may wish to adjust these chains or create others to give the students additional practice.

Explore

Distribute to each pair of students one set of activity sheets made from the blackline masters "Multiplication Chains—Sheet A" and "Multiplication Chains—Sheet B." One student in each pair should take sheet A, and the other student should take sheet B. Also give each pair of students a blank sheet of paper to use as a cover sheet.

Explain the process to the students. Each activity sheet shows two multiplication chains leading up to the problems that the chains help solve. Each pair of students should choose one member to act as student 1, with the other taking the role of student 2. Student 1 will show a multiplication chain, one problem at a time, to student 2. Student 1 should hide the remaining problem(s) in the chain under the cover sheet as student 2 works. When student 2 solves a problem, student 1 should ask how he or she arrived at the answer. Once student 2 has solved all the problems in a chain (and has found the whole product as well as the partial products), students 1 and 2 should work together to draw a rectangle that shows how the chain breaks the whole product into partial products.

Next, students 1 and 2 should switch roles and repeat the process until they have worked through all four chains on the sheets. Then the

Fig. 4.9.

A representation of a multiplication chain for $63 \times 12 = \square$

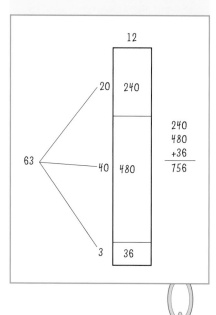

Navigating through Number and Operations in Grades 3–5

students will be set to work together to create their own multiplication chains for the two remaining problems on the sheets.

Extend

Invite several pairs of students to present their multiplication chains for the last problems on the activity sheets to the whole class. Ask them, "What break (or breaks) did you decide to make in one of the factors in the multiplication problem?" Have them explain their reasoning. Then ask them, "Can you summarize the ideas that you need to keep in mind as you consider ways to break a factor?" Emphasize to your students that the purpose of breaking a factor in this way is to make a multiplication problem easier to solve.

To extend students' reasoning about multiplication chains and the distributive property of multiplication over addition, have them work with chains that make a factor in a multiplication larger, instead of smaller, than in the original problem. In a chain that does this, the problem solver creates partial products that he or she must put together by subtraction rather than addition. Students should again consider numbers that are helpful, such as multiples of 10 or 100, but now they will be compensating for the larger size of a factor by subtracting.

Let your students examine this process in the following multiplication chains:

$23 \times 10 = \square$ $47 \times 10 = \square$
$23 \times 1 = \square$ $47 \times 1 = \square$
$- - - - - -$ $- - - - - -$
$23 \times 9 = \square$ $47 \times 9 = \square$

$54 \times 100 = \square$ $34 \times 100 = \square$
$54 \times 1 = \square$ $34 \times 2 = \square$
$- - - - - -$ $- - - - - -$
$54 \times 99 = \square$ $34 \times 98 = \square$

Figure 4.10 uses the area model for multiplication to represent the chain for $23 \times 9 = \square$. To solve the problem, one could first multiply 23 by 10, since multiplying by 10 is easier than multiplying by 9:

$$23 \times 10 = 230$$

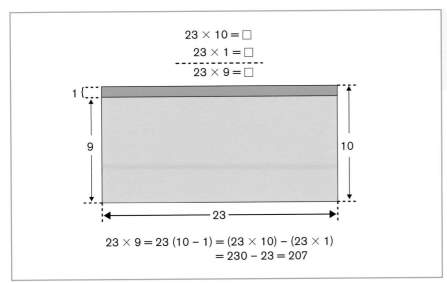

$$23 \times 9 = 23 (10 - 1) = (23 \times 10) - (23 \times 1)$$
$$= 230 - 23 = 207$$

Fig. **4.10.**

A representation of the use of a multiple of ten and a chain to solve $23 \times 9 = \square$

But then one would need to subtract 1×23, or 23, from 230, since the problem was to find the product 23×9, not 23×10. The distributive property of multiplication over *subtraction* is evident in this computation:

$$23 \times 9 = 23 \times (10 - 1) = (23 \times 10) - (23 \times 1) = 230 - 23 = 207$$

Encourage the students to see how the distributive property works in each chain given above (see fig. 4.11).

Fig. **4.11.**

Multiplication chains that make a factor larger and compensate by a subtraction

$$23 \times 10 = 230$$
$$23 \times 1 = 23$$
$$------$$
$$23 \times 9 = 207$$
$$23 \times 9 = 23 \times (10 - 1) = (23 \times 10) - (23 \times 1) = 230 - 23 = 207$$

$$47 \times 10 = 470$$
$$47 \times 1 = 47$$
$$------$$
$$47 \times 9 = 423$$
$$47 \times 9 = 47 \times (10 - 1) = (47 \times 10) - (47 \times 1) = 470 - 47 = 423$$

$$54 \times 100 = 5400$$
$$54 \times 1 = 54$$
$$------$$
$$54 \times 99 = 5346$$
$$54 \times 99 = 54 \times (100 - 1) = (54 \times 100) - (54 \times 1) = 5400 - 54 = 5346$$

$$34 \times 100 = 3400$$
$$34 \times 2 = 68$$
$$------$$
$$34 \times 98 = 3332$$
$$34 \times 98 = 34 \times (100 - 2) = (34 \times 100) - (34 \times 2) = 3400 - 68 = 3332$$

If students need to practice their skill and build their confidence in multiplying by multiples of 10, give them the following chain (devised for the purpose at hand) and have them examine the relationships among the "links":

$$1 \times 7 = \square$$
$$10 \times 7 = \square$$
$$2 \times 7 = \square$$
$$20 \times 7 = \square$$
$$5 \times 7 = \square$$
$$50 \times 7 = \square$$
$$------$$
$$88 \times 7 = \square$$

Emphasize that 10×7 is ten times 1×7, that 20×7 is ten times 2×7, and, similarly, that 50×7 is ten times 5×7. The associative property is embedded in these statements; for example, $50 \times 7 = (10 \times 5) \times 7 = 10 \times (5 \times 7)$. So, to solve $50 \times 7 = \square$, students might reason that 50×7 is ten times larger than 5×7. Thus, since $5 \times 7 = 35$, then $50 \times 7 = 350$.

This activity has demonstrated how creating multiplication chains and using the distributive property can help students solve multiplication problems efficiently, both by mental computation and by paper-and-pencil work. The next activity shows how students can use mental mathematics to solve division problems.

Using Mental Mathematics to Divide

Grades 3–5

Summary

Students use mental mathematics to solve division problems by "breaking," or decomposing, a problem's dividend into smaller parts that they can divide efficiently by the problem's divisor. Thus, they partition the whole quantity into equal parts, operate separately on each part, and use addition to compose the quotient for the original problem by summing the quotients for the parts.

Goals

- Develop flexibility in solving division problems with larger numbers
- Use known multiplication and division relationships, particularly multiples of 10
- Solve division problems by "breaking" a whole and dividing it into parts
- Use the distributive property of division over addition to solve division problems

Prior Knowledge or Experience

- Familiarity with the distributive property of division over addition
- Experience in splitting arrays (see Splitting Arrays in chapter 2 and Learning Multiplication Facts with Arrays in chapter 3)

Materials and Equipment

For each pair of students—

- Two envelopes, each containing a set of problem cards cut from copies of the following blackline masters:
  - "Drawing a Bead on Division—Card Set 1"
  - "Drawing a Bead on Division—Card Set 2"
- Paper and pencils

For the teacher—

- A copy of each of the following blackline masters:
  - "Drawing a Bead on Division—Card Set 1"
  - "Drawing a Bead on Division—Card Set 2"

Activity

Engage

Review the distributive property for multiplication over addition, and remind your students of their experiences in solving multiplication

Reproduce the blackline masters "Drawing a Bead on Division–Card Set 1" and "Drawing a Bead on Division–Card Set 2." Cut out the cards, and place each set in its own envelope. Repeat the process, making enough envelopes to give each pair of students an envelope containing all the cards from set 1 and an envelope containing all the cards from set 2.

pp. 196, 199–98

problems by splitting arrays. Then read the following problem aloud to the students:

Bruce makes key chains. He has bought a package of 140 large, special beads to hang on the chains as charms. The beads are in the shapes of soccer balls, footballs, basketballs, and baseballs. He is going to put 4 beads on each key chain. How many key chains can he complete with 140 beads?

As you read, write on the board, "140 beads," and "4 beads on a key chain." Ask the students, "Is this an addition, subtraction, multiplication, or division problem?" Be sure to follow up with the very important question, "Why do you think so?"

The underlying structure of the problem makes it a division problem, since it gives the whole quantity, 140 beads, and its solution involves separating this number of beads into equal groups of 4 beads. However, students can use their knowledge of addition, subtraction, and multiplication relationships to solve the problem.

Have the students use both specific and general language to identify each number in the problem (see fig. 4.12). In the specific context of the problem, "140" is the number of beads in the package. Speaking more generally, however, we can identify "140" as the total quantity under consideration. Likewise, in the concrete situation, "4" is the number of beads that Bruce will put on each chain. More abstractly, "4" is the number in each equal group.

Be sure to have the students characterize the solution in the same way. Specifically, the solution is the number of chains that Bruce can complete with the package of 140 beads. More generally, however, the solution is the number of equal groups, with 4 in each group, which are in 140.

Fig. **4.12.**

Using both specific and general terms to identify "140" and "4," as well as the solution, in the problem about Bruce's key chains

Number	Specific Terms	General Terms
140	Number of beads in the package	Whole amount
4	Number of beads needed for each key chain	Size of each group
Solution	Number of key chains that Bruce can make	Number of equal groups

Next, have your students write an equation for the problem. Their work on this task will show you whether they know how the numbers in the problem are related or how to represent these relationships with symbolic notation. To be sure that the students understand what the numbers mean in their equation, have them label each one as well as the undetermined solution (for example, "140 beads ÷ 4 beads per key chain = number of key chains").

Remind the students that they need to figure out how many groups of 4 beads they can make out of a total of 140 beads. Say, "You know what 100 ÷ 4 equals, don't you?" Write 100 ÷ 4 = 25 on the board when your students give the answer. Then ask, "Can you use this fact to help you figure out what 140 ÷ 4 equals?"

Give your students time to think. See if they realize on their own that because they know that there are twenty-five 4s in 100, they are partway to a solution for the problem. Completing the solution now comes down to finding how many 4s are in 40 (ten 4s), and then adding the two partial quotients (25 + 10 = 35).

Emphasize to the students the importance of using relationships that they already know to decompose a large quantity into smaller parts that they can divide easily by the divisor in their problem. For example, if after counting twenty-five 4s in 100, students find counting 4s in 40 to be challenging, they might break 40 into 20 + 20, as shown in figure 4.13. If they know that there are five 4s in 20, they can readily see that there are 5 + 5, or ten, 4s in 40. Ten 4s in 40 plus twenty-five 4s in 100 give thirty-five 4s in 140. Thus, Bruce can complete 35 key chains with the package of 140 beads.

Fig. **4.13.**

Breaking 140 into numbers that are easily divisible by 4

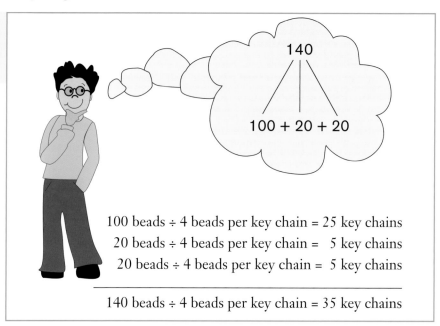

100 beads ÷ 4 beads per key chain = 25 key chains
20 beads ÷ 4 beads per key chain = 5 key chains
20 beads ÷ 4 beads per key chain = 5 key chains
_____
140 beads ÷ 4 beads per key chain = 35 key chains

Alternatively, if your students happen to know that 120 ÷ 4 equals 30, they might break 140 into 120 and 20. This fact could make it convenient for them to solve the problem in the following steps:

120 beads ÷ 4 beads per key chain = 30 key chains
20 beads ÷ 4 beads per key chain = 5 key chains

Thus, 140 beads ÷ 4 beads per key chain = 35 key chains

Explore

Assign a partner to each student, and give each pair of students an envelope containing a set of cards cut from a copy of the blackline master "Drawing a Bead on Division—Card Set 1." Say, "You are going to use division facts that you know to solve some division problems easily —maybe even in your head."

Have one student in each pair draw a card. Working together, the students in each pair should read the problem and identify the number that represents the whole amount, or total quantity. Then they should consider the "starter problem" that the card gives. This problem helps them break the total quantity—the dividend—into smaller parts that they can divide by the other number—the divisor—in the problem. The divisor tells them either the number of equal groups into which the dividend is divided or the number in each equal group. (The quotient gives whichever of these two quantities the problem does not give.)

Each card's starter problem helps the students break the dividend as they did in the problem about Bruce's key chains—into parts that will allow them to use familiar division relationships to obtain a solution efficiently. Tell the students, "By decomposing the dividend in this way, you can use mental math to help you solve the problems."

Have each pair of students take turns drawing cards for problems that they will work together to solve. They should also take turns recording their work on paper. Tell them, "Your work should show how you broke the whole amount and how you divided each of the smaller parts." The dividends in problems 3 and 4 do not divide evenly, so these quotients have *remainders*. You may want your students to be aware of the possibility of remainders as they work.

To tailor the exercise to a range of learners in your class, you can modify some of the problems on the cards to make them harder or easier for certain pairs of students. Figure 4.14 shows possible approaches and solutions for the problems in card set 1.

Fig. **4.14.**

Solutions for the problems in card set 1

Problem 1

96 beads; 8 beads on a bracelet

How many bracelets?

80 beads ÷ 8 beads/bracelet = 10 bracelets
16 beads ÷ 8 beads/bracelet = 2 bracelets
_____
96 beads ÷ 8 beads/bracelet = 12 bracelets

Problem 2

260 beads; 20 beads on a necklace

How many necklaces?

100 beads ÷ 20 beads/necklace = 5 necklaces
100 beads ÷ 20 beads/necklace = 5 necklaces
60 beads ÷ 20 beads/necklace = 3 necklaces
_____
260 beads ÷ 20 beads/necklace = 13 necklaces

Problem 3

500 beads; 15 beads on a bracelet

How many necklaces?

150 beads ÷ 15 beads/bracelet = 10 bracelets
150 beads ÷ 15 beads/bracelet = 10 bracelets
150 beads ÷ 15 beads/bracelet = 10 bracelets
45 beads ÷ 15 beads/bracelet = 3 bracelets
_____
495 beads ÷ 15 beads/bracelet = 33 bracelets

500 beads ÷ 15 beads/bracelet =
33 bracelets, with 5 beads left over

Problem 4

130 beads; 6 beads on a key chain

How many key chains?

60 beads ÷ 6 beads/key chain = 10 key chains
60 beads ÷ 6 beads/key chain = 10 key chains
6 beads ÷ 6 beads/key chain = 1 key chain
_____
126 beads ÷ 6 beads/key chain = 21 key chains

130 beads ÷ 6 beads/key chain =
21 key chains, with 4 beads left over

Problem 5

235 beads; 5 beads on a bookmark

How many bookmarks?

100 beads ÷ 5 beads/bookmark = 20 bookmarks
100 beads ÷ 5 beads/bookmark = 20 bookmarks
35 beads ÷ 5 beads/bookmark = 7 bookmarks
_____
235 beads ÷ 5 beads/bookmark = 47 bookmarks

Problem 6

850 beads; 25 beads on a necklace

How many necklaces?

100 beads ÷ 25 beads/necklace = 4 necklaces
200 beads ÷ 25 beads/necklace = 8 necklaces
500 beads ÷ 25 beads/necklace = 20 necklaces
50 beads ÷ 25 beads/necklace = 2 necklaces
_____
850 beads ÷ 25 beads/necklace = 34 necklaces

Extend

Select one or two of the problems from the card sets for the whole class to discuss. You might choose one that has a remainder, one that has a dividend in the 100s, or one that the students have solved in a variety of ways. Ask several pairs of students to write their solutions on the board. Then have the students analyze and compare the various solutions.

Distribute to each pair of students an envelope containing cards for the problems on the blackline master "Drawing a Bead on Division—Card Set 2." As before, some problems have remainders. Several problems ask explicitly if anything is left over, but other problems that have remainders give no hint of this fact. The following problem is similar to the problems in card set 2 that ask about a remainder:

Griffin has 47 beads. He needs 4 beads for each key chain that he is making. How many key chains can he make? How many beads will he have left over?

47 = 40 + 7
40 beads ÷ 4 beads/key chain = 10 key chains
7 beads ÷ 4 beads/key chain = 1 key chain, with 3 left over

or

47 = 40 + 4 + 3
40 beads ÷ 4 beads/key chain = 10 key chains
4 beads ÷ 4 beads/key chain = 1 key chain
3 beads are left over

In either case, 10 key chains + 1 key chains equals 11 key chains, with 3 beads left over.

Have the students consider the starter problems that the cards give, and encourage them to suggest others that would also facilitate solutions (fig. 4.15 shows solutions for the problems in card set 2). Urge the students to discuss the reasoning behind their suggestions, and record key ideas from their explanations on the board. Finally, ask the students, "Can you summarize the important ideas to keep in mind as you consider ways to break apart the whole amount to make it easier to solve division problems?"

Fig. 4.15.

Solutions for the problems in card set 2

Problem A	Problem B
73 beads; 9 beads on a bracelet	300 beads; 15 beads on a necklace
How many bracelets?	How many necklaces?
63 beads ÷ 9 beads/bracelet = 7 bracelets	300 beads ÷ 15 beads/necklace = 20 necklaces
9 beads ÷ 9 beads/bracelet = 1 bracelet	
72 beads ÷ 9 beads/bracelet = 8 bracelets	
73 beads ÷ 9 beads/bracelet = 8 bracelets, with 1 bead left over	

Problem C 500 beads; 50 beads in a box How many boxes? 500 beads ÷ 50 beads/box = 10 boxes	**Problem D** 100 beads; 6 beads in a kit How many kits? 60 beads ÷ 6 beads/kit = 10 kits 36 beads ÷ 6 beads/kit = 6 kits —————————— 96 beads ÷ 6 beads/kit = 16 kits 100 beads ÷ 6 beads/kit = 16 kits, with 4 beads left over
Problem E 77 beads; 5 beads on a bookmark How many bookmarks? 50 beads ÷ 5 beads/bookmark = 10 bookmarks 25 beads ÷ 5 beads/bookmark = 5 bookmarks —————————— 75 beads ÷ 5 beads/bookmark = 15 bookmarks 77 beads ÷ 5 beads/bookmark = 15 bookmarks, with 2 beads left over	**Problem F** 80 beads; 25 beads on a necklace How many necklaces? 75 beads ÷ 25 beads/necklace = 3 necklaces 80 beads ÷ 25 beads/necklace = 3 necklaces, with 5 beads left over
Problem G 720 ÷ 6 = ? 600 ÷ 6 = 100 120 ÷ 6 = 20 —————— 720 ÷ 6 = 120	**Problem H** 97 ÷ 3 = ? 90 ÷ 3 = 30 6 ÷ 3 = 2 —————— 96 ÷ 3 = 32 97 ÷ 3 = 32, with a remainder of 1
Problem J 100 ÷ 7 = ? 70 ÷ 7 = 10 28 ÷ 7 = 4 —————— 98 ÷ 7 = 14 100 ÷ 7 = 14, with a remainder of 2	**Problem K** 275 ÷ 5 = ? 250 ÷ 5 = 50 25 ÷ 5 = 5 —————— 275 ÷ 5 = 55

Fig. **4.15.** (continued)

Even though this activity focuses on subtractive (or "measurement") division problems, discuss breaking the dividend into parts to solve partitive (or "sharing") division problems. For example, give your students the following problem: "Uncle Pete wants to divide his collection of 125 baseball cards equally among his 5 nephews. How many cards will he give to each nephew?" Ask, "How could you use our strategy of breaking the dividend into parts to help Uncle Pete share the cards fairly?" Show the students how they could share the cards by breaking the 125 cards into two groups—one with 100 cards and the other with 25 cards. They could use "100 ÷ 5 = ?" as a starter problem. Then they could solve the problem as follows:

$$100 \text{ cards} \div 5 \text{ nephews} = 20 \text{ cards per nephew}$$
$$25 \text{ cards} \div 5 \text{ nephews} = 5 \text{ cards per nephew}$$

$$125 \text{ cards} \div 5 \text{ nephews} = 25 \text{ cards per nephew}$$

As the students use division to solve problems, they need to see the importance of composing and decomposing numbers. Help them begin to think of 132 ÷ 4 as (120 + 12) ÷ 4. Such decomposition allows students to use mental mathematics as a way to solve problems flexibly, as the Number and Operations Standard expects them to in grades 3–5.

If your students have difficulty in grasping the idea of partitioning the dividend, use dot arrays to show the partitioning of the whole amount and then the separating or decomposing of each part. Discuss the use of multiples of 10 as an important tactic for breaking apart the whole amount.

Be sure that your students recognize and use the inverse relationship between multiplication and division in the process of solving the problems in the activity. For example, facing a problem such as 132 ÷ 4 = □, students can turn the problem into a multiplication problem by thinking, "Four times what equals 132?" They may decide to break 132 into 120 and 12 if they know that 4 × 30 = 120 and 4 × 3 = 12. By considering these familiar factor-factor-product relationships, they can easily establish that 132 ÷ 4 equals (120 + 12) ÷ 4, or (120 ÷ 4) + (12 ÷ 4), or 30 + 3, or 33.

In the activities so far in this chapter, the students have explored strategies for finding exact answers to problems. In the next activity, however, they investigate strategies for estimating solutions.

"Students need to have many experiences decomposing and composing numbers in order to solve problems flexibly." (NCTM 2000, p. 150)

Going Over or Under to Estimate

Grades 4–5

Summary

Students' work reinforces their flexible use of strategies for making estimates. The students estimate to solve multiplication problems that do not call for exact products but require them to say whether the products would be "over" or "under" given, or "target," numbers.

Goals

- Develop estimation strategies, including flexible rounding, the use of benchmarks, and "front-end" estimation, for multiplication problems
- Use estimation strategies to determine whether a computation is greater than or less than a given reference point
- Record and write an explanation to describe the reasoning behind a chosen approach

Prior Knowledge or Experience

- An understanding of the ideas of estimating and making a "good" estimate
- Experience in making estimates
- Work with simple estimation strategies

Materials and Equipment

For each student—

- A copy of the blackline master "Over or Under—Recording Sheet"

For each pair of students—

- An envelope containing a set of problem cards cut from a copy of the blackline master "Over or Under—Problem Cards"
- A die with its faces relabeled with the following numbers: 7, 9, 12, 19, 24, and 35

For the teacher—
- An overhead projector
- A transparency of each of the following blackline masters:
  ○ "Over or under 200?"
  ○ "Over or under 500?"
- A small box containing eight items (crayons or other small items)
- A box containing twenty-four items (crayons or other small items)

Reproduce the blackline master "Over or Under–Problem Cards." Cut out the cards, and assemble the set in an envelope. Repeat the process, making enough envelopes to give one to each pair of students.

pp. 199, 200, 201, 202

Give each pair of students a die with the numbers 7, 9, 12, 19, 24, and 35 on its faces. Write one number on each face of a blank die, or tape over the numbers on a conventional die and use a pen or marker to renumber the taped faces to show these numbers.

Activity

Engage

Work in estimation builds on and strengthens students' number sense. Making estimates hones skills in mental computation and reinforces an understanding of place-value concepts. Estimating is not about following rules but rather about thinking flexibly, exploring relationships, and making decisions. Strategies depend on the situation and the numbers involved as well as the relationships that the estimator perceives among the numbers.

This activity encourages students to arrive at estimates by using—

- "front-end" estimation;
- benchmarks;
- flexible rounding.

Estimators who work with the left-most digits in a problem and then adjust their result by considering the other digits are using *front-end estimation*. Those who use *benchmarks* to arrive at estimates usually measure against multiples of 5, 10, 100, and so on, making adjustments to suit the numbers in the problem. In *flexible rounding*, estimators do not follow a prescribed set of rules but rather use the numbers and the context to decide whether to go up to a larger number or move down to a smaller number and whether to change one or both numbers when estimating the result of working with two numbers.

To engage your students in using these strategies in a very natural way, show the class a box of eight items (markers, crayons, or other small objects). Say, for example, "Suppose that every student in this class has a box of eight markers just like this one. I am wondering whether the total number of markers is greater than or less than (or equal to) 200." On the board, write a statement of the problem, including the number of students in the class. For example, in a class of twenty-four students, you might write, "Each student has a box of 8 markers. There are 24 students in all. Is the total number of markers over or under 200?"

Ask the students, "Do we need to find an exact answer to solve this problem? Or will an estimate do?" Emphasize that an estimate will suffice because the problem asks only whether the number is over or under 200—it doesn't call for an exact number. Give the students about twenty seconds to use mental math—not paper and pencil—to make their estimates. Ask them to show a "thumbs up" if they think the total would be over 200 or a "thumbs down" if they think it would be under 200.

The students will reason in various ways. Have a few of them explain their thinking. Summarize their strategies, and if a student has used one of the three strategies identified above, give its customary name. The reasoning of two students follows:

- Bryan uses 25 as a benchmark: "It's like having 8 quarters. I know 4 quarters is one dollar, or 100 pennies, and 8 quarters would be two dollars, or 200 pennies. And I know the total's under 200 because the actual number isn't 25, it's only 24, so the markers would be fewer than 200." ($8 \times 25 = 200$, so $8 \times 24 < 200$)

• Natasha uses front-end estimation: "I know that 20 × 8 is 160, and that's 40 away from 200. And I know that 4 × 8 is less than 40, so the total number of markers is under 200." [24 × 8 = (20× 8) + (4 × 8) < 200]

Next, show the class a box of 24 items (markers, crayons, etc). Say, for example, "Suppose that every student in this class has a box of twenty-four markers just like this one. I am wondering whether the total number of markers will be greater than or less than 500." On the board, write a statement of the problem, including the number of students in the class. For example, in a class of twenty-four students, you might write, "Each student has a box of 24 markers. There are 24 students in all. Is the total number of markers over or under 500?"

Again, ask the students to show a "thumbs up" if they think the total is over 500 markers and a "thumbs down" if they think the total is under 500. As before, have a few students explain their reasoning. The reasoning of one student follows:

Aubrey uses flexible rounding: "I multiplied 20 × 24. That's 480. So 20 students would already have 480 crayons, and that's only 20 away from 500, and I would still have to include markers for 4 other students. So the total's got to be over 500." [(20 × 24) + (4 × 24) = 480 + 96 > 500]

Present the problems on the blackline master "Over or under 200?" one at a time to the whole class. (You can write them on the board or make a transparency from the blackline master and show the problems one by one on an overhead projector.) Show each problem for about fifteen to twenty seconds. Have the students make estimates and show a "thumbs up" or "thumbs down" to signal whether they think the solution is "over" or "under" the target number of 200. Then discuss how they made their decisions. Figure 4.16 shows possible ways of estimating to determine solutions to the problems.

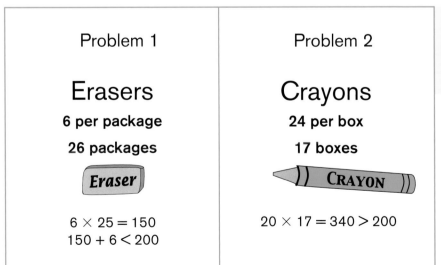

Fig. **4.16.**

Estimating to solve the problems on the blackline master "Over or under 200?"

Fig. **4.16.** (continued)

Problem 3	Problem 4
Sidewalk chalk	**Pencils**
15 pieces per bucket	**9 per package**
12 buckets	**19 packages**

$15 \times 10 = 150$ $150 + (15 \times 2) < 200$	$9 \times 20 = 180 < 200$

Repeat the procedure, this time using the problems on the blackline master "Over or under 500?" Figure 4.17 shows ways of estimating to determine solutions.

Fig. **4.17.**

Estimating to solve the problems on the blackline master "Over or under 500?"

Problem A	Problem B
Small binder clips	**Pens**
48 per box	**16 per box**
8 boxes	**41 boxes**
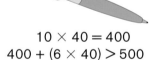	
$50 \times 8 = 400 < 500$	$10 \times 40 = 400$ $400 + (6 \times 40) > 500$
Problem C	Problem D
Film	**Crayons**
24 exposures per roll	**32 per box**
17 rolls	**19 boxes**

$25 \times 20 = 500$ $24 \times 17 < 500$	$30 \times 20 = 600 > 500$

Explore

Distribute to each student a copy of the blackline master "Over or Under—Recording Sheet." Pair the students, and give each pair an envelope with a set of cards made from the blackline master "Over or Under—Problem Cards." Also give each pair a die with the faces renumbered 7, 9, 12, 19, 24, and 35. Tell the students, "Today you are going to work in pairs to make estimates to solve multiplication problems. You will not be figuring out an exact product but instead will be making a quick estimate to determine whether the product is over or under a certain target number."

Walk the students through the process. One student in each pair should draw a problem card. Then the other student should roll the die. The number that appears on the die will give the two students the number of packages, boxes, buckets, or other units referred to on the problem card. Both students should then enter the information on their recording sheets and make estimates to determine whether the total number is over or under the target number given on the card.

For example, suppose student 1 draws problem 5:

Also suppose that student 2 rolls 19 on the die. This signifies that there are 19 buckets of chalk, each containing 15 sticks. Both students must then make estimates to determine whether the total number of sticks of chalk is over or under 200. The students might round 19 to 20, for example, and then multiply 15 × 20 to get 300 quickly and easily. Then they might reason that 15 × 19 would be less than 300, but only 15 less—and still much greater than 200.

First, however, each student should record the item, the quantity per unit (box, bucket, etc.), the number of units (number rolled on the die) and the target number on his or her recording sheet (see fig. 4.18). After both students make their estimates, they should circle "over" or "under" on the sheet and write out an explanation of their reasoning.

Fig. **4.18.**

Row 1 of the "Over or Under Recording Sheet," filled in to show work on the problem, "If we have 19 buckets of chalk, each containing 15 sticks, is the total number of sticks of chalk over or under 200?"

Item	Quantity per Unit (Number of items in a box, a bucket, etc.)	Number of Units (Number rolled on the die)	Is the total number of items over or under the target?	How did you reason?
Stick of chalk	15 sticks per bucket	19	(Over) or Under <u>200</u> ?	I knew 15 x 20 would be 300 sticks of chalk, which would be a whole hundred more than 200, and 15 x 19 would be only a little bit less.

When both students have completed their explanations, they should compare their reasoning. Ask them to consider the following questions:

- "Did you and your partner think about the solution in the same way? In different ways?"
- "If you and your partner made estimates in two different ways, which way seems easier?
- "Did you get stuck as you reasoned through the problem? If so, can you and your partner help each other figure out a good way to think about the problem?"

Then the students should pick another card, roll the die again, and repeat the process.

As in previous activities, you can tailor the exercise to a range of learners in your class by modifying some of the problems on the cards to make them harder or easier for certain pairs of students. (You might also need to change the numbers on the die to correlate with the new set of problems.)

Extend

Have each pair of students look over the problems on their recording sheets. Ask them to identify a problem that they both thought was easy to solve by estimating, and have them write "easy" next to it. Then ask them to identify a problem that they both thought was difficult to solve by estimating, and have them write "hard" next to it. As the students identify the problems, they should discuss what makes a problem easy or hard to solve with an estimate. On the backs of the recording sheets, have one student describe what makes a problem that calls for an estimate easy and have the other describe what makes such a problem hard.

List on the board some of the problems that the students have identified as "easy" and some that they have identified as "hard." Have the students discuss the characteristics of "easy" and "hard" problems. Summarize these characteristics on the board. Students may notice, for example, that a problem is "easy" if they can round down (multiplying 20×15, for instance, instead of 21×16) and obtain a result that is "over" the target number—say, 200. Then they know immediately that the exact product is also greater than 200.

You can also help the students extend their reasoning by having them solve problems involving money. "Over" and "under" target numbers could include $1.00, $5.00, $10.00, $20.00, $50.00, or $100.00. A few sample problems follow:

- A video game costs $29.99. Suppose you have $100.00. Can you buy 3 games?
- Collectable characters cost $5.49 each. Sean needs 4 more characters to complete his set. He has $20.00. Can he buy all the characters he needs to complete his set?
- Pencil grips sell for 69 cents apiece. Janice has $5.00. Can she buy 5 pencil grips?

In this activity, solving practical problems by making estimates reinforces the students' skills in mental computation and their concepts of place value. The next activity consolidates their understanding of common fractions by relating these fractions to the minutes in an hour on the face of an analog clock.

"Estimation is … a practical skill. It can guide students' use of calculators, especially in identifying implausible answers, and is a valuable part of the mathematics used in everyday life." (Kilpatrick, Swafford, and Findell 2001, p. 215)

Taking an Hour for Clock Fractions

Grades 4–5

Summary

Students relate groups of minutes on the face of an analog clock to the common fractions $\frac{1}{2}$, $\frac{1}{4}$, $\frac{1}{3}$, $\frac{1}{6}$, and $\frac{1}{12}$, and through their work with these "clock fractions," they gain skill and flexibility in adding and comparing fractions.

Goals

- Demonstrate the fractions $\frac{1}{2}$, $\frac{1}{4}$, $\frac{1}{3}$, $\frac{1}{6}$, and $\frac{1}{12}$, on the face of an analog clock
- Relate commonly used fractions to the number of minutes in one hour
- Use visual models, benchmarks, and equivalent forms to add or subtract commonly used fractions

Prior Knowledge or Experience

- An understanding of fractions as parts of unit wholes
- A knowledge of the factors of 60

Materials and Equipment

For each student—

- A copy of the blackline master "Ways to Use an Hour"
- A sheet or two of paper

For each group of four students—

- A sheet of chart paper
- One or two marking pens

For the teacher—

- An overhead projector
- A transparency of the blackline master "Clock Face"
- A marking pen with ink that rubs off a transparency easily
- A cloth or tissue to wipe ink from a transparency

pp. 203, 204

Engage

Begin by asking your students, "How many minutes are in an hour?" Display a transparency of the blackline master "Clock Face" on an overhead projector (or draw a clock face on the board). To open an investigation of the relationships between the minutes marked on the clock face and the fractions $\frac{1}{2}$, $\frac{1}{4}$, $\frac{1}{3}$, $\frac{1}{6}$, and $\frac{1}{12}$, ask the following

30 minutes = $\frac{1}{2}$ hour

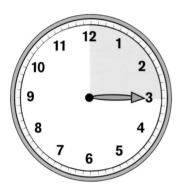

15 minutes = $\frac{1}{4}$ hour

question: "How many minutes after the hour is it when the minute hand is pointing to the 6?" Use a marking pen to draw a minute hand in this position on the transparency.

After a student correctly responds, "Thirty minutes," follow up by asking, "What are some ways that you can use to figure this out?" Emphasize counting by 5s (5, 10, 15, 20, 25, 30) and be attentive to any other reasoning that the students suggest. For example, a student may say something like, "It takes 60 minutes for the minute hand to go completely around the clock from 12 to 12, so it takes half as long for it to go from the 12 to the 6, and this means that it's 30 minutes after the hour when the minute hand is pointing to the 6."

Such a response will make your next question an easy one. Ask, "So what fraction of an hour are we talking about when the minute hand is on the 6?" The students should be ready to relate "30 minutes past the hour" to the fraction $\frac{1}{2}$.

Move on to a new fraction— $\frac{1}{4}$. Rub the minute hand from the clock face on the transparency, and draw a new one, this time pointing to the 3. Ask, "How many minutes after the hour is it when the minute hand is pointing to the 3?" Once someone has given the correct response of 15 minutes, probe all the students' reasoning, as before: "How did you figure this out?"

The students' thinking will be similar to that in the first example, and this time they may also have thought something like, "The minute hand has traveled only half the way to the 6, and the time to 6 was 30 minutes, and I know that $\frac{1}{2} \times 30 = 15$, so when the minute hand is on the 3, it is 15 minutes after the hour." Again, follow up by asking, "What fraction of an hour is 15 minutes?" Emphasize that there are 4 equal parts—four groups of 15 minutes— in one hour, so 15 minutes is $\frac{1}{4}$ of an hour.

Using the same process, guide the students in investigating relationships between three other positions of the minute hand and common fractions:

- A minute hand pointing to the 4 and the fraction $\frac{1}{3}$ (20 minutes after the hour)

- A minute hand pointing to the 2 and the fraction $\frac{1}{6}$ (10 minutes after the hour)

- A minute hand pointing to the 1 and the fraction $\frac{1}{12}$ (5 minutes after the hour)

In each case, again ask the following questions in turn:

- "How many minutes after the hour is it when the minute hand is pointing to this number?"
- "How did you figure this out?"
- "What fraction of an hour is this?"

So far, your students have been thinking about fractions only in terms of minutes after the hour on a clock face. The students can of course think about these fractions in other positions on the face of a clock, where the fractions represent other rotations of the figure.

Explore

To begin to expand the student' thinking about the relationships between common fractions and various blocks of minutes in an hour, draw a circular clock face on the board and shade in one-half of it as shown in the margin.

Ask the students, "If music class begins at 10:20 a.m. and ends at 10:50 a.m., what fraction of an hour does music class last?" (10:50 – 10:20 = 0:30, or $\frac{1}{2}$ hour) Be sure to elicit your students' thinking by asking, "How do you know?" Have the students suggest other ways to show half an hour on a clock face. Have them verify each response by relating the thirty-minute period that they identify on the clock face with one-half of an hour. Record several of the students' responses on the board.

Draw another clock face on the board, this time shading the sector defined by the minute hand as it moves from 2 to 6 (see the margin). Ask the students, "If recess begins at 2:10 p.m. and ends at 2:30 p.m., what fraction of an hour is recess?" (2:30 – 2:10 = 0:20, or $\frac{1}{3}$ hour) Follow up by asking, "How do you know?"

Ask the students, "Can you suggest other ways to show one-third of an hour on the clock face?" They might suggest drawing sectors to show the time elapsed from 2:30 to 2:50, 2:15 to 2:35, or 2:05 to 2:25, to give just a few examples from the hour between two and three o'clock. Record several ideas on the board. Extend this work by asking the students how many minutes would be in $\frac{2}{3}$ of an hour.

When the students are relating groups of minutes easily to fractional parts of the hour, take the opportunity review all the factor pairs for the number 60. Ask the students, "What pairs of numbers can we multiply together to get a product of 60?" Have the students work with partners to find all the pairs of factors (see fig. 4.19).

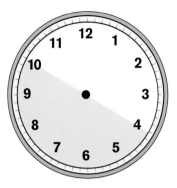

30 minutes = $\frac{1}{2}$ hour

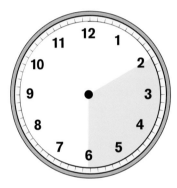

20 minutes = $\frac{1}{3}$ hour

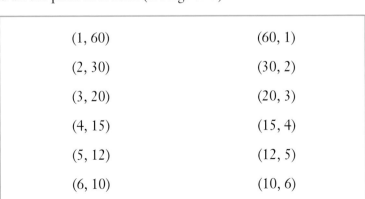

(1, 60)	(60, 1)
(2, 30)	(30, 2)
(3, 20)	(20, 3)
(4, 15)	(15, 4)
(5, 12)	(12, 5)
(6, 10)	(10, 6)

Fig. **4.19.**

Pairs of factors for 60

To give additional support to the students' thinking about the relationship between a particular number of minutes and a fraction of an hour, use the list of factor pairs to make a chart like that in figure 4.20. Column 1 shows all the two-number factorizations of 60. Column 2 represents each factorization as a particular number of equal groups. Column 3 gives the size of each group as a number of minutes and expresses that number as a fraction of an hour. (Rows 1–6 illustrate a whole and the common fractions $\frac{1}{2}, \frac{1}{4}, \frac{1}{3}, \frac{1}{6}$, and $\frac{1}{12}$, which are the focus of the activity. Rows 7–12 illustrate the remaining common fractions of an hour— $\frac{1}{5}, \frac{1}{10}, \frac{1}{15}, \frac{1}{20}, \frac{1}{30}$ and $\frac{1}{60}$ —that are associated with two-number factorizations of 60.)

Fig. **4.20.**

Two-number factorizations of 60 expressed as particular numbers of equal groups, with the sizes of the groups related to minutes and fractions of an hour

Factorization	How Many Equal Groups? How Many in a Group?	How Many Minutes in a Group? What Fraction of an Hour Is This?
1 × 60	1 group of 60	60 minutes $= \frac{1}{1}$, or 1, hour
2 × 30	2 groups of 30	30 minutes $= \frac{1}{2}$ hour
3 × 20	3 groups of 20	20 minutes $= \frac{1}{3}$ hour
4 × 15	4 groups of 15	15 minutes $= \frac{1}{4}$ hour
6 × 10	6 groups of 10	10 minutes $= \frac{1}{6}$ hour
12 × 5	12 groups of 5	5 minutes $= \frac{1}{12}$ hour
5 × 12	5 groups of 12	12 minutes $= \frac{1}{5}$ hour
10 × 6	10 groups of 6	6 minutes $= \frac{1}{10}$ hour
15 × 4	15 groups of 4	4 minutes $= \frac{1}{15}$ hour
20 × 3	20 groups of 3	3 minutes $= \frac{1}{20}$ hour
30 × 2	30 groups of 2	2 minutes $= \frac{1}{30}$ hour
60 × 1	60 groups of 1	1 minute $= \frac{1}{60}$ hour

Give each student a copy of the blackline master "Ways to Use an Hour," and assign the students to groups of four. Distribute a sheet of chart paper and one or two marking pens to each group.

Introduce the activity by saying, "Suppose that everyone in the class has earned one hour of free time, and the whole class is going to use the time together. But each of you must propose at least three plans for how the class should use this hour. The only guidelines are that each plan must include at least three different activities, the activities must take at least three different fractions of the hour, and the time must add up to exactly one hour."

As you continue to explain the activity, write all the numerical information in the following scenario on the board: "For example, you may suggest spending $\frac{1}{3}$ of an hour playing games, $\frac{1}{2}$ of an hour doing free reading, and $\frac{1}{6}$ of an hour watching a video. An equation for this plan might look like this: '20 minutes (or $\frac{1}{3}$ hour) + 30 minutes (or $\frac{1}{2}$ hour) + 10 minutes (or $\frac{1}{6}$ hour) = 60 minutes (or 1 hour).'"

When you are sure that your students understand the example, continue: "After everyone in your group has come up with three plans, each of you will present your plans, and then your group will select two plans to show on chart paper. Afterward, each group will display and explain its proposals to the class, and the class will vote to select a winning plan."

Have the students look at their copies of "Ways to Use an Hour." Tell them, "When you make your one-hour plans, use the clock faces on the activity sheet to show and label the times that you plan to spend on each activity. Then write an equation for your plan, as we did in the example on the board. Finally, you must explain how you know that the activities in your plan will take exactly one hour altogether."

Observe your students while they develop their plans. Do they work with minutes first and then relate these to fractions? Or do they focus first on fractions and then use minutes to verify that their fractions add up to exactly one hour? Which fractions are difficult for them to combine?

The students should begin to demonstrate a sense of related fractions. For example, they should see that thirds and sixths are related ($\frac{2}{6}$ of an hour = 2 × $\frac{1}{6}$ of an hour = 2 × 10 minutes = 20 minutes, which is the same as $\frac{1}{3}$ of an hour). They should also see that fourths and twelfths are related ($\frac{3}{12}$ of an hour = 3 × $\frac{1}{12}$ of an hour = 3 × 5 minutes = 15 minutes, which is the same as $\frac{1}{4}$ of an hour). Are your students able to explain their reasoning clearly? When each group presents its two plans to the class, can they verify that the fractions of an hour for their activities total to a whole by relating each one to minutes in an hour?

You can modify the task to suit learners who have less experience with fractions by limiting the fractions that they use. For example, let these students begin with halves and fourths. Then include thirds, sixths, and twelfths. To provide additional challenge for other students, include other fractions, such as fifths, tenths, or fifteenths.

Extend

Challenge the students to use clock fractions to plan ways to use up to two hours. You might suggest that your students plan activities for a birthday party, a trip to a water park, or the school's open-house night. Working alone or with a partner, the students should draw two clock faces on paper and use them to show their work. They should also use fractions in an equation that represents their allocation of the time. Impose some of the following restrictions on the students' planning:

- Plan activities for halves, fourths, and sixths of an hour but for no other fractions of an hour

- Plan activities for thirds, fourths, and twelfths of an hour but for no other fractions of an hour

- Plan activities for exactly 6 fourths of an hour

- Plan activities for exactly 7 sixths of an hour

- Plan activities for exactly 15 twelfths of an hour

- Plan activities for at least 5 sixths of an hour

- Plan activities for at least 9 twelfths of an hour

- Plan activities for four different fractions of an hour

Another way to extend your students' thinking about common fractions and skill in manipulating them is to have them use clock faces and clock fractions to solve a variety of subtraction, addition, and multiplication story problems. Four examples follow (fig. 4.21 shows solutions):

- Brianna had $\frac{3}{4}$ of an hour to clean up her room and watch television. She finished cleaning the room in 10 minutes. How many minutes did she have left to watch television? Write Brianna's television time as a fraction of an hour.

- Quentin had $\frac{3}{4}$ of an hour of soccer practice. He spent $\frac{1}{2}$ hour doing soccer drills and the rest of the time playing a game. How long was the game? Give the time both in minutes and as a fraction of an hour.

- Chase ran for 10 minutes and then walked for 5 minutes. Then he ran for 10 more minutes and walked for 5 more minutes. What fractional part of an hour did Chase run? What fractional part of an hour did he walk? What fractional part of an hour did he run *and* walk?

- Paige spent $\frac{1}{6}$ of an hour riding her bike to school each day. How much time did Paige spend riding her bike to school in one school week? Write your answer as a fraction of an hour and in minutes.

As another approach to extending your students' understanding of these concepts, you might allow the students to use fifths, tenths, fifteenths, twentieths, thirtieths, and sixtieths of an hour to make combinations of one whole hour or two whole hours.

Fig. **4.21.**

Solutions to problems involving clock fractions

• Brianna spent $\frac{3}{4}$ hr $= 3 \times \frac{1}{4} = 3 \times 15$ min $= 45$ min cleaning

her room and watching TV. She spent 10 min cleaning her room.

$(45 - 10)$ min $= 35$ min remaining to watch TV.

35 min $= (30 + 5)$ min $= \left(\frac{1}{2} + \frac{1}{12}\right)$ hr $= \left(\frac{6}{12} + \frac{1}{12}\right)$ hr $=$

$\frac{7}{12}$ hr for TV.

• Quentin practiced soccer for $\frac{3}{4}$ hr, or 45 min. He spent $\frac{1}{2}$ hr, or 30 min, on drills.

He spent $(45 - 30)$ min $= 15$ min, or $\frac{1}{4}$ hr, in a game.

• Chase ran for $(10 + 10)$ min $= 20$ min, or $\frac{1}{3}$ hr.

He walked for $(5 + 5)$ min $= 10$ min, or $\frac{1}{6}$ hr.

He walked and ran for $(20 + 10)$ min $= 30$ min, or $\frac{1}{2}$ hr.

• Paige spent $\left(\frac{1}{6} \text{ hr/day} \times 5 \text{ days}\right)$, or $\frac{5}{6}$ hr, riding her bike to school.

$\frac{1}{6}$ hr $= 10$ min, so $\frac{5}{6}$ hr $= 5 \times 10$ min, or 50 min biking to school.

Conclusion

This chapter has introduced activities that can provide students with opportunities to explore mental mathematics, estimation, and a variety of strategies for computing with multidigit numbers and fractions. These strategies can help build a solid foundation for computational fluency and flexibility with numbers and operations.

NAVIGATIONS
SERIES

GRADES 3–5

NAVIGATING *through* NUMBER *and* OPERATIONS

Looking Back and Looking Ahead

"In grades 3–5, students should focus on the meanings of, and relationship between, multiplication and division." (NCTM 2000, p. 151)

Grades 3–5 are years in which a deep understanding of number and operations develops. Multiplication and division of whole numbers become central, and students gain fluency with basic number combinations, or *facts*—particularly multiplication facts and their division counterparts. Understanding and recall of these basic facts are essential to computational fluency. Students' comprehension of the meanings of multiplication and division grow as they consider an array of problems and representations involving these operations and their properties, which serve as links to important algebraic ideas.

When students enter grade 3, their work in mathematics focuses on understanding multiplication and division. Students encounter varied representations of multiplication—particularly the area model, which allows students to make connections readily to division. In working with division, third graders consider situations that they can represent by sharing or partitioning as well as by repeated subtraction.

Students in grade 3 begin developing strategies for establishing basic multiplication facts. The use of patterns and other thinking strategies greatly simplifies this important task. As students progress through grades 4 and 5, they gain experience with and an understanding of these facts, moving on to problems involving larger numbers, and they use algorithms for multiplication and division.

As students move through grades 3–5, their work with larger whole numbers, important benchmarks (such as 1,000), and decimals reinforces and extends their concepts of numeration and place value. They also spend a great deal of time investigating fractions. Their experiences help

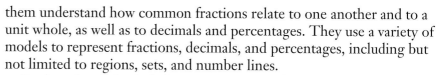

them understand how common fractions relate to one another and to a unit whole, as well as to decimals and percentages. They use a variety of models to represent fractions, decimals, and percentages, including but not limited to regions, sets, and number lines.

Students in grades 3–5 also encounter negative integers in informal ways, through the use of such common models as the thermometer and number line. Their study of numbers expands to include work with classes of numbers and beginning work with factors, square numbers, prime numbers, and composite numbers.

The goal of mathematics instruction by the end of grade 5 is for students to achieve fluency in whole-number computation and develop a well-established sense of number. On completing grade 5, students should understand that each operation helps them solve many types of problems. They should be capable of solving some problems mentally and others by estimation, and they should recall or be able to derive the basic number facts for each operation efficiently. In addition, they should understand equivalent expressions for fractions, decimals, and percentages and be able to interpret and explain the information that each type of expression communicates.

A look ahead to grades 6–8 shows students deepening their understandings of fractions, decimals, and percentages and increasing their computational fluency with these representations. The study of numbers expands again, as students extend their ability to handle number theory tasks involving factors, multiples, prime numbers, and divisibility.

Students in grades 6–8 encounter problems involving multiplicative comparisons (for example, miles per hour), gaining experience in working with ratios, rates, and percentages—representations that introduce the important idea of proportionality. The students' understanding of number and operations deepens as they encounter problems involving many middle-grades mathematics topics, including measurement, probability, and algebra.

Students' work in grades 6–8 thus continues the vital work of grades 3–5. The Number and Operation Standard suggests that instruction at all levels, pre-K–grade 12, be designed to help students—

- Understand numbers, ways of representing numbers, relationships among numbers, and number systems;
- Understand meanings of operations and how they relate to one another; and
- Compute fluently and make reasonable estimates. (NCTM 2000, p. 148)

This book has provided ideas for meeting these goals in grades 3–5. The mathematics experiences that students have in grades 3–5 lay an essential foundation for the more advanced ideas to come in grades 6–8. Students who receive a solid grounding in number and operations in grades 3–5 are prepared for success in grades 6–8 and beyond.

NAVIGATIONS SERIES

GRADES 3–5

NAVIGATING *through* NUMBER *and* OPERATIONS

Appendix

Blackline Masters and Solutions

Spin to Win

Name _____

Below are circles for two games of "Spin to Win." For each game, your teacher will spin a spinner five times. After every spin, you must write the number that comes up on the spinner in an empty circle. Your goal is to make the largest four-digit number that you can.

You may reject any one number by placing it in the "Reject Circle." But once you have written a number in a circle, you cannot move or erase it!

Game 1

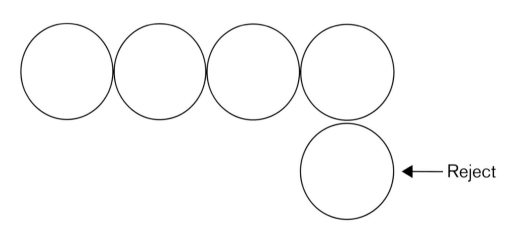

Game 2

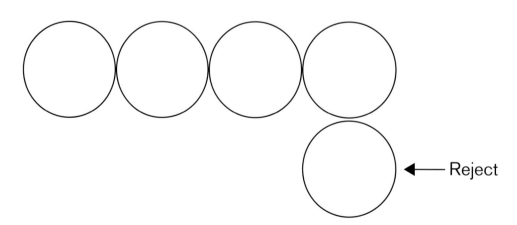

Spinner Master

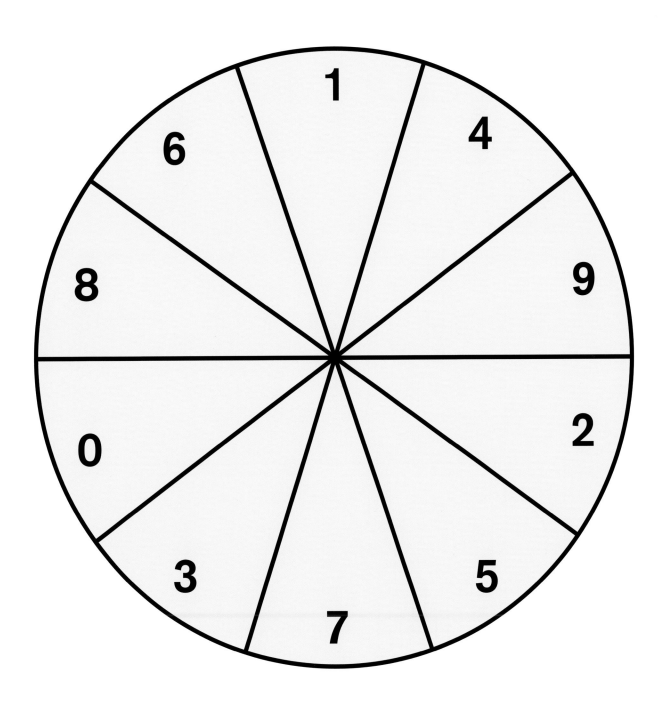

Place Value Mat—Whole Numbers

Name _____

Hundreds	Tens	Ones

Place Value Mat–Decimals

Name _____

Ones	Tenths	Hundredths

Tile Rectangles

Name _____

Number of Tiles	Dimensions of Rectangles	Total Number of Rectangles
1		
2		
3		
4		
5		
6		
7		
8		
9		
10		
11		
12		
13		
14		
15		
16		
17		
18		
19		
20		
21		
22		
23		
24		
25		

Navigating through Number and Operations in Grades 3–5

Parallel Number Lines

Name _____

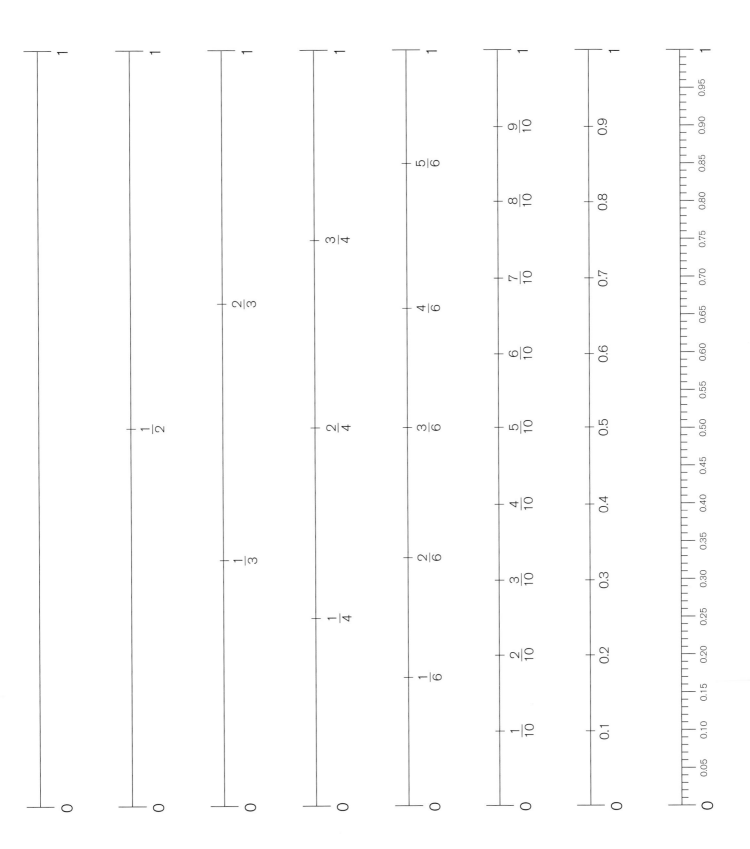

Decimal Grids–Tenths

Name _____

Decimal Grids—Hundredths

Name _____

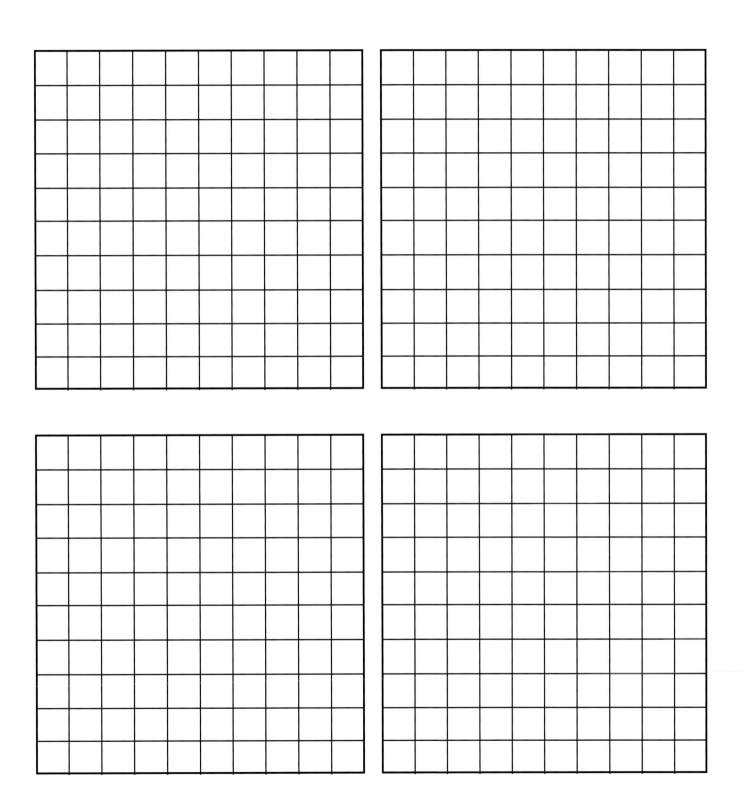

Multiplication Work Mat

Name _____

Navigating through Number and Operations in Grades 3–5

Multiplication Recording Sheet

Name _____

Problem 1

Equation(s)

Problem 2

Equation(s)

Problem 3

Equation(s)

Problem 4

Equation(s)

Can You Solve It with Multiplication?

Name _____

1. James and his dad made cupcakes as a birthday surprise for James's sister, who just turned 8. They decided to put 8 gumdrops on the top of each of the 6 cupcakes that they made. How many gumdrops did they put on the cupcakes in all?

2. Ankara and Simone sorted all the mystery books out of their book collections. Ankara had only 4 mysteries. Simone said, "I've got 9 times as many as you have." How many mystery books did Simone have?

3. Renaldo and Benny are picking apples to earn some extra money. Renaldo has picked 7 apples, but Benny has picked 6 times as many as Renaldo. How many apples has Benny picked?

4. One summer, Tracy helped her dad plant flowers in their garden. Altogether, they planted 4 rows of flowers. Each row produced 8 flowers. How many flowers did the garden have in all?

Navigating through Number and Operations in Grades 3–5

Division Work Mat

Name _____

Division Recording Sheet

Name _____

Problem 1

Equation(s)

_____

_____

Problem 2

Equation(s)

_____

_____

Problem 3

Equation(s)

_____

_____

Problem 4

Equation(s)

_____

_____

Can You Solve It with Division?

Name _____

1. Sonya was sorting her pencils. She had 30 pencils, which she put into 6 equal piles. How many pencils did she put in each pile?

2. Mrs. Smith is arranging transportation for a class trip. She plans to drive, and some parents will, too. Mrs. Smith has 24 students in her class, and she plans to assign 4 children to each car. How many cars, including her own, will Mrs. Smith need for the trip?

3. Kevin has $15.00 to use to buy rubber balls that cost $3.00 apiece. How many balls can Kevin buy?

4. Katy is decorating goody bags for her birthday party. She has 5 goody bags that she must decorate in the next 35 minutes. How many minutes should she spend on each bag?

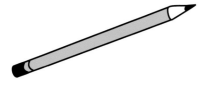   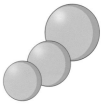

10 × 10 Dot Array

Name _____

Navigating through Number and Operations in Grades 3–5

30 × 36 Dot Array

Name _____

Multiplying by Special Numbers

Name _____

Table 1

×	8	26	B = ___
1			$1 \times B =$
1.1	$1.1 \times 8 =$		
1.15		$1.15 \times 26 =$	
A = ___			

1. In bottom row of table 1, find "A = _____" in column 1. Choose a number for A that is slightly greater than 1 and write it in the blank in the table.

2. In the top row of table 1, find "B = _____" in column 4. Choose a number for B that is greater than 50 and write it in the blank in the table.

3. Using your calculator, complete column 2 in table 1 by multiplying each number in column 1 by 8. Write each product in the appropriate row in column 2.

4. Compare the products in column 2 with the number 8. What do you notice?

5. Using your calculator, complete column 3 in table 1 by multiplying each number in column 1 by 26. Write each product in the appropriate row in column 3.

Name _____

6. Compare the products in column 3 with the number 26. What do you notice?

7. On the basis of your results in steps 3–6, what do you predict will be true of the products in column 4 compared with the number that you chose for *B*?

8. Use your calculator to determine the products in column 4, and write them in the appropriate rows.

9. Compare the products in column 4 with the number that you chose for *B*. What do you notice?

Table 2

$\times$	8	26	$D =$ _____
1		$1 \times 26 =$	
0.9			
0.85	$0.85 \times 8 =$		
$C =$ _____			

10. In the bottom row of table 2, find "$C =$ _____" in column 1. Choose a number for *C* that is slightly less than 1 and write it in the blank in the table.

11. In the top row 1 of table 2, find "$D =$ _____" in column 4. Choose a number for *D* that is greater than 60 and write it in the blank in the table.

Name _____

12. Using your calculator, complete column 2 in table 2 by multiplying each number in column 1 by 8. Write each product in the appropriate row in column 2.

13. Compare the products in column 2 with the number 8. What do you notice?

14. Using your calculator, complete column 3 in table 2 by multiplying each number in column 1 by 26. Write each product in the appropriate row in column 3.

15. Compare the products in column 3 with the number 26. What do you notice?

16. On the basis of your results in steps 12–15, what do you predict will be true of the products in column 4 compared with the number that you chose for D?

17. Use your calculator to determine the products in column 4, and write them in the appropriate rows.

18. Compare the products in column 4 with the number that you chose for D. What do you notice?

$$\times \; = \; \times \; = \; \times \; = \; \times \; = \; \times \; = \; \times$$

Dividing by Special Numbers

Name _____

Table 1

÷	4	17	$F =$ _____
1			
1.1	$4 \div 1.1 =$		
1.15		$17 \div 1.15 =$	
$E =$ _____			

1. In the bottom row of table 1, find "$E =$ _____" in column 1. Choose a number for E that is slightly greater than 1 and write it in the blank in the table.

2. In the top row of table 1, find "$F =$ _____" in column 4. Choose a number for F that is greater than 70 and write it in the blank in the table.

3. Using your calculator, complete column 2 in table 1 by dividing 4 by each number in column 1. Write each quotient in the appropriate row in column 2.

4. Compare the quotients in column 2 with the number 4. What do you notice?

5. Using your calculator, complete column 3 in table 1 by dividing 17 by each number in column 1. Write each quotient in the appropriate row in column 3.

Dividing by Special Numbers (continued)

Name _____

6. Compare the quotients in column 3 with the number 17. What do you notice?

7. On the basis of your results in steps 3–6, what do you predict will be true of the quotients in column 4 compared with the number that you chose for *F*?

8. Use your calculator to determine the quotients in column 4, and write them in the appropriate rows.

9. Compare the quotients in column 4 with the number that you chose for *F*. What do you notice?

Table 2

÷	4	17	$H =$ _____
1			
0.9		$17 \div 0.9 =$	
0.75	$4 \div 0.75 =$		
$G =$ _____			

10. In the bottom row of table 2, find "$G =$ _____" in column 1. Choose a number for *G* that is slightly less than 1 and write it in the blank in the table.

11. In the top row of table 2, find "$H =$ _____" in column 4. Choose a number for *H* that is greater than 80 and write it in the blank in the table.

Name _____

12. Using your calculator, complete column 2 in table 2 by dividing 4 by each number in column 1. Write each quotient in the appropriate row in column 2.

13. Compare the quotients in column 2 with the number 4. What do you notice?

14. Using your calculator, complete column 3 in table 2 by dividing 17 by each number in column 1. Write each quotient in the appropriate row in column 3.

15. Compare the quotients in column 3 with the number 17. What do you notice?

16. On the basis of your results in steps 12–15, what do you predict will be true of the quotients in column 4 compared with the number that you chose for *H*?

17. Use your calculator to determine the quotients in column 4 and write them in the appropriate rows.

18. Compare the quotients in column 4 with the number that you chose for *H*. What do you notice?

$$\div \; = \; \div \; = \; \div \; = \; \div \; = \; \div \; = \; \div$$

Addition and Subtraction Word Problems

Name _____

1. Jefferson Elementary School has 231 students. On Monday, only 228 students were present in the school. How many students were absent?

2. The Bobcats scored 31 points in the first half of the basketball game. They scored 29 points in the second half. How many points did the Bobcats score in all?

3. Mrs. Wilson had $63 in her wallet. She went to the store and bought a few groceries. Later she looked in her wallet and found that she had only $56. How much money did she spend at the store?

4. So far during the basketball season, Jo has made 38 consecutive free throws. If she makes 3 more free throws without missing any, how many consecutive free throws will she have made?

5. Jamie is saving money to buy a DVD player. She has already saved $68. On Saturday she will earn $8 more. How much money will she then have?

6. Mr. and Mrs. Johnson are writing thank-you notes for their wedding gifts. They bought a box of 72 note cards. On Monday, they used 3 cards to write 3 notes. How many thank-you cards are left in the box?

$+ \quad - \quad + \quad - \quad + \quad - \quad + \quad - \quad + \quad - \quad +$

Navigating through Number and Operations in Grades 3–5

Multiplication and Division Word Problems

Name _____

1. Marci has 14 nickels. How much money does Marci have in dollars and cents?

2. Four girls earned $280 by painting rooms in a house. If they divide the money equally, how much money will each girl receive?

3. Tom's uncle said, "I have 120 pounds of mulch in the trunk of my car. Will you help me unload it?" The mulch was in 40-pound bags. How many bags did Tom and his uncle unload from the car?

4. Kayla bought 4 shirts that cost $15 each. How much money did she spend?

5. Kim is reading a book with 80 pages. She plans to read the same number of pages each day for 5 days. How many pages should she read each day to finish in 5 days?

6. Steve loaded bags of cement onto his truck for a small construction job. He made 3 trips, carrying one 50-pound bag each time. How many pounds of cement did Steve put on his truck?

$\times$ $\div$ $\times$ $\div$ $\times$ $\div$ $\times$ $\div$ $\times$ $\div$ $\times$

Make Ten to Add

Name _____

Your teacher will show you how to use base-ten blocks and a "'Make Ten' Work Mat" to solve the problems below. For each problem, write a sentence explaining how you added to make the next ten and then counted the remaining ones to find the sum.

1. $48 + 8 =$

2. $27 + 9 =$

3. $49 + 7 =$

4. $35 + 7 =$

5. $28 + 4 =$

6. $48 + 6 =$

7. $56 + 8 =$

8. $18 + 6 =$

9. $36 + 6 =$

10. $28 + 7 =$

11. $64 + 8 =$

$+$ $=$ $+$ $=$ $+$ $=$ $+$ $=$ $+$ $=$ $+$

Navigating through Number and Operations in Grades 3–5

"Make Ten" Work Mat

Name _____

For each addition, show the larger number by placing tens-blocks on the left side of the mat (under "Tens") and ones-blocks in the top ten-frame (under "Ones"). Show the other number by placing ones-blocks in the lower ten-frame (under "Additional Ones"). Move ones-blocks from the lower frame into the top frame until it has ten ones-blocks. Then replace all ten ones-blocks in the top frame by a new tens-block on the left. Now solve the problem by counting up all the tens and ones on your mat.

Tens   **Ones**

Additional Ones

Dime Array

Name _____

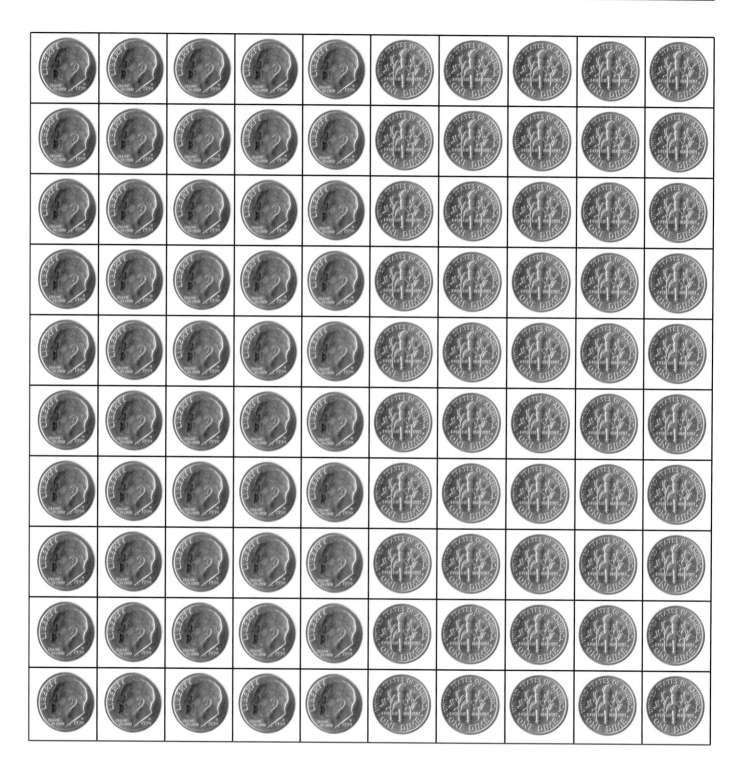

Navigating through Number and Operations in Grades 3–5

Splitting Arrays

Name _____

Look at the arrays of circles below. Can you state a multiplication fact that each array shows? Write the multiplication fact on the line underneath the array. Suppose that someone is having trouble finding a multiplication fact for an array. Draw a line to show how you can split each array into pieces to find a multiplication fact more easily.

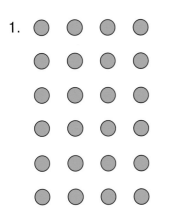

1.

Fact _____

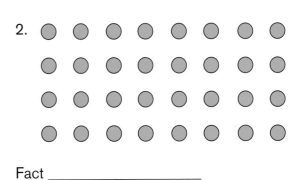

2.

Fact _____

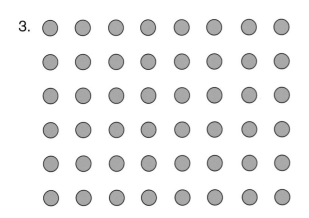

3.

Fact _____

4.

Fact _____

Name _____

5.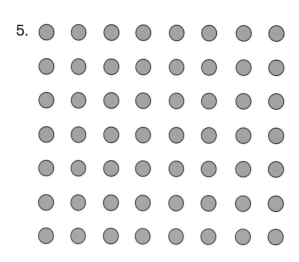

Fact _____

6.

Fact _____

Splitting More Arrays

Name _____

Look at the arrays of circles below. Can you state a multiplication fact that each array shows? Write the multiplication fact on the line underneath the array. Draw one or more lines to show how you can split each array into pieces to find a multiplication fact by using facts that you know. Tell how you can determine the total number of dots in the array by knowing the number in each smaller array.

1.

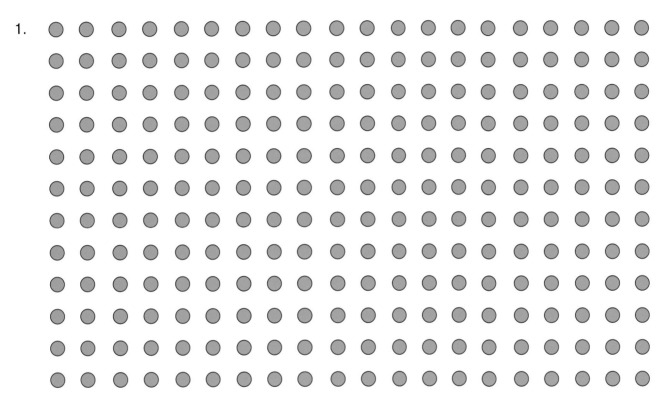

Fact _____

2.

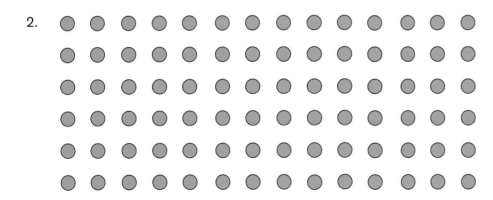

Fact _____

Splitting More Arrays

Name _____

3.

Fact _____

4.

Fact _____

Navigating through Number and Operations in Grades 3–5

Facts and Factors

Name _____

1. Each of the numbers below is the product of two single-digit numbers. Complete each multiplication fact by filling in appropriate single-digit numbers. For example, if you had "20 = _____ × _____," you would write in 4 and 5, but not 2 and 10, or 20 and 1, because 10 and 20 are two-digit numbers. If you had "25 = _____ × _____," you would write in two 5s. Each number that you write is a single-digit *factor* of the corresponding product.

a. 15 = _____ × _____

d. 27 = _____ × _____

b. 14 = _____ × _____

e. 24 = _____ × _____

c. 54 = _____ × _____

f. 35 = _____ × _____

2. One digit is missing from each two-digit product below. Sometimes, the missing digit is the ones digit, and sometimes it is the tens digit. Can you fill in the missing digit and complete each multiplication fact by supplying two single-digit factors? For example, if you had "7___ = _____ × _____," you would enter 2 as the missing digit and 8 and 9 as the single-digit factors, because 8×9 (or 9×8) $= 72$. *Note:* For some statements, there is more than one way to fill in the blanks.

a. 6___ = _____ × _____

e. ___1 = _____ × _____

b. 5___ = _____ × _____

f. ___8 = _____ × _____

c. 8___ = _____ × _____

g. ___9 = _____ × _____

d. ___3 = _____ × _____

h. ___6 = _____ × _____

× = × = × = × = × = ×

Mystery Multiplication Facts

Name _____

The statements below describe two-digit numbers. *Each number is the product of two single-digit factors.* For each statement, find a number that the statement accurately describes, and write the basic multiplication fact (or facts) in which that number is the product. *Note:* Some statements describe more than one number. For these statements, more than one answer is correct.

1. One of the digits in this two-digit number is 7. The number is larger than 20.

   A number that fits this description is _____

   Multiplication fact(s):

2. One of the digits in this two-digit number is 8. The sum of the digits is greater than 11.

   A number that fits this description is _____

   Multiplication fact(s):

3. The difference between the larger digit and the smaller digit in this two-digit number is 7.

   A number that fits this description is _____

   Multiplication fact(s):

4. One of the digits in this two-digit number is 5, but the number is not divisible by 5. Nor is it divisible by 9.

   A number that fits this description is _____

   Multiplication fact(s):

Navigating through Number and Operations in Grades 3–5

Mystery Multiplication Facts (continued)

Name _____

5. The sum of the digits in this two-digit number is 9. The difference between the digits is 3.

    A number that fits this description is _____

    Multiplication fact(s):

6. The tens digit in this two-digit number is one-fourth of the ones digit. The sum of the digits is an even number.

    A number that fits this description is _____

    Multiplication fact(s):

7. If you switch the digits of this two-digit number, you form a smaller two-digit number that is also the product of two one-digit factors. The sum of the digits is an even number.

    A number that fits this description is _____

    Multiplication fact(s):

8. One of the digits in this two-digit number is 9.

    A number that fits this description is _____

    Multiplication fact(s):

Traveling in the City–Spinners

Name _____

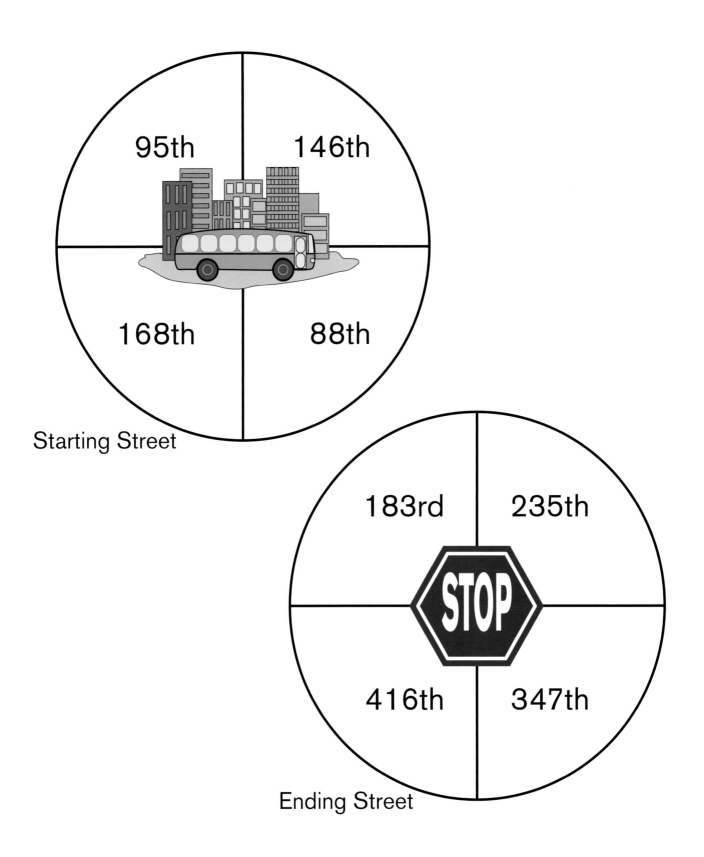

95th   146th

168th   88th

Starting Street

183rd   235th

416th   347th

Ending Street

Navigating through Number sand Operations in Grades 3–5

Traveling in the City– Open Number Lines

Name _____

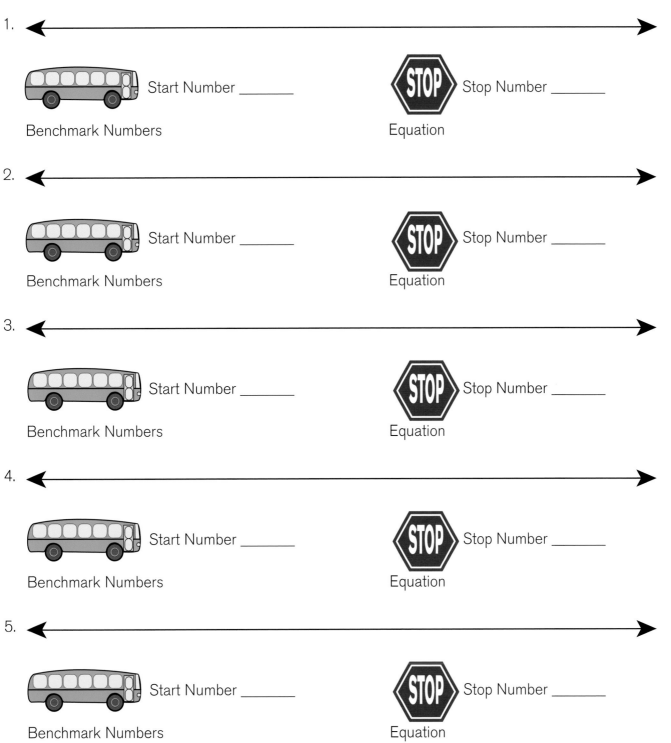

1. ←——————————————————————→

   Start Number _____   Stop Number _____

   Benchmark Numbers   Equation

2. ←——————————————————————→

   Start Number _____   Stop Number _____

   Benchmark Numbers   Equation

3. ←——————————————————————→

   Start Number _____   Stop Number _____

   Benchmark Numbers   Equation

4. ←——————————————————————→

   Start Number _____   Stop Number _____

   Benchmark Numbers   Equation

5. ←——————————————————————→

   Start Number _____   Stop Number _____

   Benchmark Numbers   Equation

Multiplication Chains—Sheet A

Name _____

Multiplication Chain	Draw a Rectangle and Break It Apart
$4 \times 6 =$ $40 \times 6 =$ _ _ _ _ _ $44 \times 6 =$ $6 \times 5 =$ $20 \times 5 =$ $50 \times 5 =$ _ _ _ _ _ $76 \times 5 =$	

Create your own multiplication chain for the following problem:

$$42 \times 7 = \square$$

Multiplication Chains–Sheet B

Name _____

Multiplication Chain	Draw a Rectangle and Break It Apart
6 X 3 = 60 X 3 = — — — — — 66 X 3 = 6 X 7 = 10 X 7 = 30 X 7 = — — — — — 46 X 7 =	

Create your own multiplication chain for the following problem:

$$56 \times 6 = \square$$

Drawing a Bead on Division– Card Set 1

Name _____

Set 1–Problem 1

A package of beads contains 96 beads. James makes and sells bracelets with 8 beads on each bracelet. How many bracelets can James make?

Starter problem: $80 \div 8 =$ ____

Set 1–Problem 2

Keisha makes necklaces, and she strings 20 beads on each one. She has a box with 260 beads. How many necklaces can Keisha make with the beads in the box?

Starter problem: $100 \div 20 =$ ___

Set 1–Problem 3

Bryan is in charge of helping the children in daycare make bracelets. He has a bag of 500 beads. Each bracelet uses 15 beads. How many bracelets can the children make?

Starter problem: $150 \div 15 =$ ____

Set 1–Problem 4

Moira is making key chains to sell at the craft fair. She has 130 beads, and she will put 6 beads on each chain. How many key chains can Moira make?

Starter problem: $60 \div 6 =$ ____

Set 1–Problem 5

Derrick is making bookmarks as holiday presents. He wants to hang a string of 5 beads from the end of each bookmark. He has 235 beads. How many bookmarks can Derrick make?

Starter problem: $100 \div 5 =$ ____

Set 1–Problem 6

The guests at Sahar's birthday party will make necklaces with 25 beads on each. Sahar will set a jar of 850 beads in the middle of the table. How many necklaces can her guests make?

Starter problem: $100 \div 25 =$ ____

Drawing a Bead on Division–Card Set 2

Name _____

Set 2–Problem A

Heather has 73 beads. She makes bracelets and puts 9 beads on each one. How many bracelets can she make? How many beads will she have left over?

Starter problem: $63 \div 9 =$ ____

Set 2–Problem B

Paige buys a bag of 300 beads to use in making necklaces with 15 beads on each one. How many necklaces can she make?

Starter problem: $300 \div 15 =$ ____

Set 2–Problem C

Brett orders 500 beads from a catalog. The beads arrive at his house in boxes with 50 beads in each. How many boxes of beads does Brett receive?

Starter problem: $500 \div 50 =$ ____

Set 2–Problem D

Chase sells kits for key chains. He has 100 beads, and he puts 6 beads in each one. How many key-chain kits can Chase make? Will he have any beads left over?

Starter problem: $60 \div 6 =$ ____

Set 2–Problem E

Quinn finds 77 beads in a drawer and decides to use them in making book-marks. He will attach a string of 5 beads to each bookmark. How many bookmarks can Quinn make?

Starter problem: $50 \div 5 =$ ____

Set 2–Problem F

Cara has 80 beads to use in necklaces for herself and her sisters. She decides to put 25 beads on each necklace. How many necklaces can Cara make?

Starter problem: $75 \div 25 =$ ____

Name _____

Set 2–Problem G

$720 \div 6 =$ ____

Starter problem: $600 \div 6 =$ ____

Set 2–Problem H

$97 \div 3 =$ ____

Starter problem: $90 \div 3 =$ ____

Set 2–Problem J

$100 \div 7 =$ ____

Starter problem: $70 \div 7 =$ ____

Set 2–Problem K

$275 \div 5 =$ ____

Starter problem: $250 \div 5 =$ ____

Over or under 200?

Name _____

Problem 1

Erasers
6 per package
26 packages

Problem 2

Crayons
24 per box
17 boxes

Problem 3

Sidewalk chalk
15 pieces per bucket
12 buckets

Problem 4

Pencils
9 per package
19 packages

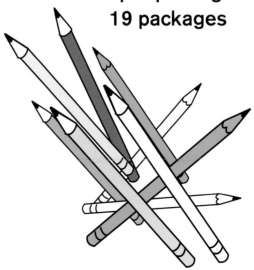

Over or under 500?

Name _____

Problem A

Small binder Clips
45 per box
8 boxes

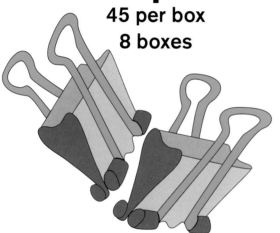

Problem B

Pens
16 per box
41 boxes

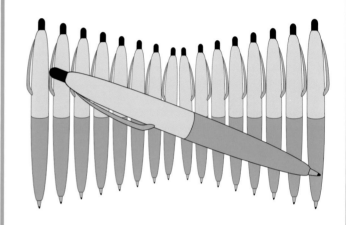

Problem C

Film
24 exposures per roll
17 rolls

Problem D

Crayons
32 per box
19 boxes

Over or Under–Recording Sheet

Name _____

Record the information in each problem and circle "over" or "under" in column 4.

Item	Quantity per Unit (Number of items in a box, a bucket, etc.)	Number of Units (Number of units rolled on the die)	Is the total number of items over or under the target?	How did you reason?
			Over or Under _____?	
			Over or Under _____?	
			Over or Under _____?	
			Over or Under _____?	
			Over or Under _____?	

Over or Under–Problem Cards

Name _____

Problem 1
Markers

8 markers per box
Over or under 100?

Problem 2
Binder clips

45 per package
Over or under 700?

Problem 3
Pencils

12 per package
Over or under 200?

Problem 4
Pencil grips

48 per box
Over or under 1000?

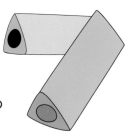

Problem 5
Sidewalk chalk

15 sticks per bucket
Over or under 200?

Problem 6
Paper clips

72 per box
Over or under 1000?

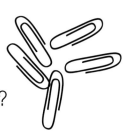

Problem 7
Pens

18 per box
Over or under 500?

Problem 8
Crayons

96 per box
Over or under 2000?

Problem 9
Film

24 exposures per roll
Over or under 500?

Problem 10
Erasers

144 per package
Over or under 2000?

Clock Face

Ways to Use an Hour

Name _____

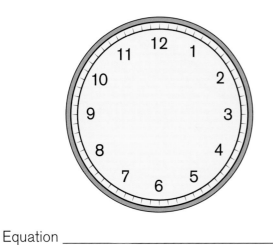

Explanation:

Equation _____

Explanation:

Equation _____

Explanation:

Equation _____

Navigating through Number and Operations in Grades 3–5

Solutions for the Blackline Masters

Blackline masters not listed by name either call for no solutions or have solutions that are discussed in the text.

Solutions for "Make Ten to Add"

A sample sentence appears in the discussion on page 106.

Solutions for "Splitting Arrays"

1. $6 \times 4 = 24$, or $4 \times 6 = 24$. Students' ideas about splitting the array will vary, but many students will probably suggest splitting it into halves, either vertically or horizontally, to give $2 \times (2 \times 6)$ or $2 \times (4 \times 3)$.

2. $4 \times 8 = 32$, or $8 \times 4 = 32$. Students' ideas about splitting the array will vary.

3. $6 \times 8 = 48$, or $8 \times 6 = 48$. Students' ideas about splitting the array will vary.

4. $7 \times 6 = 42$, or $6 \times 7 = 42$. Students' ideas about splitting the array will vary.

5. $7 \times 8 = 56$, or $8 \times 7 = 56$. Students' ideas about splitting the array will vary.

6. $9 \times 7 = 63$, or $7 \times 9 = 63$. Students' ideas about splitting the array will vary.

Solutions for "Splitting More Arrays"

1. $12 \times 20 = 240$, or $20 \times 12 = 240$. Students' ideas about splitting the array will vary; one way is shown below:

$$(2 \times (10 \times 10)) + (2 \times (2 \times 10)) =$$
$$(2 \times 100) + (2 \times 20) =$$
$$200 + 40 =$$
$$240$$

2. $6 \times 14 = 84$, or $14 \times 6 = 84$. Students' ideas about splitting the array will vary; one way is shown below:

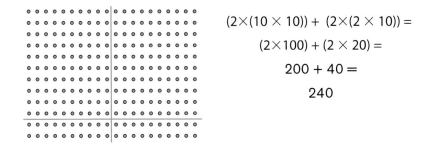

$$(6 \times 6) + (6 \times 6) + (6 \times 2) =$$
$$36 + 36 + 12 =$$
$$84$$

3. $15 \times 8 = 120$, or $8 \times 15 = 120$. Students' ideas about splitting the array will vary; one way is shown below:

$$(5 \times 8) + (5 \times 8) + (5 \times 8) =$$
$$40 + 40 + 40 =$$
$$120$$

4. $9 \times 16 = 144$, or $16 \times 9 = 144$. Students' ideas about splitting the array will vary; one way is shown below:

$$(9 \times 10) + (9 \times 3) + (9 \times 3) =$$
$$90 + 27 + 27 =$$
$$90 + 54 =$$
$$144$$

Solutions for "Facts and Factors"

1. a. $15 = 3 \times 5$ (or 5×3).
   b. $14 = 2 \times 7$ (or 7×2).
   c. $54 = 6 \times 9$ (or 9×6).
   d. $27 = 3 \times 9$ (or 9×3).
   e. $24 = 4 \times 6$ (or 6×4).
   f. $35 = 5 \times 7$ (or 7×5).
2. a. $6\underline{3} = 7 \times 9$ (or 9×7).
      $6\underline{4} = 8 \times 8$.
   b. $5\underline{4} = 6 \times 9$ (or 9×6).
      $5\underline{6} = 7 \times 8$ (or 8×7).
   c. $8\underline{1} = 9 \times 9$.
   d. $6\underline{3} = 7 \times 9$ (or 9×7).
   e. $\underline{2}1 = 3 \times 7$ (or 7×3).
      $\underline{8}1 = 9 \times 9$.
   f. $\underline{1}8 = 2 \times 9$ (or 9×2).
      $\underline{2}8 = 4 \times 7$ (or 7×4).
      $\underline{4}8 = 6 \times 8$ (or 8×6).
   g. $\underline{4}9 = 7 \times 7$.
   h. $\underline{1}6 = 2 \times 8$ (or 8×2).
      $\underline{3}6 = 4 \times 9$ (or 6×6 or 9×4).
      $\underline{5}6 = 7 \times 8$ (or 8×7).

Solutions for "Mystery Multiplication Facts"

1. A number that fits this description is 27.
   Multiplication facts:
   $3 \times 9 = 27$; $9 \times 3 = 27$

   Another number that fits this description is 72.
   Multiplication facts:
   $8 \times 9 = 72$; $9 \times 8 = 72$

2. The number that fits this description is 48.
   Multiplication facts:
   $6 \times 8 = 48$; $8 \times 6 = 48$

3. A number that fits this description is 18.
   Multiplication facts:
   $2 \times 9 = 18$; $9 \times 2 = 18$

   Another number that fits this description is 81.
   Multiplication fact:
   $9 \times 9 = 81$

4. The number that fits this description is 56.
   Multiplication facts:
   $7 \times 8 = 56$; $8 \times 7 = 56$

5. A number that fits this description is 36.
   Multiplication facts:
   $4 \times 9 = 36$; $6 \times 6 = 36$; $9 \times 4 = 36$

   Another number that fits this description is 63.
   Multiplication facts:
   $7 \times 9 = 63$; $9 \times 7 = 63$

6. The number that fits this description is 28.
   Multiplication facts:
   $4 \times 7 = 28$; $7 \times 4 = 28$

7. The number that fits this description is 42.
   Multiplication facts:
   $6 \times 7 = 42$; $7 \times 6 = 42$

8. The number that fits this description is 49.
   Multiplication fact:
   $7 \times 7 = 49$

Solutions for Multiplication Chains—Sheets A and B

Sheet A

Multiplication Chain	Draw a Rectangle and Break It Apart
$4 \times 6 = 24$ $40 \times 6 = 240$ – – – – – $44 \times 6 = 264$	 4 40 6 | 24 | 240 | 6 ← 44 →
$6 \times 5 = 30$ $20 \times 5 = 100$ $50 \times 5 = 250$ – – – – – $76 \times 5 = 380$	6 20 50 5 | 30 | 100 | 250 | 5 ← 76 →

A possible chain for the problem $42 \times 7 = \square$ follows:

$$2 \times 7 = 14$$
$$20 \times 7 = 140$$
$$20 \times 7 = 140$$
$$- - - - - - - -$$
$$42 \times 7 = 294$$

Sheet B

Multiplication Chain	Draw a Rectangle and Break It Apart
$6 \times 3 = 18$ $60 \times 3 = 180$ – – – – – $66 \times 3 = 198$	6 60 3 | 18 | 180 ← 66 →
$6 \times 7 = 42$ $10 \times 7 = 70$ $30 \times 7 = 210$ – – – – – $46 \times 7 = 322$	6 10 30 7 | 42 | 70 | 210 ← 46 →

A possible chain for the problem $56 \times 6 = \square$ follows:

$$6 \times 6 = 36$$
$$50 \times 6 = 300$$
$$- - - - - - - -$$
$$56 \times 6 = 336$$

Solutions for "Over or Under–Problem Cards"

Solutions and ways to think about each problem follow:

1. 8 markers per box; over or under 100?

    For 7 boxes: 10 boxes × 8 markers in a box = 80 markers; 80 < 100, so the total number of markers in 7 boxes will also be **under** 100.

    For 9 boxes: 10 boxes × 8 markers in a box = 80 markers; 80 < 100, so the total number of markers in 9 boxes will also be **under** 100.

    For 12 boxes: 10 boxes × 8 markers in a box = 80 markers; 2 more boxes will add 8 × 2, or 16, markers, so the total number of markers in 12 boxes (80 + 16) is still **under** 100.

    For 19 boxes: 20 boxes × 8 markers in a box = 160 markers, a total that is so far over 100 that it guarantees that the total number of markers in 19 boxes will also be **over** 100.

    For 24 boxes: 25 boxes × 8 markers in a box = 200 markers, a total that is two times 100 and guarantees that the total number of markers in 24 boxes will also be **over** 100.

    For 35 boxes: 30 boxes × 8 markers in a box = 240 markers, a total that is so far over 100 that it guarantees that the total number of markers in 35 boxes will also be **over** 100.

2. 45 binder clips per package; over or under 700?

    For 7 packages: 7 packages × 50 clips in a package = 350 clips, a total that is far under 700 and guarantees that the total number of clips in 7 packages with 45 clips in a package will also be **under** 700.

    For 9 packages: 10 packages × 45 clips in a package = 450 clips, a total that is far under 700 and guarantees that the total number of clips in 9 packages will also be **under** 700.

    For 12 packages: 12 packages × 50 clips in a package = 600 clips, a total that is under 700 and guarantees that the total number of clips in 12 packages with 45 clips in a package will also be **under** 700.

    For 19 packages: 20 packages × 45 clips in a package = 900 clips, a total that is far enough over 700 to guarantee that the total number of clips in 19 packages will also be **over** 700.

    For 24 packages: 20 packages × 45 clips in a package = 900 clips, a total that is over 700, and the total number of clips in 24 packages will also be **over** 700.

    For 35 packages: 10 packages × 45 clips in a package = 450 clips; 20 packages will be 900 clips, a total that is already over 700 and thus guarantees that the total number of clips in 35 packages will also be **over** 700.

3. 12 pencils per package; over or under 200?

    For 7 packages: 10 packages × 12 pencils in a package = 120 pencils, a total that is under 200, so the total number of pencils in 7 packages will also be **under** 200.

    For 9 packages: 10 packages × 12 pencils in a package = 120 pencils, a total that is under 200, so the total number of pencils in 9 packages will also be **under** 200.

    For 12 packages: 10 packages × 12 pencils in a package = 120 pencils. This means that 5 packages hold 60 pencils, so 15 packages will hold 120 + 60, or 180 pencils, a total that is still under 200; thus, the total number of pencils in 12 packages is also **under** 200.

    For 19 packages: 20 packages × 12 pencils in a package = 240 pencils, a total that is over 200; taking away one package (leaving 19 packages) removes only 12 pencils, so the total number of pencils in 19 packages will also be **over** 200.

For 24 packages: 20 packages × 12 pencils in a package = 240 pencils, a total that is over 200, so the total number of pencils in 24 packages will also be **over** 200.

For 35 packages: 10 packages × 12 pencils in a package = 120 pencils; 20 packages = 240 pencils, a total that is already over 200, so the total number of pencils in 35 packages will also be **over** 200.

4. 48 pencil grips per box; over or under 1000?

For 7 boxes: 10 boxes × 48 pencil grips in a box = 480 pencil grips; 480 < 1000, so the total number of pencil grips in 7 boxes will also be **under** 1000.

For 9 boxes: 10 boxes × 48 pencil grips in a box = 480 pencil grips; 480 < 1000, so the total number of pencil grips in 9 boxes will also be **under** 1000.

For 12 boxes: 10 boxes × 48 pencil grips in a box = 480 pencil grips; 5 more boxes will add 240 pencil grips, and the total number of pencil grips in 15 boxes (480 + 240) will still be under 1000, so the total number of pencil grips in 12 boxes will also be **under** 100.

For 19 boxes: 20 boxes × 50 pencil grips in a box = 1000 pencil grips. The problem on the card involves 1 fewer box and 2 fewer pencil grips in each box, so the total number of pencil grips in 19 boxes will be **under** 1000.

For 24 boxes: 20 boxes × 48 pencil grips in a box = 960 pencil grips, a total that is so close to 1000 that it guarantees that the total number of pencil grips in 24 boxes [960 + (4 × 48)] will be **over** 1000.

For 35 boxes: 20 boxes × 48 pencil grips in a box = 960 pencil grips, a total that is so close to 1000 that it guarantees that the total number of pencil grips in 35 boxes will be **over** 1000.

5. 15 sticks of sidewalk chalk per bucket; over or under 200?

For 7 buckets: 10 buckets × 15 sticks in a bucket = 150 sticks; 150 < 200, so the total number of sticks of chalk in 7 buckets will also be **under** 200.

For 9 buckets: 10 buckets × 15 sticks in a bucket = 150 sticks; 150 < 200, so the total number of sticks of chalk in 9 buckets will also be **under** 200.

For 12 buckets: 10 buckets × 15 sticks in a bucket = 150 sticks; 2 more boxes will add 30 sticks of chalk, and the total number of sticks of chalk (150 + 30) will be **under** 200.

For 19 buckets: 20 buckets × 15 sticks in a bucket = 300 sticks, a total that is far enough over 200 to guarantee that the total number of sticks of chalk in 19 buckets (300 − 15) will also be **over** 200.

For 24 buckets: 20 buckets × 15 sticks in a bucket = 300 sticks, a total that is over 200, so the total number of sticks of chalk in 24 buckets will also be **over** 200.

For 35 buckets: 30 buckets × 15 sticks in a bucket = 450 sticks, a total that is over 200, so the total number of sticks of chalk in 35 buckets will also be **over** 200.

6. 72 paper clips per box; over or under 1000?

For 7 boxes: 10 boxes × 72 paper clips in a box = 720 paper clips; 720 < 1000, so the total number of paper clips in 7 boxes will also be **under** 1000.

For 9 boxes: 10 boxes × 72 paper clips in a box = 720 paper clips; 720 < 1000, so the total number of paper clips in 9 boxes will also be **under** 1000.

For 12 boxes: 10 boxes × 72 paper clips in a box = 720 paper clips; 2 more boxes will add fewer than 150 paper clips, and the total number of paper clips (720 + 144) will be **under** 1000.

For 19 boxes: 20 boxes × 72 paper clips in a box = 1440 paper clips, a total that is far enough over 1000 to guarantee that the total number of paper clips in 19 boxes (1440 − 72) will also be **over** 1000.

For 24 boxes: 20 boxes × 72 paper clips in a box = 1440 paper clips, a total that is over 1000, so the total number of paper clips in 24 boxes will also be **over** 1000.

For 35 boxes: 20 boxes × 72 paper clips in a box = 1440 paper clips, a total that is over 1000, so the total number of paper clips in 35 boxes will also be **over** 1000.

7. 18 pens per box; over or under 500?

For 7 boxes: 10 boxes × 18 pens in a box = 180 pens; 180 < 500, so the total number of paper clips in 7 boxes will also be **under** 500.

For 9 boxes: 10 boxes × 18 pens in a box = 180 pens; 180 < 500, so the total number of pens in 9 boxes will also be **under** 500.

For 12 boxes: 10 boxes × 18 pens in a box = 180 pens; 2 more boxes will add just 36 pens, and the total number of pens (180 + 36) will be **under** 500.

For 19 boxes: 20 boxes × 18 pens in a box = 360 pens; 360 < 500, so the total number of pens in 19 boxes will also be **under** 500.

For 24 boxes: 20 boxes × 18 pens in a box = 360 pens; 2 more boxes will add 36 pens, so 4 more boxes will add 72 pens, and the total number of pens in 24 boxes (360 + 72) will still be **under** 500.

For 35 boxes: 20 boxes × 18 pens in a box = 360 pens; another 10 boxes will add 180 more pens, and the total for 30 boxes (360 + 180) will be over 500, so the total number of pens in 35 boxes will also be **over** 500.

8. 96 crayons per box; over or under 2000?

For 7 boxes: 10 boxes × 96 crayons in a box = 960 crayons; 960 < 2000, so the total number of crayons in 7 boxes will also be **under** 2000.

For 9 boxes: 10 boxes × 96 crayons in a box = 960 crayons; 960 < 2000, so the total number of crayons in 9 boxes will also be **under** 2000.

For 12 boxes: 10 boxes × 96 crayons in a box = 960 crayons; 2 more boxes will add a few less than 200 more crayons, and the total number of crayons (960 + 192) will be **under** 2000.

For 19 boxes: 10 boxes × 96 crayons in a box = 960 crayons; 20 boxes will hold twice that many crayons, but the total (960 + 960), though close to 2000, will still be under it, so the total number of crayons in 19 boxes will also be **under** 2000.

For 24 boxes: 10 boxes × 96 crayons in a box = 960 crayons; 20 boxes will hold twice that many crayons, and the total for 20 boxes (960 + 960) will be close enough to 2000 to guarantee that the total number of crayons in 24 boxes (960 + 960 + 384) will be **over** 2000.

For 35 boxes: 10 boxes × 96 crayons in a box = 960 crayons; 30 boxes will hold three times that many crayons, or close to 3000 crayons. Thus, the total number of crayons in 35 boxes (960 + 960 + 960 + 480) will be well **over** 2000.

9. 24 exposures per roll of film; over or under 500?

For 7 rolls: 10 rolls × 24 exposures on a roll = 240 exposures; 240 < 500, so the total number of exposures on 7 rolls of film will also be **under** 500.

For 9 rolls: 10 rolls × 24 exposures on a roll = 240 exposures; 240 < 500, so the total number of exposures on 9 rolls of film will also be **under** 500.

For 12 rolls: 10 rolls × 24 exposures on a roll = 240 exposures; 2 more rolls will add just 48 exposures, and the total number of exposures on 12 rolls of film (240 + 48) will be **under** 500.

For 19 rolls: 20 rolls × 24 exposures on a roll = 480 exposures; 480 < 500, so the total number of exposures on 19 rolls of film will also be **under** 500.

For 24 rolls: 20 rolls × 24 exposures on a roll = 480 exposures; each additional roll will contribute 24 exposures to that total, so the total number of exposures on 24 rolls of film (480 + 24 + 24 + 24 + 24) will be **over** 500.

For 35 rolls: 20 rolls × 24 exposures on a roll = 480 exposures; each additional roll will contribute 24 exposures to that total, so the total number of exposures on 35 rolls of film [480 + (15 × 24)] will be **over** 500.

10. 144 erasers per package; over or under 2000?

For 7 packages: 10 packages × 144 erasers in a package = 1440 erasers, a total that is under 2000, so the total number of erasers in 7 packages will also be **under** 2000.

For 9 packages: 10 packages × 144 erasers in a package = 1440 erasers, a total that is under 2000, so the total number of erasers in 9 packages will also be **under** 2000.

For 12 packages: 10 packages × 144 erasers in a package = 1440 erasers. Two more packages will add fewer than 300 erasers, so the total number of erasers in 12 packages [1440 + (2 × 144)] will still be **under** 2000.

For 19 packages: 10 packages × 144 erasers in a package = 1440 erasers; 20 packages will hold twice that many erasers, and the total (1440 + 1440) will be so far over 2000 that it guarantees that the total number of erasers in 19 packages (1440 + 1440 − 144) will also be **over** 2000.

For 24 packages: 10 packages × 144 erasers in a package = 1440 erasers; 20 packages will have twice that many erasers, and the total (1440 + 1440) will be over 2000, so the total number of erasers in 24 packages will also be **over** 2000.

For 35 packages: 10 packages × 144 erasers in a package = 1440 erasers; 30 packages will hold three times that many erasers, and the total (1440 × 3) will be so far over 2000 that it guarantees that the total number of erasers in 35 packages will also be **over** 2000.

Navigating through Number and Operations in Grades 3–5

References

Brownell, William A., and Charlotte B. Chazal. "The Effects of Premature Drill in Third-Grade Arithmetic." *Journal of Educational Research* 29 (September 1935): 17–28.

Fosnot, Catherine Twomey, and Martin Dolk. *Young Mathematicians at Work: Constructing Number Sense, Addition, and Subtraction*. Portsmouth, N.H.: Heinemann, 2001.

Fraivillig, Judith. "Strategies for Advancing Children's Mathematical Thinking." *Teaching Children Mathematics* 7 (April 2001): 454–59.

Fuson, Karen C. "Research on Learning and Teaching Addition and Subtraction of Whole Numbers." In *Analysis of Arithmetic for Mathematics Teaching*, edited by Gaea Leinhardt, Ralph Putnam, and Rosemary A. Hattrup, pp. 53–188. Hillsdale, N.J.: Lawrence Erlbaum Associates, 1992.

Gabriele, Anthony J., Edward C. Rathmell, and Larry Leutzinger. "Augmenting the Curriculum with a Reform Approach to Learning Basic Facts." Final report submitted to the Iowa Space Grant Consortium, January 1998.

Graeber, Anna O. "Misconceptions about Multiplication and Division." *Arithmetic Teacher* 40 (1993): 408–11.

Isaacs, Andrew C., and William M. Carroll. "Strategies for Basic-Facts Instruction." *Teaching Children Mathematics* 5 (May 1999): 508–15.

Kilpatrick, Jeremy, Jane Swafford, and Bradford Findell, eds. *Adding It Up: Helping Children Learn Mathematics*. Washington D.C.: National Academy Press, 2001.

Leutzinger, Larry. Follow-up interview with randomly selected students from the study by Gabriele, Rathmell, and Leutzinger, September 1998.

National Council of Teachers of Mathematics (NCTM). *Curriculum and Evaluation Standards for School Mathematics*. Reston, Va.: NCTM, 1989.

———. *Principles and Standards for School Mathematics*. Reston, Va.: NCTM, 2000.

———. *Curriculum Focal Points for Prekindergarten through Grade 8 Mathematics: A Quest for Coherence*. Reston, Va.: NCTM, 2006.

Philipp, Randolph A. "Multicultural Mathematics and Alternative Algorithms." *Teaching Children Mathematics* 3 (November 1996): 128–33.

Ron, Pilar. "My Family Taught Me This Way." *In The Teaching and Learning of Algorithms in School Mathematics*, 1998 Yearbook of the National Council of Teachers of Mathematics, edited by Lorna J. Morrow, pp. 115–119. Reston, Va.: NCTM, 1998.

Ross, Susan, and Mary Pratt-Cotter. "Subtraction in the United States: An Historical Perspective." *The Mathematics Educator* 10 (Summer 2000): 49–56.

Thornton, Carol A. "Strategies for the Basic Facts." In *Mathematics for the Young Child*, edited by Joseph N. Payne, pp. 133–51. Reston, Va.: National Council of Teachers of Mathematics, 1990.

Thornton, Carol A., and Paula J. Smith. "Action Research: Strategies for Learning Subtraction Facts." *Arithmetic Teacher* 35 (April 1988): 8–12.

Yeatts, Karol L., Michael T. Battista, Sally Mayberry, Denisse R. Thompson, and Judith Zawojewski. *Navigating through Problem Solving and Reasoning in Grade 4. Principles and Standards for School Mathematics* Navigations Series. Reston, Va.: National Council of Teachers of Mathematics, 2005.

Suggested Reading

Alcaro, Patricia C., Alice S. Alston, and Nancy Katims. "Fractions Attack! Children Thinking and Talking Mathematically." *Teaching Children Mathematics* 6 (May 2000): 562–67.

Baek, Jae-Meen. "Children's Invented Algorithms for Multidigit Multiplication Problems." In *The Teaching and Learning of Algorithms in School Mathematics*, 1998 Yearbook of the National Council of Teachers of Mathematics (NCTM), edited by Lorna J. Morrow, pp. 151–60. Reston, Va.: NCTM, 1998.

Berman, Barbara, and Fredda Friederwitzer. *Fraction Circle Activities*. Palo Alto, Calif.: Dale Seymour Publications, 1988.

Bove, Sandra P. "Place Value: A Vertical Perspective." *Teaching Children Mathematics* 1 (May 1995): 542–46.

Burns, Marilyn. *Lessons for Introducing Fractions: Grades 4–5*. Sausalito, Calif.: Math Solutions Publications, 2001.

Cohen, Patricia Cline. *A Calculating People: The Spread of Numeracy in Early America*. Chicago: University of Chicago Press, 1982.

Cramer, Kathleen, and Apryl Henry. "Using Manipulative Models to Build Number Sense for Addition of Fractions." In *Making Sense of Fractions, Ratios, and Proportions*, 2002 Yearbook of the National Council of Teachers of Mathematics (NCTM), edited by Bonnie Litwiller, pp. 41–48. Reston, Va.: NCTM, 2002.

Dearing, Shirley Ann, and Boyd Holtan. "Factors and Primes with a T Square." *Arithmetic Teacher* 34 (April 1987): 34.

De Francisco, Carrie, and Marilyn Burns. *Lessons for Decimals and Percents: Grades 5–6*. Sausalito, Calif.: Math Solutions Publications, 2002.

Fosnot, Catherine Twomey, and Martin Dolk. *Young Mathematicians at Work: Constructing Fractions, Decimals, and Percents*. Portsmouth, N.H.: Heinemann, 2002.

Glasgow, Robert, Gay Ragan, Wanda M. Fields, Robert Reys, and Deanna Wasman. "The Decimal Dilemma." *Teaching Children Mathematics* 7 (October 2000): 89–93.

Hamel, Thomas, and Ernest Woodward. *Fraction Concepts: Using Fraction Circles and the Math Explorer Calculator*. Portland, Maine: J. Weston Walch, 1995.

Hillen, Judith. *Fabulous Fractions*. Fresno, Calif.: AIMS Education Foundation, 2000.

Huinker, DeAnn. "Examining Dimensions of Fraction Operation Sense." In *Making Sense of Fractions, Ratios, and Proportions*, 2002 Yearbook of the National Council of Teachers of Mathematics (NCTM), edited by Bonnie Litwiller, pp. 72–78. Reston, Va.: NCTM, 2002.

Huinker, DeAnn M. "Multiplication and Division Word Problems: Improving Students' Understanding." *Arithmetic Teacher* 37 (October 1989): 8–12.

Juraschek, Bill, and Amy S. Evans. "Ryan's Primes." *Teaching Children Mathematics* 3 (May 1997): 472–74.

Kouba, Vicky L., and Kathy Franklin. "Multiplication and Division: Sense Making and Meaning." In *Research Ideas for the Classroom: Early Childhood Mathematics*, edited by Robert J. Jensen, pp. 103–26. Reston, Va.: National Council of Teachers of Mathematics; New York: Macmillan, 1993.

———. "Multiplication and Division: Sense Making and Meaning." *Teaching Children Mathematics* 1 (May 1995): 574–77.

Litwiller, Bonnie L., ed. *Making Sense of Fractions, Ratios, and Proportions,* 2002 Yearbook of the National Council of Teachers of Mathematics (NCTM). Reston, Va.: NCTM, 2002.

Long, Lynette. *Delightful Decimals and Perfect Percents: Games and Activities That Make Math Easy and Fun.* New York: John Wiley & Sons, 2002.

Martinie, Sherri L., and Jennifer M. Bay-Williams. "Investigating Students' Conceptual Understanding of Decimal Fractions Using Multiple Representations." *Mathematics Teaching in the Middle School* 8 (January 2003): 244–47.

Moss, Joan, and Robbie Case. "Developing Children's Understanding of the Rational Numbers: A New Model of an Experimental Curriculum," *Journal for Research in Mathematics Education* 30 (1999): 124–48.

Moyer, Patricia S., and Elizabeth Mailley. "*Inchworm and a Half:* Developing Fraction and Measurement Concepts Using Mathematical Representations." *Teaching Children Mathematics* 10 (January 2004): 244–52.

Moyer, Patricia Seray. "*A Remainder of One:* Exploring Partitive Division." *Teaching Children Mathematics* 6 (April 2000): 517–21.

Oppenheimer, Lauren, and Robert H. Hunting. "Relating Fractions and Decimals: Listening to Students Talk." *Mathematics Teaching in the Middle School* 4 (February 1999): 318–21.

Patriarca, Linda, Marilyn Scheffel, and Sheila Hedeman. *Decimals: A Place Value Approach.* Palo Alto, Calif.: Dale Seymour Publications, 1998.

Powell, Carol A., and Robert P. Hunting. "Fractions in the Early Years Curriculum: More Needed, Not Less." *Teaching Children Mathematics* 10 (September 2003): 6–7.

Rathmell, Edward C. "Using Thinking Strategies to Teach the Basic Facts." In *Developing Computational Skills,* 1978 Yearbook of the National Council of Teachers of Mathematics (NCTM), edited by Marilyn N. Suydam, pp. 13–38. Reston, Va.: NCTM, 1978.

Reys, Barbara J., Ok-Kyeong Kim, and Jennifer M. Bay. "Establishing Fraction Benchmarks." *Mathematics Teaching in the Middle School* 4 (May 1999): 530–32.

Ross, Sharon R. "Place Value: Problem Solving and Written Assessment." *Teaching Children Mathematics* 8 (March 2002): 419–23.

Sowder, Judith. "Place Value as the Key to Teaching Decimal Operations." *Teaching Children Mathematics* 3 (April 1997): 448–53.

Steffe, Leslie P., and John Olive. "The Problem of Fractions in the Elementary School." *Arithmetic Teacher* 38 (May 1991): 22–24.

Stump, Sheryl L. "Designing Fraction-Counting Books." *Teaching Children Mathematics* 9 (May 2003): 546–50.

Sweeney, Betsy. "Connecting Fractions, Decimals, and Percents." *Mathematics Teaching in the Middle School* 5 (January 2000): 324–28.

Thompson, Charles S., and Vicki Walker. "Connecting Decimals and Other Mathematical Content." *Teaching Children Mathematics* 2 (April 1996): 496–502.

Watanabe, Ted. "Representations in Teaching and Learning Fractions." *Teaching Children Mathematics* 8 (April 2002): 457–63.

Whitin, David J. "More Patterns with Square Numbers." *Arithmetic Teacher* 33 (January 1986): 40–42.

Witherspoon, Mary Lou. "Fractions: In Search of Meaning." *Arithmetic Teacher* 40 (April 1993): 482–85.

Yolles, Arlene. "Making Connections with Prime Numbers." *Mathematics Teaching in the Middle School* 7 (October 2001): 84–86.

Children's Literature

Teachers may wish to incorporate appropriate literature into the activities in this book. To identify children's books that are suitable for particular mathematics topics, teachers may refer to The Wonderful World of Mathematics: A Critically Annotated List of Children's Books in Mathematics, *by Diane Thiessen, Margaret Matthias, and Jacqueline Smith (Reston, Va.: NCTM, 1989). The examples of children's literature that are cited in the text follow:*

Gifford, Scott. *Piece = Part = Portion: Fractions = Decimals = Percents.* Berkeley, Calif.: Tricycle Press, 2003.

Leedy, Loreen. *Fraction Action.* New York: Holiday House, 1994.

LoPresti, Angeline Sparagna. *A Place for Zero.* Watertown, Mass.: Charlesbridge, 2003.

Neuschwander, Cindy. *Amanda Bean's Amazing Dream: A Mathematical Story.* New York: Scholastic Press, 1998.

Pallotta, Jerry. *The Hershey's Milk Chocolate Fractions Book.* New York: Scholastic Press, 1999.

———. *Twizzlers Percentages Book.* New York: Scholastic Press, 2001.

———. *Apple Fractions.* New York: Scholastic Press, 2002.

Peterson, Ivars, and Nancy Henderson. *Math Trek: Adventures in the Math Zone.* San Francisco: Jossey-Bass, 1999.

Schwartz, David M. *On Beyond a Million.* New York: Dragonfly Books, 2001.

Wells, Robert E. *Can You Count to a Googol?* Morton Grove, Ill.: Albert Whitman, 2000.

The following books may also be useful:

Aker, Suzanne. *What Comes in 2's, 3's, and 4's?* New York: Simon & Schuster, 1990.

Anno, Mitsumasa. *Anno's Mysterious Multiplying Jar.* New York: Putnam, 1983.

Dyrk, Marti. *The Fraction Family Heads West.* Manchaca, Tex.: Bookaloppy Press, 1997.

Emberley, Ed. *Ed Emberley's Picture Pie: A Circle Drawing Book.* New York: Little Brown, 1984.

Enzensberger, Hans M. *The Number Devil.* New York: Henry Holt, 1997.

Friedman, Aileen. *The King's Commissioners.* New York: Scholastic Press, 1994.

Froman, Robert. *The Greatest Guessing Game: A Book about Dividing.* New York: Crowell, 1978.

Geringer, Laura. *A Three Hat Day.* New York: HarperCollins, 1985.

Hong, Lily Toy. *Two of Everything.* Morton Grove, Ill.: Albert Whitman & Co., 1993.

Hulme, Joy. *Counting by Kangaroos.* New York: W. H. Freeman, 1991.

Hulme, Joy, and Carol Schwartz. *Sea Squares.* New York: Hyperion, 1991.

Hutchins, Pat. *The Doorbell Rang.* New York: HarperCollins, 1989.

Juster, Norton. *The Phantom Tollbooth.* New York: Random House, 1971.

Mathews, Louise. *Bunches and Bunches of Bunnies.* New York: Scholastic Press, 1978.

———. *Gator Pie.* Littleton, Mass.: Sundance Publishing, 1995.

McMillan, Bruce. *Eating Fractions.* New York: Scholastic Press, 1991.

Pinczes, Elinor J. *Arctic Fives Arrive.* Boston: Houghton Mifflin, 1996.

———. *A Remainder of One.* Boston: Houghton Mifflin, 2001.

———. *Inchworm and a Half.* Boston: Houghton Mifflin Company, 2001.

———. *One Hundred Hungry Ants.* Boston: Houghton Mifflin, 2001.

Slobodkina, Esphyr. *Caps for Sale.* W. R. Scott, 1940.

Tang, Greg. *The Best of Times.* New York: Scholastic Press, 2002.

Teachers may also wish to refer to the following for additional suggestions about using children's literature to teach mathematics in grades 3–5:

- *Exploring Mathematics through Literature: Articles and Lessons for Prekindergarten through Grade 8*, edited by Diane Thiessen (NCTM 2004). This book provides classroom examples of the use of children's literature to teach problem solving, representation, and reasoning.

- *New Visions for Linking Literature and Mathematics*, by David J. Whitin and Phyllis Whitin (NCTM/National Council of Teachers of English 2004). This book helps teachers find and use age-appropriate children's books with mathematical content.

DATE DUE